&Albert Square & Me

THE ACTORS OF EASTENDERS

An unauthorised 25th anniversary tribute
Exclusive interviews from the pages of the Walford Gazette

Edited by Larry Jaffee
with contributions from Tim Wilson and Dan Abramson

iUniverse, Inc.
New York   Bloomington

Albert Square & Me
The Actors of EastEnders

Copyright © 2009 Larry Jaffee

The *Walford Gazette* is not associated with, nor is an official publication of BBC Worldwide Americas, which owns the copyright and trademark *EastEnders*. Content contained within *Albert Square & Me* was previously published in the *Walford Gazette*, which has permission from BBC Worldwide Americas for usage of the name *EastEnders, Walford Gazette* and the programme's plots, characters, etc.

iUniverse books may be ordered through booksellers or by contacting:

iUniverse
1663 Liberty Drive
Bloomington, IN 47403
www.iuniverse.com
1-800-Authors (1-800-288-4677)

ISBN: 978-1-4401-5987-9 (pbk)
ISBN: 978-1-4401-5986-2 (ebk)

Printed in the United States of America and the UK

iUniverse rev. date: 8/3/2009

Cover Photo: PETER MACDIARMID/Rex USA

Front cover design by Anne Trauben

Wendy Richard and Barbara Windsor show Queen Elizabeth II around the *EastEnders* set, November 2001.

Dedication

This book is dedicated to my parents Skip and Ruth Jaffee, who have supported and encouraged my various endeavours, as well as to my children Jake and Annie, who have put up with my obsession with *EastEnders* since they were infants.

Preface

This book was seventeen years in the making. Since November 1992, the *Walford Gazette* has been published continuously on a quarterly basis as the world's only periodical dedicated to *EastEnders*. The newspaper has run interviews with more than eighty of the current and past cast members. It was co-founded by Larry Jaffee and Dan Abramson, who died in 1999, and has since been published and edited by Jaffee, who has worked as a journalist since graduating from college in 1980. Among his professional accomplishments is writing regularly for *The New York Times* at the age of 23 and being published in *Rolling Stone* at 24. He also has been the editor-in-chief of several magazines, newspapers, and websites. But he's most proud of the *Walford Gazette*.

Acknowledgements

I would like to thank the late Dan Abramson for convincing me that the world needed a newspaper dedicated to *EastEnders*, and also Tim Wilson for his many interviews to the *Walford Gazette*. I would also like to thank the many *EastEnders* actors who granted us their time to provide insights into the programme, the craft of acting, and their careers. I would like to thank the many agents and publicity staff at *EastEnders* who set up the interviews.

Among the BBC executives who have been helpful to me in publishing the newspaper over the years, I'd like to thank *EastEnders* company manager Carolyn Weinstein, BBC Head of Drama John Yorke, as well as former executive producers Matthew Robinson, Mal Young, and Louise Berridge. I would like to thank Pamela Knight for her expert copy-editing skills, and tremendous help in shepherding this book through the publication process. I'd also like thank Anne Trauben for her tremendous support during the creation of this book and particular help with the cover.

Wikipedia.org and imdb.com were helpful in assembling the epilogue of what the interviewees have done since talking to the *Walford Gazette*. All photos in the book were either taken by Larry Jaffee or provided to the *Walford Gazette* except where noted.

And finally, I'd like to thank the *Walford Gazette* subscribers and numerous contributors, who have come from all walks of life to share in the comings and goings of Albert Square.

Contents

List of Interviews:

The Den & Angie Years

The Mitchell Era

Introduction

In Great Britain, *EastEnders* needs no introduction. For more than twenty-four years, BBC One's longest-running serial has captured the British public's fancy, delving into the intertwined lives of the inhabitants of a fictional working-class neighbourhood in east London. The machinations of the television business (especially a programme that airs four new half-hour episodes a week year-round) make it impractical to keep the ensemble together. Contracts expire, actors want to test waters so they're not pigeonholed as one-trick ponies, and characters often run their course in fictional TV. Only one actor remains from *EastEnders'* original February 1985 cast.

The *Walford Gazette*, published continuously on a quarterly basis since 1993 from New York, has chronicled the comings and goings of more than eighty actors who have played past and present characters on the show. Many of these actors don't talk to the British press because of the tabloids' typically scandalous coverage of their personal lives. But they have granted exclusive interviews to the *Walford Gazette,* which respects their privacy and focuses instead on the craft of acting. Our articles deal with how they became actors, what they did before and after *EastEnders,* as well as providing insights into the characters that made them famous.

Little did Dan Abramson and I know when we hatched the *Gazette* in late 1992 that not only would our publication be eagerly read by stateside fans but also by the actors themselves. Dan, who died in 1999, would send copies of the newspaper to the studio. One day, Steve McFadden (Phil Mitchell) picked up an issue and liked so much what he read that he called Dan from his dressing room to tell him so. What started out as a transatlantic non-interview because McFadden wasn't inclined to do so became one, thanks to Dan's professional cajoling.

Nick Berry (Wicksy) granted the *Gazette* its first in-person interview because he was visiting New York on holiday with his brother, and Dan's friend, Freddie Hancock, the widow of the great comedian Tony Hancock, tipped us off of his availability. The five of us had breakfast at a swanky Central Park South restaurant.

My first solo interview with an *EastEnders* actor in London came about a year later in 1994 when I visited Gretchen Franklin, whose agent assured me that his client would gladly welcome me. Gretchen sounded exactly like Ethel when she answered the phone. We saw each other at her flat in Barnes, just outside London, and exchanged letters regularly between visits over the next eleven years. She became the British gran I never had.

When Gretchen died on 11 July 2005, BBC Radio 5 interviewed two individuals for its weekly obituary programme, *Brief Lives* (about notable people who passed) – June Brown, whom I met the previous year at the studio, and myself. Ms. Brown some years earlier had granted Tim Wilson an exclusive interview for the *Gazette*. When I was introduced to June, she remembered: "That young man Tim Wilson interviewed me for your newspaper. He used to write me letters, and was a big fan." I assured her that he remained so.

Tim, an American actor and fellow Anglophile, quickly became an integral third wheel in Dan's and my labour of love, landing memorable interviews with the likes of Anita Dobson, Gillian Taylforth, Martine McCutcheon, Sid Owen, Patsy Palmer, and Danniella Westbrook, to name only a few.

I myself became close with a few other cast members, such as Deepak Verma (Sanjay Kapoor), who stayed with me for about a week in the mid-1990s; he's since reciprocated several times when I needed a place to stay in London. Treating Deepak to a Bob Dylan concert in London, I witnessed first-hand what a hassle it was being so closely identified with an *EastEnders* character. "Where's Gita?" enquired a cheeky concert-goer, even though Deepak hadn't been on the show in six years.

Once, as Deepak and I climbed the stairs at the London club Soho House for a drink, we passed Michelle Collins (Cindy Beale). The two hadn't seen each other in a while. Michelle and I subsequently became fast friends, and she didn't hesitate when I enlisted her help a few years later to be the special guest at a meet-and-greet hastily organised to save *EastEnders* from being cancelled locally in New York.

When John Altman (Nick Cotton) was visiting New York, I surprised the local fan club by strolling in with the bloke they know as "Nasty Nick." A year later we spent the entire day together in Richmond, where he lives. We drove around in his car and he pointed out the homes of Sir Richard Attenborough, Sir Mick Jagger, and Pete Townshend. Walking along the Thames, a ragamuffin bicyclist almost sideswiped John, who responded with his Nick Cotton persona, "OI!!!" He then transformed back into John, suggesting we see Hampton Court, where King Henry VIII lived. Its majestic gardens attract many visitors. At home, John turned out to have quite a green thumb himself. Who knew?

Perhaps my most interesting personal relationship with an *EastEnders* actor has been with Wendy Richard (Pauline Fowler). How it came about was somewhat unusual. One day in early 2000 I received an email from John Burns, then Wendy's boyfriend, later her husband, saying that they would be in New York and would I fancy a drink? I was surprised, since over the years her agent had repeatedly turned down the requests Dan Abramson had made for an interview. When I arrived at their Upper East Side hotel, off Central Park, I was half expecting to be read the riot act about something that had offended her in the *Gazette*.

I do remember them both being bothered by a paparazzo for the British tabloids milling around the hotel lobby (we met at the bar), and wondering who had tipped the man off. (I didn't have anything to do with it, and thankfully they believed me.)

Wendy was glad to hear that I had been selling the hardcover of her autobiography, which had been published earlier in the year. In fact, her book was selling way faster than the memoirs of either Barbara Windsor or Mike Reid, both issued around the same time. This surprised me somewhat because I thought that Peggy and Frank were more popular characters. I kept that first meeting casual (I never pulled out a tape recorder or notebook), which seemed to be what Wendy preferred. Interestingly, that was how the relationship remained over a half-dozen or so meetings in New York and London (at her local pub, the Beehive in Marble Arch) that she, John and I would have in the ensuing years. I never did a formal, career-spanning interview with her, which I now, of course, regret.

Wendy was always friendly, and asked about my family, whom she met in 2001 when I organised a dinner party in her honour with about 15 New York-area fans at a good Indian restaurant. Wendy was always quick to offer support or a first-hand quote when something came up in the U.S. regarding *EastEnders*, such as the BBC America cancellation in September 2003. And she also told me how devastated she was by the 9/11 attacks. New York was their home away from home. I once gave Wendy as a gift a rare promotional DVD of *Everyone Loves Raymond*, her favourite American TV show.

I realised that it was largely because of John Burns that I had such a great relationship with Wendy. He was constantly thinking of ways for her to get closer to her many fans. In fact, a few years ago John and I discussed the possibility of mounting an *EastEnders* convention in the U.S. with Wendy as the star attraction. Sadly, that never came to fruition.

Most of all, I was so touched by Wendy calling my mother in December 2007 to offer words of encouragement right before she was to have cancer surgery. My mom was so moved that someone famous would take the time to speak with her. I miss you, Wendy; you're a peach!

Just a word about the interviews contained within: Most U.S. fans watch *EastEnders* via regional public television stations, and the episodes are more than five years behind what's current in the U.K. Consequently, readers may find *Albert Square & Me* lacking in today's stars. So, don't be surprised if there's eventually a Volume 2. Of the interviews we did conduct, about half the time the actors had already left the show. In any case, the year of the interview is noted after the character's name.

I hope you have as much fun reading as I did selecting from seventeen years of interviews. Cheers,

–Larry Jaffee, May 2009

Foreword to the Den & Angie Years

by Leonard Fenton (Dr. Legg)

Leonard Fenton and Gretchen Franklin at Nigel's wedding
(Polaroid from Gretchen's personal collection)

EastEnders, when it was first transmitted in February 1985, was an instant success – a phenomenon in British television. We who took part in it had no idea that it would appeal to such a wide range of viewers. Apart from its following in homes throughout the U.K., university students would flock to their common rooms to watch it. And then there was the Christmas episode, which had 30 million viewers – half the population.

We actors were proud to be involved in the project, and I remember how we wanted to influence the behaviour of our characters. My wish was that Dr. Legg would marry and become part of a family like the others on the Square, but alas that was not to be. He would remain a loner.

And that is how he was when WNYC introduced the programme to New York. Those were heady days. Five of the cast were delighted to be invited over in January 1989 to meet fans at Harvey's Chelsea Restaurant. Our hands went into overdrive as we signed photographs and were dazzled by flashing cameras. The folks at WNYC welcomed us warmly and introduced us to many fans – one of whom was special – she threw a splendid party in my honour about 10 years later in her large apartment on Broadway when Larry Jaffee and I became friendly.

It was exhilarating to find that we had such a loyal fan-base in New York, with fans that responded enthusiastically when Larry and Dan Abramson published the first issue of the *Walford Gazette* in 1992. I met Larry when he came over to England on *Gazette* business about seven years later. We had a meal, exchanged news about *EastEnders* in New York and London, and he came to see a stage play, *Zadie's Shoes*, that I was in at the time.

Since that time he has followed the happenings in *EastEnders* with great dedication and kept in touch with the cast. I personally appreciate all the fine work Larry has done and wish him every success in his future endeavours.

Foreword to The Mitchell Era

By Deepak Verma (Sanjay Kapoor)

Jake Jaffee (son of the author) and Deepak Verma, London, 1995

I am delighted to be able to write a few words about how I came to know Larry Jaffee. Larry is a true fan of *EastEnders,* and there's nobody quite as obsessed as he is about the intricacies of the show and the people who have been in it over the years. It is people like Larry who have really made the experience of having been in the series a remarkable and warming one. We have become close friends over the years, and periodically have stayed at each other's flats. We've often chuckled over the irony that he would prefer to be in London while I'd live in Manhattan. Just a month ago, we rekindled our friendship while I was visiting New York.

I met Larry in 1995 when I was planning a trip to New York. I adventurously phoned up the *Walford Gazette* to see if anybody would put me up – this was my mum's idea as she had recently read the newspaper and thought I shouldn't go to such a scary place on my own. New York was somewhere that I hadn't been before, the thought of spending time on my own was frightening, and I had only recently come across these crazy Yanks who were lovers of the show. Since I agreed to tape some promotional spots for the local *EastEnders* broadcast outlet on Long Island, I eventually ended up staying with Larry Lombardo, an ex-cop who lived nearby and told me that he slept with a gun under his pillow. The only problem I had was that, as I was on the ground floor and he was on the top floor, it was me that would end up dead first!

At a party thrown in my honour at Chez Jaffee, I ended up cooking with Larry's now ex-wife Teri my special Chicken Bhuna (just like mamma makes!) and a few veggie dishes while a group of the *Walford Gazette* contingent watched the latest episodes of 'Enders. Those were my shy days, and I just hung out in the kitchen all evening as I was too embarrassed to face the crowd who were full of questions about being a "soapstar." Larry just laughed at this in his usual way whilst downing a spoonful of Bhuna. Among the party guests were renowned musician Lenny Kaye and his lovely wife Stephanie (both diehard *EastEnders* fans). Larry introduced us, and we have remained in touch over the years.

Larry has continued to cover my career, and I really look forward to reading his chronicles of me and my *EastEnders* colleagues. We alumni do indeed belong to a special club. My tenure on the show gave me the freedom and the opportunities that I now am fortunate enough to enjoy. I am eternally grateful to the series for changing my life.

I hope you enjoy the book and keep watching *EastEnders*. It is a true British institution and always will be.

June Brown (Dot Cotton), 2002

"I won't hear a word said against my Nick. He's a good boy – most of the time. He's simply a cross Dot's had to bear."

All right, let me state this upfront. Meeting and interviewing June Brown (Dot Cotton) has been, without a doubt, a highlight of my life – and I am no longer a young man. Dot has always been my favourite *EastEnders* character, and June has been one of my favourite actresses PERIOD in any medium. I've admired her work for so long.

When we met at the *EE* studio I was keenly aware of how privileged I was to have this opportunity and was determined to savour the moment. I like to think I did. We first met very briefly in her dressing room as she was preparing to go on set. There, June was in full Dot regalia – that extremely familiar, plain brown coat and that plastic rain hat. The infamous umbrella with the duck handle was leaning against June's dressing room table. I could barely contain my excitement.

She beamed broadly at me and remarked that she remembered when we were in correspondence with each other back in 1989 and 1990. I told her I still had the Christmas card she sent. She said she still had the letters I sent – somewhere! She apologised profusely for the "frightful" schedule the show has been putting its actors through to get four episodes of the show a week in the can – as it would hinder our interview time somewhat. She had to go off and do a bit in the Square – where Dot is bumped into by some hooligans – and she couldn't believe she was being dragged in tonight just for *that*.

I was initially dropped off in the actors' green room where actress Lucy Benjamin (Lisa) was thoroughly enjoying a tape of new *Friends* episodes I'd brought in for her and Natalie Cassidy (Sonia).

June popped in briefly to ask if, after she was done shooting, we could meet up in the actors' smoking room, which was down the hall from the green room. It's a good thing I'm not averse to second-hand smoke. Even so, I'd have had serious problems with being cooped up in there for too long. She finally returned, after around a half-hour, with actor John Bardon (Jim Branning) in tow. These two are a hysterically funny double act on-screen *and* off.

Much of the initial repartee between them was about an upcoming charity ball, with John suggesting that she wear a nice blue dress she'd already worn to another event and June shooting back with, "Don't be so daft, Jim, uhhhh, I mean John. Of course, I can't do that, you silly bugger! You can just wear the same suit with a clean shirt but with us ladies it's different. Oh, you can be a right old fool at times." There was obvious affection underneath the bickering between these two.

June does sound an awful lot like Dot in person, but I'm still not sure she was doing it because she liked to stay "in character." In any event, she was thoroughly delightful. She bid John good night and settled down with me to enjoy one of her cherished cigarettes. Since she was still in full Dot Cotton drag I had to remind myself not to blur the lines between the two ladies and thus not to ask Dot Cotton questions.

June Brown: Oh, finally – away from that set. I thought it would never end, dear. I couldn't believe they had me come in for just that silly little bit. And it might not even make it when the show goes out! (*Writer's note: She was right. It didn't!*) At least it's Friday and now I can sit here and enjoy me fag!

Walford Gazette: I'd be very disillusioned if you didn't smoke like Dot does. When Wendy Richard was in New York she told us all about how the two of you are like a pair of chimneys.

JB: Poor Dot's tried to quit, poor thing, but I certainly haven't. Haven't got the willpower, I suppose – at least with this.

WG: I still remember an early episode when Dot was chewing on nicotine gum to cut down on the cravings when she first tried to quit, and somebody in the Vic had told her that non-smokers were "antisocial."

JB (laughs): Oh, that's right! That must have been when Angie was behind the bar, bless her.

WG: Yes, and Wendy was in the scene. Pauline was asked by Dot if she was being antisocial and Pauline responded with a weary "Oh, just leave me out of it, Dot, eh?" and walked away.

JB: That sounds like Pauline, all right. Grumpy thing. And then Dot would go around trying to get rid of the smoke in the Vic with that aerosol can, right? Air freshener?

WG (laughs): Yes – that was so funny.

JB: Hmmmm… the good old days.

WG: I can't let another moment pass without bringing up what I think is one of the funniest things I've ever seen – Dot putting on a posh voice to dispatch OzCabs in the cafe.

JB: Shall I do a bit for you? "Oh, OzCab Five, OzCab Five, where is your destination, please? Marylebone Road? Oh, that'll do very nicely. Over and out." I loved that bit.

WG: And so did I and everyone else who saw it. Looking at you, I'm so pleased that with Dot very little seems to change… like her wardrobe!

JB: It's called consistency, dear. Yes, that is so true about Dot. I've had this coat here for seventeen years. They always try to get me to wear new things but I graciously but firmly decline. I have a fur coat that Angie gave Dot when she went to Spain, which was used for a very important recent episode set on board the London Eye – that Ferris wheel thing built for the millennium.

WG: I saw that episode – it was very touching. And you looked great!

JB: Well, Dot thinks she looks right smart in her wardrobe so there's no need for her to march down to Marks & Spencers or Selfridge's to get herself decked out. There's no need at all. And of course Dot's hair never really changes. Everyone always thinks it's a wig but it's not. It's all to do with curlers, dear. Curlers and patience. It takes about three quarters of an hour, which can be very tiresome indeed but I endure it for dear old Dot.

WG: I don't quite know where to begin with Dot. She's been in so many great storylines and had such wonderful lines.

JB: My favourite line of all time with Dot was, "Well, I hope you're satisfied. My Nick's gone and I've come out in a rash." That was to her beloved Charlie. I was so angry when they decided to kill him off, having him get run over by that lorry. Dot and Charlie still had so much left to go through together, I thought. But I think it was because they had to come up with a way for Dot to once again accept Nick into her life after he tried to poison her. Still, I wish they could have waited a bit longer.

WG: If it's all right, let's just backtrack a bit – like, to the beginning. Well, the beginning of Dot, actually.

JB: The first time we saw Dot she was standing alongside Ethel outside the Vic watching the funeral cortege of poor little Hassan. I think Dot was probably smoking a fag and tetching away to Ethel. Her character was immediately established as something of a busybody, wasn't she? Nick's mother had been talked about right from the very start of the show – she lived in the same block of flats as Pete, Kathy, and Ian Beale and was always doing the other shift in the laundrette after Pauline had gone home to that rowdy bunch of Fowlers.

WG: Hey, hey, hey. Nick was no day at the beach.

JB: Now, now, now, I won't hear a word said against my Nick. He's a good boy – most of the time. (laughs) He's simply a cross she's had to bear. A rather large one, I'm afraid.

WG: At an AOL *EastEnders* chat I suggested *The Crosses I Had to Bear* as the would-be title of Dot's autobiography.

JB: Oh, really? How apt. Dot hasn't said that in a long time, though. Thank you for reminding me – I must put one of those Bible quotations into one of my scenes with Wendy next week. Well, the character of Jim Branning is swiftly becoming one of the crosses Dot must bear. Hmmmm...d'you mind if we go across the hall for a hot chocolate and then to my dressing room so I can begin the process of getting out of this place?

–Tim Wilson

John Altman (Nick Cotton), 2003

"I think they keep him like an ace card up their sleeve. When it gets a bit quiet, [time to bring back] Nick Cotton."

"There were three," rattles off John Altman, when asked how many people on *EastEnders* his alter ego "Nasty Nick" Cotton has killed since February 1985 when the series debuted in the U.K. "Reg Cox, Eddie Royle, and accidentally my son Ashley. And don't forget I tried to poison [to death] my dear old ma [the long-suffering Dot Cotton]. Not too bad, eh?"

In person, Altman turns out to be nothing like Nick and looks great for his 51 years. He usually doesn't reveal his age to the U.K. press, he confides. Nick's tattoos, he smiles, were make-up, as were the needle marks during Nick's heroin-shooting days. Altman visited New York in late June on a holiday to the States with his 16-year-old daughter Rosanna. Staying at the Long Island home of an expatriate friend he's known since schooldays, Altman paid a visit to the local public TV station, WLIW, to tape a commercial spot to help them promote on-air the then impending *EastEnders* switch to Saturday nights. WLIW's Matthew Digirolamo was good enough to tip off the *Walford Gazette* of Altman's local presence and how he might be up for an interview.

"I feel quite lucky to have played Nick Cotton for so many years," says Altman, in the Irish pub Fiddlesticks in New York's Greenwich Village. "Some actors never get anywhere. And every time I've been on *EastEnders,* they have quite meaty storylines for me. From an acting point of view, it's been a good experience. It's a bit of a cross to bear sometimes though – him being so nasty. When they're casting, I tend to get overlooked for parts like the warm, loving father, which as you can see I am in real life. It's [playing Nick] a double-edged sword really because I've been labelled Nick Cotton for the rest of my life. But it's been great because I've been in and out [of *EastEnders*] the last couple of years. And in the theatre I have been able to play Billy Flynn in a U.K. tour of *Chicago.*"

A BBC reviewer of a Norwich performance last November wrote: "Altman certainly looks the part, and his performance as the silver-tongued courtroom attorney draws on his recent TV experience as Dot Cotton's smooth-talking son."

As far as coming back again as Nick is concerned, Altman says, "They've left it open." *They* being the various creative teams that have run *EastEnders* over the past eighteen years. "I think they keep him like an ace card up their sleeve. When it gets a bit quiet, [time to bring back] Nick Cotton."

Indeed, Nick has probably returned to the Square more than any other character, not to mention that he was there from the very first episode in February 1985. I tell him how *EastEnders* fans often vividly remember the show's first ever scene of Den Watts kicking in Reg Cox's door; I remember better the last part of that episode with Den throwing Nick out of the Vic after getting into a fight with Ali.

"And Nick's fist comes through the window," Altman adds, finishing my thought.

Asked whether he thought that the *EastEnders* creative teams ever went too far with his evilness, such as poisoning Dot, Altman responds, "Not really. I try to find anything really nice about Nick." He thinks a moment. "Well, he gave his leather jacket to his son Ashley. He did love his son, you know? And when his son dies, he was actually grief-stricken looking over at the coffin. I don't know if you seen that episode yet?"

I tell him no, and explain the time warp Americans who appreciate *EastEnders* find themselves in and how I wasn't yet getting BBC America when that storyline hit.

Even though Nick was responsible for Ashley's death, explains Altman, Nick's warped mind still blames it on Mark Fowler. "I don't know what else Nick could do really, other than go out like James Cagney. Personally I wouldn't want to see him as a nice guy. I don't think the viewers would want to either. He's 99 per cent rotten Cotton, yeah." On the Nick Cotton scale, Altman comments that *EastEnders'* Trevor was a "good bad guy."

Altman's acting credits also include small parts in the *Star Wars* sequel *The Empire Strikes Back* and the 1979 film *Quadrophenia*, based on Pete Townshend's 1973 concept album by The Who. "For *Jedi*, I was only working on it for a couple of days. It's easy to miss me, but I did work on it. *Quadrophenia* was [an acting] learning curve for me. That's a cult movie in the U.K."

In the U.S., too, I point out. Another major role outside of *EastEnders* for Altman was playing George Harrison in a 1979 TV movie called *Birth of the Beatles*. A musician in real life, Altman felt at ease playing Harrison, whom he closely resembles physically.

Asked whether he ever met Harrison, Altman regrets that he never did, but remembers that Ringo Starr once recognised Nick Cotton in public.

Of what's on U.S. telly, Altman comments, "*24* is damn good television; there's so much going on at the same time."

He mentions playing one of the leads in a play called *Bouncers*, a satire about nightclub life that's booked for major U.K. cities through January. *Bouncers*, written by respected playwright John Godber, was first performed in 1977 at the Edinburgh Fringe Festival and recently enjoyed a successful run in the West End's Whitehall Theatre. The production of the play also stars Terry Duckworth, an actor in *EastEnders'* rival, *Coronation Street*, in an obvious ploy by the producers to bring the punters to the theatre.

The four leads in *Bouncers* play a total of forty-seven parts – from lager louts to handbag-clutching girls, reminiscent of the acting trio who comprise the BBC's bizarre series *The League of Gentlemen*.

Altman described his *Bouncers* characters to the British newspaper *The Independent* in a recent interview: "I switch constantly between three characters: Eric, Maureen, and Baz. I was told it would stretch me! There is Lucky Eric, a bouncer, so-called because he always finds a fiver on the dance floor. Maureen, a bit busty, but not a bag, likes a drink and a bit of a laugh. And a young yob called Baz, fit for a fight Friday night, get down there, have a skinful, maybe a Chinese chicken-in-a-basket, and try to pull a bird. The music will change – different disco numbers – one minute I'm a woman, then suddenly I'm a man. It's quite bizarre."

Following *Bouncers*, Altman tells the *Walford Gazette*, he's set to appear in a pantomime production of *Peter Pan*, which he also did last holiday season.

And after that, who knows?

With Dirty Den coming back, I mention that there's probably an opportunity to bring back Nick yet one more time given their history (I point out their gripping prison scenes) and the fact that there's no love lost between the two characters. "Yes, that was when Nick confessed to murdering Reg Cox, thinking that Dirty Den would be impressed. I haven't heard anything [about coming back]. And I'm pretty booked doing plays."

–Larry Jaffee

Leslie Grantham (Dennis Watts), 2006

"The fact is I've been killed off twice – you can't go back a third time."

Without a doubt, Leslie Grantham's portrayal of Den Watts, the first owner of the Queen Vic, created one of *EastEnders'* most memorable characters. He mouthed the show's very first words, "Something stinks in 'ere!" as Den, Ali, and Arthur broke into an Albert Square flat to find Reg Cox dead.

While Grantham left *EastEnders* in the late 1980s and went on to play characters in numerous other U.K. television series as well as regularly working the British theatre circuit, it's his "Dirty Den" that resonates most. Women wanted to be with Den, and men wanted to be him.

Grantham reprised the Den role in 2004 for 18 months. His second go-round on the show was blemished by an unfortunate Internet sex incident, detailed in his autobiography, *Life and Other Times* (Timewell Press). The book also goes into great detail about his continued remorse after accidentally killing a German taxi driver while he was in the British army. He learned to act in prison while serving eleven years of a life sentence for murder, and was released at the age of 29.

Timewell's publicist sought out the *Walford Gazette* for a telephone interview at 5.30 a.m., New York time. Grantham started the conversation by apologising: "Sorry about getting you up so early."

Walford Gazette: That's okay. I make exceptions when I get to talk to somebody I've admired for a long time. We were actually supposed to meet a few years ago when I was at the studio but the publicity department could not get it arranged.

Leslie Grantham: I can't remember now what happened. My brain's dead. I'm travelling around the country doing a book signing, so I don't quite know if it's Saturday, Sunday, Monday, or Thanksgiving.

WG: When I first became hooked on *EastEnders*, Den immediately reminded me of a Humphrey Bogart-type character.

LG: Well, you flatter me, Larry, but thank you.

WG: I'm serious about that, and it was interesting to me that later you played his *Casablanca* character in the West End stage production of *Rick's Bar*.

LG: I'm a huge Humphrey Bogart fan. The film was based on the play, *Rick's Bar*. It was tremendous for me because I know I always felt that Bogart or Rick is actually akin to, if you like and it should sound very blasphemous, but he's the sort who wants to save the world. So he has a bit of Jesus Christ in him in the fact that he sacrificed himself for love, and especially when he helps the young Jewish refugee to get the exit papers to get out of the country.

WG: Den and Angie in *EastEnders* also reminded me of Richard Burton and Elizabeth Taylor in *Who's Afraid of Virginia Woolf?*

LG: That's very much how [series co-founder] Julia Smith saw it. I saw it a bit more like James Cagney and Jean Harlow in *Public Enemy* when he smashed the grapefruit in her face. That's the sort of thing that Den would do. He's sort of unpredictable.

WG: How close were you to Julia?

LG: I was fortunate enough to see her just shortly before she died. She came to see me in a pantomime in Richmond, and she said that she was having a yearly check-up in hospital soon. And it wasn't long after that that she went. So it was very sad, a loss for me because although I only worked with her for a short period of time we did become mates. Julia became a sort of surrogate mother to me.

WG: I met Anita Dobson a few years ago after a play that she was doing. I always wondered whether the BBC might have wasted the Den comeback, and they should have brought Angie back at the same time.

LG: Yes. The trouble is that the BBC, unfortunately, is not in tune with its audience. The fact is that the viewing figures are possibly the lowest they've ever been at the moment on *EastEnders*. People are saying to me everywhere I go around the country, "Oh, hurry up and get back in there and sort that lot out again." You know, the fact is I've been killed off twice – you can't go back a third time. They're getting rid of Wendy's Pauline. Besides Dot and Pat, there's not one stable character that the audience of all ages actually identifies with. It's sad. I mean Ian Beale is not a character that the audience actually warms to because he's never had a rock solid basis. They tried to make him Dirty Den. They tried to make him J.R. from *Dallas*. There's no dependability in his character. He's very, very flighty. And the audience wants someone rock solid. Whether they're evil or whether they're good or whether they're in between, the audience identifies with someone who has a true purpose. It's not sour grapes. And I honestly believe that some of the actors in *EastEnders* at the moment – the full gamut from A to Z – really don't know anything about their characters, and the audience actually can't keep up with the changes of their characters.

WG: What do you think Julia Smith would have said if she saw what happened to her creation?

LG: I think she'd be turning in her grave now. I mean I have tremendous respect for the lady. I mean she, and also Tony Holland, what made the Julia Smith and Tony combination so good was the fact that Julia had been working at the BBC on things like *The Railway Children* and daytime television, so she understood about making quality television. And this was in the days when the BBC really was the best broadcasting company in the world. Tony Holland was an actor who could write. So he understood acting. He understood how actors work. It doesn't matter how good a script is on paper, if it doesn't go from the brain to the tongue, then there's something wrong, especially when you've got a quick turnover. And what's happening now on the show – this is when I went back – the writers don't meet the actors. You got hooked on *EastEnders*, and you do this wonderful *Walford Gazette,* which is a brilliant, a brilliant idea and a brilliant conception. It's very well written. I'm sure, and please correct me if I'm wrong, I'm sure that you've got a literary background of some sort.

WG: I'm a journalist, actually.

LG: So, therefore, you didn't suddenly go, "Oh, I love *EastEnders*. I'm gonna now churn out a paper every week." The fact you have a journalistic background helps you understand your market, what you're gonna write about. Otherwise, it turns into a *National Enquirer*-type newspaper, doesn't it?

WG: Exactly. In fact, over the years we've interviewed more than seventy-five of the cast members, many who would not give interviews to the U.K. newspapers for the reasons you just gave.

LG: That's good. So that's what I'm trying to say, going back to you, is that Tony Holland understood actors and understood writing. A lot of these writers in the beginning were ex-actors. So he nurtured them. He taught them. Even if their scripts weren't very good, he said, "Listen, now the basic premise there..." and he would spend time going through it. Now, the script editors on the show really are glorified secretaries. Anyone can read a script. Anyone can write a script, but the point is it's the finished product. It's like having a Rolls-Royce with a Suzuki engine. You know, it's all style over content, and that's the trouble with *EastEnders* at the moment.

Even when Den went back, he'd suddenly gone from being a ducker and a diver. He's slightly on the edge. He'd do a deal here and do a deal there, and it always sort of ends up coming back on him. He never really wins. And when he came back, they turned him into some Machiavellian gangster that had a deep side. Den's problem was he was a big fish in a little pond. And that was all it was. If he had a load of dodgy or snide watches for sale, they would always end up going wrong. So in the end he'd have to give back any money that he made out of it. You know, he was just a guy who ducked and dived. And suddenly he came back and he was some sort of big gangster. He never was. He wasn't a Mitchell either. He was just a guy who lived on his wits.

WG: Any regrets about coming back?

LG: No. The only regret coming back was that the scripts didn't actually live up to the promises made. I originally came back just for the 20th anniversary. When Louise [Berridge, the *EastEnders* executive producer who convinced him to come back] was gone, it was pointless staying. Everyone tells me that they miss me in the show. And maybe that is the regret – that I've actually let them down. I think they expected a new dawn of *EastEnders*, and it never happened.

WG: Were you surprised at how much things had changed when you came back? I mean obviously there were only a few familiar faces.

LG: I think I was. It was lovely to see Wendy and Letitia [Dean] (Sharon) obviously, and also meet Nigel Harman, who was playing my son, as well as June Brown (Dot Cotton), Pam St. Clement (Pat). There were some mates I'd done television shows with like John Bardon (Jim Branning), Derek Martin (Charlie Slater).

Twenty-five years ago, Larry, if we'd have been having this conversation and you'd have said to me, "British television is the best in the world and American television is rubbish," I would have said, "Yeah, you're probably right." Now you'd have to go, "American television is knocking spots off everything around the world, you know, whether it's *24, Lost, Law & Order, CSI*." It's because of the quality of the scripts, the quality of the acting, and the casting is superb. We get the American comedies. We have *Everyone Loves Raymond*, *The King of Queens*, and *Seinfeld* and all these sorts of things, they're all on at a ridiculous time over here, nine in the morning. Our own British drama or comedy is on at night, and it's not a patch on the American stuff. Maybe you'll go to me, "Oh, no. We think we prefer such-and-such; we think the American stuff rubbish." But it isn't. At the moment, I'm a great *Law & Order* fan, and now your Jerry Orbach is sadly no longer with us. That's the sort of show I would love to get into, much more than doing British drama, because British dramas are only style over content. There's no meat to it.

WG: Have you ever tried to work in the States?

LG: I did. But there are too many good actors out there. I'm not gonna rock the boat. If I come over, I'll just be hanging around the pool all day. If you're talkin' about the film stars, you know, sadly, there are no more Bogarts or Cagneys, but you do have Hackman, Eastwood, De Niro, Pacino, and James Woods, you know. I did a series called *The Paradise Club*. Someone said, I was sort of England's answer to Jack Nicholson, and someone else said, "No, I think he's England's answer to James Woods." And I took both those things as a compliment. Well, if you've got the original, why would you want some peanut like me, you know? It's up to you, Larry. If you get around those casting directors and you say, "Hey, we've got this guy Leslie Grantham. He'd be fantastic." (laughs)

WG: Okay. I'll see what I can do.

LG: All right, mate.

WG: Let's get to the book a little bit. Had you thought about writing this book previously?

LG: No. Everyone has said to me over the years, "You really should write the book," and I went, "No, no, no." I wrote it basically as therapy really. I've got sixty years of craft inside my head, and I put some stuff down on paper. I was doing a tour with an actor who I was sharing a cottage with, and he said, "Hey, this is really good. You should put it into a book." Then someone else read it and said, "Look, I'll introduce you to someone." My old agent introduced me to a publisher, who said, "Listen, I think this is brilliant. Why don't you write it?" So I did. I wrote 327,000 words. I got rid of all the boring bits and I just left the not-so-boring bits. I've tried to be as honest and truthful in the book as I am in my acting.

And I learned that from probably one of the greatest American actors of all time. I was very fortunate to meet James Cagney when he doing a terrible film called *Ragtime* in England. And I said, "Mr. Cagney, Mr. Cagney," and he said he's had a long day filming. And I said, "Well, I'm a drama student." And he said, "Acting is about walking through the door, planting your feet, and telling the truth." And I learned more in that that one sentence than I did at three years at drama school. I mean that's stayed with me the whole time, and if someone as wonderful and iconoclastic as Cagney says that to a peanut like me, I've got to take it on-board. And hopefully I have.

WG: Some of the people you talk about in your book I know personally. For example, I had a very close relationship with Gretchen Franklin.

LG: Yeah, she's one of the loveliest people I've ever worked with. And I used to take her backwards and forwards to work every day, and she was just a joy to be with.

WG: When my son was born and we named him Jake, Gretchen wrote me a letter and had mentioned to me that you had a son named Jake as well.

LG: My first television job was something called *Jake's End*, but that's not why we named him that. My eldest son is Michael, but he's called Spike. Jake, I just thought was such a lovely name. And when you look it up in the baby book, it says, "the follower." Well, he came second, so it was quite apt really. And I've got a third son called Danny, who is just a joy; he's got Down's syndrome – he's an absolutely wonderful child.

WG: And another person in the book I've interviewed was Matthew Robinson (former *EastEnders* executive producer and director).

LG: He saw me in a play that he'd written, and then he cast me in *Doctor Who*. And then he snapped me up for *EastEnders*. We still keep in touch. He is a very creative person, and I'm sure that he should be running a television company rather than sort of working for one, if you understand what I mean.

WG: Getting back to *EastEnders*, for the scenes that they had to shoot in prison, to what extent did you inform the writers about the way it should be done because you know from first-hand experience?

LG: Bill Lyons wrote all the [prison] stuff. Bill and I were very close. He was a child actor, and then he got into writing. He used to come and ask me when we were doing certain scenes. "You know, I've written this scene. I'm not quite sure." He's a very giving writer, a very good writer, but he said, "Look, I'm sure you can make it better," which was quite flattering. So I would look at it and say, "Well, Bill, I think we need to lose that line." So he used to chat to me all the time, and he did say, "Look, Julia's asked me to ask you would you mind if you did some stuff in prison?" I said, "No, I don't mind at all." I think if I hadn't had such a big workload, he probably would have picked my brains really.

WG: Another person I know pretty well is Wendy Richard. Did she ask for any advice on what it's like to finally leave *EastEnders*?

LG: We've been chatting for a while, and she was getting unhappy the way it was going. And I said, "Wendy, you don't actually need to be in the show. You know, if you feel that you're unhappy, you're a certain age now. You've had health scares. You know, just take some time out. You know, it's not as if you're short of a few dollars, Wendy." And she said something very apt to me. She said, "Once you'd gone (*Editor's note, referring to Leslie's leaving a second time*) I knew that it was it was pointless staying." She wasn't enjoying it, and she was enjoying it when I came back. And a lovely lady is Gary Oldman's sister, Laila Morse, who plays Mo.

WG: In fact, Wendy helped secure an interview with Laila that was in my last issue.

LG: Laila's doing it because she enjoys the show and she's doing it for fun and for remuneration. But she said, you know, "When you came back, it was fantastic," and we got on very well and we've become great mates. She said, "I used to love sitting in the green [room] with you. We'd just have a laugh all day. I speak to Laila once or twice a week. And when I had the book launch party, she and Wendy came. They would come down to see me in plays and pantomimes and stuff like that.

WG: I had a theory about what happened in your dressing room, which you deal with pretty explicitly in the book. It reminded me of Pee Wee Herman, the American actor, how he wanted to get rid of that kid show because he knew it wasn't who he really was and he went into that adult theatre.

LG: No. I think mine's slightly different. The thing is that I had a stalker for years. The more and more I tried to get away from her she became so bitter and twisted. I only ever met her once. It wasn't a spur-of-the-moment thing. I'd been in conversation with someone for a long, long, long time, but in the end it became a stupid event. It was totally stupid; it was entrapment. I think the press knew that they were on a sticky wicket. They then came up with several other people out of the woodwork who I was supposed to have had an affair with, which was totally untrue. But you can't sue for one without dragging the other thing up.

And that would then turn into a Gillian Taylforth situation [the *EastEnders* actress who played Kathy, and unsuccessfully sued a tabloid for libel]. Gillian never told a lie in her life. She's just a straight working-class girl, very, very, straight. She was always late in *EastEnders*, and Julia finally said, "One more late arrival and I will sort of suspend you or spank you." Well, the very next day Gillian came in late and we said, "Tell her your car broke down, or someone rear-ended your car." So we rehearsed it all with her. She went down to Julia, and Julia said, "You're late." And Gillian said, "Yes, I know. I overslept." (laughs)

So you can't win, you know, and it was a stupid thing that I did, but it wasn't anything other than me sort of thinking that some 23-year-old was marvellous. But that's not the reason, contrary to popular belief, that I got sacked. I actually went back to *EastEnders* only for 18 months. The option was on my side. I decided the way the show was going, it wasn't worth me staying. And I wasn't enjoying it, Larry. I was leaving home at six o'clock in the morning, getting to work at half-past seven, quarter to eight, leaving at half-past eight at night, getting home at ten o'clock, and learning 30 to 40 to 50 pages of dialogue. And the show was going completely different. The viewing figures shot up when I went back, high on my last episode, and they've now gone down. So I think the proof's in the pudding actually.

But I do have a huge affinity with the show, and that's only because I was in at the beginning of a wonderful, wonderful event, the wonderful show, which has brought a lot of pleasure to a lot of people in a lot of countries around the world. And here I am on a Saturday morning talking to you, and I mean that I'm not giving you any B.S. I actually mean that. It's a pleasure to be actually talking to the person who actually created the *Walford Gazette*. If there's anything you ever want me to do for your publication in the future, please don't hesitate to ask.

WG: Thank you, Leslie. I appreciate that very much.

–Larry Jaffee

Anita Dobson (Angie Watts), 1995

"Leslie [Grantham] and I would just ad-lib away. A lot of good stuff was our ad-libs, to be truthful. Sorry, all you stunning writers!"

My conversation with Anita Dobson was interrupted by a bomb scare. But let's first concentrate on the conversation, which was far more interesting.

Ms. Dobson is a virtual tornado of energy, wonderfully theatrical and funny and sweet. We met last winter at her agent's office near London's Charing Cross Road shortly after a snowstorm, quite rare in these parts. The erstwhile Angie was then in the midst of a United Kingdom tour of Chekhov's *Three Sisters* and had generously set aside part of her one day off in town to grant an interview for the *Walford Gazette*.

When I entered the agent's office, Dobson was at stage centre, entertaining the staff with stories about the previous night's Brit Awards, which she had attended with her long-time companion, Brian May of the rock group Queen. I was introduced to Anita, and then quickly ushered into the anteroom by her agent. As there were no telephones, fax machines or anxious actors to disturb us there, we were able to get down to the serious business of celebrating Anita.

Walford Gazette: First of all, thank you very much for showing up at all, what with the snowstorm. I know most Londoners don't react well to extreme weather conditions.

Anita Dobson: Yes, well, I skied through Hyde Park as Diane Keaton did in *Reds*, to make it over here. Wait a minute – she skied through Gorky Park, didn't she? Or was it Siberia?

WG: Whatever! We at the *Walford Gazette* are honoured by your presence. In the last issue, I wrote that Angie was one character I would really like to see make a return visit to Albert Square. (*Editor's note: This interview took place prior to the creative team killing off the character.*) And I am positive that I am not alone in that sentiment.

AD: It is a lovely sentiment. But I'm terribly sorry to say that I wouldn't hold out too much hope for that if I were you. The thing about *EastEnders* which you may or may not know is that once somebody leaves it, he or she usually do not come back. It's on to other things, away from the crazy ride of being on that show.

WG: Could anything or anybody persuade you to make a brief return?

AD: All right! Maybe I'd think about doing something if it could be done on location – in New York or Florida maybe – and on film, like the Venice episodes we shot in 1986. I remember watching those episodes and saying to myself, Hey, I look *good*!!! It was hard going back to videotape after that experience. I kid you not.

WG: The Venice episodes were great, and you, Leslie Grantham (Den) and Jane How (Jan) looked gorgeous on film.

AD (laughs): Didn't we? Hello, gorgeous! I think it was [series executive producer/creator] Julia Smith's idea to send us to Venice and we filmed everywhere – St. Mark's Square... all these fabulous shops... getting on and off the actual Orient Express. I was a complete nut about Italy even before that location shoot. I'd been there on a tour of *The Rocky Horror Picture Show*. I just love everything about it: the people, the language, the climate. We had a very happy time in Venice, despite the efforts of the British paparazzi to drive us crazy. I want to go back right now!

WG: It's been widely chronicled that you replaced another actress just before taping began on the first episode of *EastEnders*. Did you get a call in the middle of the night?

AD: Almost. I was on tour with the Oxford Playhouse doing Shakespeare – starving for my Art, darling – and there was this TV show getting started called *EastEnders*. All my family and friends kept on asking why I hadn't been seen for it, because I'm East End born and bred. All that I could tell them was that my then agent told me that I was too young for the "mature" roles.

Anyway, I get this call from my agent, who said that Julia Smith wanted to see me. She had taught me drama technique at drama school, and my name had suddenly popped into her head. I was told that the first actress cast in the role wasn't working out, because although she could play the blowsy and played-out aspect of Angie, she couldn't find the *flash* that Julia wanted. So the first thing I was worked on was Angie's look. This Italian girl I knew from my *Rocky Horror* days kept shouting, "You musta' use da hair gel." So I gelled my hair into a stupor.

My mum had sent me a bit of money with a note that read, "For God's sake, darling, get yourself some decent clothes!" because I was usually rigged out in ripped jeans and pullovers. So I'd already gone out and bought a few terrific little 1940s suits at antique shops during the last leg of the Oxford tour. When I walked into meet Julia decked out in this little nipped-waist, streamlined skirt, high heels with lots of make-up, I must have looked exactly like what she had in her head.

There were about a half-dozen other actresses there reading for the part that day. So I read for Julia and [co-creator] Tony Holland, thought I did pretty well and left clutching four scripts in my hand, still not knowing if I really got the part! On the way home my car broke down, and always – *always*!! – before something good happens to me a disaster takes place. Either I get kicked in the head with a football, or somebody hits me or I lose a job... it's still a bearer of glad tidings. In this case it was the car. And that afternoon I was told the part was mine.

WG: Did you wind up wearing any of those forties suits in the show?

AD: No, but Julia called me the next day and said: "I don't think Angie should wear slacks. Tell me what you think." I replied that Angie should never wear slacks unless they were form-fitting ski pants. Julia asked if I was comfortable with high-heeled shoes, and I said that not only was I comfortable in them, but that Angie should only wear high heels. She trusted me to shop for Angie's wardrobe and shop I did. I shopped myself into a... a... a....

WG: A stupor?

AD (laughs): A coma!!! And I walked into the rehearsal room to meet the cast and get to work, and after we rehearsed the first scene, Leslie Grantham said, "Yes, brilliant!" because it all just clicked. Letitia Dean then walked up to me and said, "Would you like a cup of tea, Mum?" And of course, I melted and got a bit misty-eyed because there I was, 36 years old with no kids, and this adorable little blonde fluffball had suddenly been thrust into my arms and was calling me "Mum." It was great.

WG: It certainly did click between you and Leslie. Den and Angie are, for my money, an incredibly interesting and exciting couple.

AD: What a flatterer you are! But Den and Angie were actually quite a sad couple, don't you think? I mean, she pines for him, a guy who practically flaunts his mistress about! And, when *EastEnders* began, they hadn't slept with each other for ten years.

WG: True. I mean the phenomenal chemistry between you and Leslie was interesting and exciting. Did you and he socialize off-screen?

AD: It's the weirdest thing because we didn't. Actually it made sense in a funny kind of way that we always went our separate ways after work. I usually went out with Gilly, Tish, and Sue [Taylforth, Dean, and Tully] to a wine bar or somewhere to unwind. I think Den and Angie's on-screen relationship was so fantastic, extraordinary, and intense that we never felt the need to feed into it when we weren't at the studio. There was a tremendous understanding between us as acting partners.

WG: Please tell us about the special "two-hander" in which Angie tells Den that she only has six months to live – as a ploy to keep him from leaving her.

AD: We enjoyed doing it. Right before we started, I walked up to Leslie and asked him, "Have you learned the script yet?" And he whispered, "No, have you?" And I said, "Well, I have a rough idea." And he said, "All right, then. So when you stop talkin' my mouth opens, and when I stop talking your mouth opens." *And we did it!* We even decided between the two of us that the emotional climax of the episode should be in a different place. So we sort of ad-libbed it into the right place.

WG: Wasn't the writer a bit annoyed with you for taking liberties with her material?

AD: She was literally on the studio soundstage with us, smiling and thumbing her way through the script – of which she was justifiably proud – and she suddenly had this rather confused look on her face when we changed bits. However, she loved what we did and told us so.

WG: Angie's relationship with Sharon was also fascinating. Would you describe Angie as guilty of emotional child abuse?

AD: My God! That never entered my mind. Do you think she was?

WG: I don't mean to imply that Angie was abusive in that she physically battered Sharon or that she committed verbal abuse through demeaning taunts. But I do think that she used Sharon as an emotional punching bag on many occasions. Sharon ran away once because she was unhappy. And she did choose Grant as a husband, even though she knew he had serious problems with controlling his violent nature. Grant is a loose cannon, just like Den and Angie.

AD: Well, all right, she wasn't a good mother. She didn't know which end was up! I think someone handed Sharon over to her one day, and Angie thought of her like this glistening Christmas present. I think she never really thought it through beforehand. I do believe she really wanted a child and she loved Sharon, but eventually found the competition pretty difficult to deal with in regard to Den's attentions. She was pretty rough on Sharon because of her drinking. But abusive? No. Maybe that's a bit of a strong description.

At this point Anita's agent enters the room and informs us that there is a security alert under way, due to reports of a bomb having been placed at Foyles bookshop, just across the road. Apparently, in cases, like this the thing to do is move to the stairwell, since it is in the back of the building and, therefore, as far as possible from the threatened explosion. I feel rather panicked myself. Anita makes a game of it, with a reference to a favourite entertainer of the 1940s: "Oh, isn't this exciting. I can make like Vera Lynn and sing 'The White Cliffs of Dover' for everybody and boost morale!"

We make our way to the stairwell, along with the rest of the staff, and sit it out for ninety minutes. Anita plays not only Vera Lynn, but also Mrs. Miniver and Bette Midler as well. The Dobson performance is so screamingly funny that I thought I would explode, rather than the bookshop. It turns out to be a false alarm, however, and I follow Anita's charisma back to the anteroom.

AD: Where were we before all the excitement? Oh yes, the abuse question! Certainly, I think Angie was into abuse in an unconscious way. Both generally and to herself.

WG: Would you call her a malicious character?

AD: Angie was not cold and calculating. She could be vicious, but not malicious. If she felt she'd been backed into a corner by somebody – and there was no justice – she would absolutely go straight for the jugular. Malicious people think things through, don't they? Angie didn't. She always blew hot and cold, and she was distracted by other things. She basically only reacted in the heat of the moment, especially after a few drinks.

WG: One of my favourite Angie moments is when she's moving out of the Vic. She's storming down the stairs holding a box. Then she sees a little picture on the wall that she suddenly wants. So she growls, "I'll have it!" and tosses the picture into the box. Do you remember that?

AD: I do. Ad-lib, Tim! A lot of it was very me, I'm afraid (laughs). If a lot of stuff looks spontaneous, it's because it was. If there was still a bit of time left at the end of a scene – which we'd know by the stage manager's hand signals – Leslie and I would just ad-lib away. A lot of good stuff was our ad-libs, to be truthful. Sorry, all you stunning writers!

WG: Have you and Leslie seen much of each since working together?

AD: No, not really. I did see him when I attended the opening night party of his play in the West End – the one where he played Rick from *Casablanca*. It turned out to be a major photo opportunity for the press. They went mad. It was lovely to see Leslie again. He was extremely good in the play.

WG: What about Letitia Dean (Sharon)?

AD: I love that girl. She's a wonderful person. Last year, when she left the show, she rang me up and asked, "Mum, could you please come to my going-away party?" The BBC had already rung up with an invitation and I told them I'd go, but keep it a secret from Tish. Then I told Tish that unfortunately I had to work on a TV movie that day. So I hired a big stretch limo, got the hugest bouquet of flowers I could find, got all done up and motored off to Elstree. Timing was on my side, because the party was being held outside on the Albert Square lot. And it was that awkward moment after Tish had opened her presents and didn't think she could keep from bursting into tears unless someone else did or said something. At that very moment my limo slowly pulled into

Albert Square. I got out, Tish screamed "Mum!" and everybody cheered. A fantastic moment. She was so pleased, and I was so glad I could do it for her.

WG: Was that the first time you'd been back since your last day on the show?

AD: Yes, it was. And it was the best occasion to return because it was Tish's big day, not mine.

WG: I remember being very disappointed with the choice of the actor to play Sonny, the man with whom Angie ran away to Spain. I thought he was too old and wimpy.

AD: The actor was a lovely, sweet man. But I must agree. I remember thinking, "Where's my toy boy? Where is my Italian waiter?" Angie should've gone off with an Italian waiter on a motorcycle. That would have really cranked Den's chain!

WG: What is Angie is up to in Florida, in your estimate?

AD: I have a fantasy that she's made good. She's swathed head to foot in furs and has just had her first of many facelifts.

WG: Is she married again?

AD: Yes, and he's more than a bit younger than her. He's also more than a bit dodgy. And he's got these horrible stepchildren from hell! That's her punishment for not phoning or writing postcards [to Albert Square] often enough.

WG: Is Angie still drinking?

AD: Of course she is! Luckily she's got the Betty Ford Clinic to check into every so often. She's in paradise! In all seriousness, I'm actually very interested in what people think happen to Angie. Start up a competition.

WG: After *EastEnders* you did a beautiful job in a play about the Holocaust entitled *A Shayna Maidel*.

AD: A wonderful play. It didn't get a chance to build an audience during its run because of the recession, unfortunately. This also happened with other shows I did in the West End like *Eurovision* and *Budgie*. *Eurovision* was a scream. It was set against the backdrop of the annual Eurovision Song contest, and I played this mad Italian. It was produced under the Andrew Lloyd Webber banner, and because it didn't have the earmarks of an immediate smash hit, it was put to sleep like a dog. *Budgie* had script problems, but the songs were terrific. I played Hazel, this laughing-through-tears survivor who keeps standing by her man, who's a dodgy bloke. Sound familiar? That may have been a mistake to do, typecasting-wise, since it was the first thing I did after *EastEnders*. You think maybe I should play a nun?

WG: You would have been swell in *Sister Act*. What was *Split Ends*?

AD: *Split Ends* was [a TV series] written by a great pal of mine, Lee Richmond, who's an American. It was a sitcom set in a beauty salon, and I played the head honcho beautician and I was blonde! It pulled in 10 million viewers per week, which is not too shabby. But the new regime at ITV had their own ideas. So it wasn't commissioned for a second series. Talk about luck of the damned, eh? At least I got to keep the clothes.

WG: Unfortunately, I didn't get to see you as the beautician. But I did get to see you play a gangster's moll in *Someone to Watch Over Me*. That was a very interesting television movie, and I thought you were excellent.

AD: It was originally called *Rudkin's Fetch*, which I thought was a more quirky, distinctive title. "Fetch" is an archaic word for a spectral vision – or a ghost. It was this really scary story about this creepy, vengeful gangster named Rudkin, who is able to astrally project himself out of his cell to keep tabs on his brother – who framed him – and his mistress, who I played. The brother and the mistress, it turns out, have an ongoing affair. My character realises too late that she's being watched by Rudkin and dies a rather nasty death.

WG: I recorded it and could only watch it once because it was too scary. It would have made a great segment for *The Twilight Zone* or *Night Gallery*.

AD: I thought the leopard-skin skirt was a triumph. Didn't you?

WG: Again back to the wardrobe! Speaking of which, Patti LuPone was reported to have kept her clothes after she left *Sunset Boulevard*. Would you like to do the show?

AD: Would I? Let me at it! A good friend of mine, Elaine Paige, played it here in London, and she's making her Broadway debut with it in the fall. I would love to take a crack playing Norma Desmond. After all, mad divas are my speciality – see, I am one!

–Tim Wilson

Anna Wing (Lou Beale), 1996

"[EastEnders] could use some older people, who are very experienced with life; old bags give weight."

"We have to make it quick!" Anna Wing bluntly makes it clear over the telephone from her London home. "*EastEnders* starts in fifteen minutes."

Although it's been eight years at the time of this interview in 1996 since she graced Albert Square as Lou Beale, matriarch of the clan, "I wouldn't dream of missing an episode," Wing explains. "After all, I'm an East Ender," she says, noting that not only did she grow up in the Hackney section of the East End, but so did her parents and grandparents.

During the audition process, the veteran actress implored the producers: "You must give me the job. I have the pedigree. I succeeded in the end [in convincing the producers that she should play Lou Beale]. I remember the [East End, circa early 1900s] children, all the sounds, the noise, the market. It's part of my birthright."

Wing was instructed by the show's creators "to bring something from your background" in developing the character of Lou Beale. As it turned out, the name of Wing's father was "Albert," the name of Beale's deceased husband and the fictional neighbourhood Square.

She remembers that on the first day of shooting *EastEnders*, the set was "all tensed up." Susan Tully, who was to play Lou's granddaughter Michelle Fowler, "came up to me" for some encouragement, while Wing was psyching herself up. "I told her never speak to me before we start." Luckily, Tully realised Wing was only kidding, and the two actresses went on to have many memorable scenes. "I was terribly fond of Tully, and loved them all," Wing says of her fellow cast members, whom she praised for their professionalism.

Lou Beale's passing in 1988 sort of started the exodus of the original *EastEnders*. "I'm always sorry to see them go."

Although Wing never misses an episode, even in 1996, she believes that Walford could use "some older people, who are very experienced with life; old bags give weight" to the proceedings.

Wing still stays in contact with some former *EastEnders* colleagues like Gretchen Franklin (Ethel) and Edna Dore (Mo Butcher). "Gretchen is a wonderful dancer and very clever lady. She once broke her leg, but no one could keep her away from the set. She's an absolute trouper." Wing noted that "Edna and I trained together [as actresses]."

These days, the [then] 82-year-old Wing still acts occasionally, and recently appeared in a play with her son Mark (who's a theatre director living in San Francisco). "It was wonderful; we had a kind of rapport."

Wing is also quite busy with various charitable activities, specifically for underprivileged people. "The phone never stops ringing."

She also never misses an episode of *Coronation Street*, Britain's other favourite soap, in which her daughter-in-law, Anita Kelly, plays a character.

Hardly a day does not go by that somebody recognizes Wing as Lou Beale. She'll hear whispering in a supermarket, "That lady used to be on television. People still come up to me; so I'm very lucky."

–Larry Jaffee

Wendy Richard (Pauline Fowler), 2008

"I left with my head held high. I've never slagged off the show, nor would I."

No trip to London for me is complete without a visit with Wendy Richard and her partner John Burns at their "local" (Britspeak for favourite pub). Tucked away on a corner street, this hideaway bar is located off Edgware Road, a busy section of central London. The pub is far smaller than the Queen Vic.

Awaiting their arrival, I was treated to the jukebox blasting my favourite British hits of the 1980s from the likes of Frankie Goes to Hollywood, Duran Duran, and Culture Club. We hadn't seen each other in three and a half years, and much has happened for all of us since.

Wendy finally left the series in November 2006 after nearly twenty-two years continuously playing Pauline Fowler. But with the U.S. public TV stations nearly five years behind the U.K. storylines, the character should be with us as long as the show is still on the air.

John arrives first at the pub, holding the lead of their new, well-behaved year-and-a-half dog, Lily. A tanned Wendy soon after entered the pub, and she explains that they had just returned from holiday in Malta. She tells me she's loving the freedom of not being tied to *EastEnders*, and has regularly appeared on various TV programmes since.

EastEnders still means a lot to her, and she notes she declined the BBC's offer for a farewell party, and instead held a "thank you" do in July 2007 at her own expense for the crew whom she worked with over the years on the show. Among the 120 attendees to her event were the behind-the-scenes workers, including sound, camera operators, props, costume and set designers, all whom are key in mounting a successful series and seldom get invited to industry events, she notes. A few of her acting colleagues showed up as well, including Todd Carty (Mark), James Alexandrou (Martin) and Natalie Cassidy (Sonia).

"It felt right since I resigned," explains Wendy. "I left with my head held high. I've never slagged off the show, nor would I. I have too many friends on both sides of the camera."

John and Wendy also recently appeared on a game show called *All Star Mr & Mrs*. She received favourable newspaper reviews the week of my trip for a sitcom, ITV1's sitcom *Benidorm*, playing a "loud-mouthed, rude," wheelchair-bound character. The morning after our meeting she appeared as a special guest on the Paul O'Grady talk show. At the pub, Wendy pets Lily and says, "You're going to be on telly tomorrow." Sure enough, Lily was on the show.

Wendy's also starring in the pilot of a new series called *Here Comes the Queen*, produced by David Croft, for whom the actress co-starred as Miss Brahms in *Are You Being Served?*

Wendy tells me with pride about how Natalie Cassidy was in rehearsals for a West End-destined play, Chekhov's *The Cherry Orchard*, in which she will be co-starring with Dame Diana Rigg, and how her now-svelte former *EE* colleague recently had a best-selling fitness DVD.

Both she and John watch a lot of American television, with their favourites being *The Sopranos, Mad Men, King of Queens*, and *Family Guy*.

–Larry Jaffee

Bill Treacher (Arthur Fowler), 1995

"The only way to make money in this business is as a soap star or a film star, and I'm not a film star."

In the beginning, Bill Treacher did not want to commit himself to a long-term portrayal of Arthur Fowler. "I thought I'd never see my family," says Treacher from his agent's office in a building called The Old School House, located near his home in suburban Suffolk. That's a long way from his boyhood in the real East End of London.

He adds, "it's a couple of hours drive" from the Albert Square stage set where he has been emoting in Arthurian tones for ten years now. "I asked the producer, Julia Smith, 'Am I really right for this role?' She said, 'It was written with you in mind'."

Smith offered Treacher a one-year contract. "I said, 'Good God! I can't sign up for a year!'" He preferred six months after which he signed the first of a series of renewals "for one year, with an option on their side for one more year."

This is the sort of employer/employee relationship that Arthur Fowler would truly understand. As Treacher explains the renewal system, "It means that they can either pick up your option or tell you to bugger off."

He admits that on one occasion, however, he almost quit voluntarily. "That was when Arthur had his breakdown. I wanted to get out then. I'd had enough." It was an old friend, actress Muriel Pavlov, who wrote Treacher. She convinced him to continue playing Arthur. "I'm glad I didn't quit. The only way to make money in this business is as a soap star or a film star, and I'm not a film star."

For the record, Pavlov actually was a film star back in the 1950s when she teamed with Dirk Bogarde in the *Doctor in the House* movies. Fans of that series should have little trouble imagining the nice young woman Pavlov portrayed taking time out from her busy schedule to advise Arthur Fowler to stay steadily employed.

Treacher grew up in the East End community of Bethnal Green. "This was many years ago," he quips, "just after Cromwell fell." He recalls the pre-World War II East End as an ethnic melting pot. "There were a lot of Russian Jewish people and then Jewish refugees from Hitler."

The fictitious Walford, in Treacher's view, captures much of the reality of his home turf, but not all of it.

"East Enders are rather sharp dressers. Arthur looks like he was clothed by Oxfam."

There was never any question as to which career the young Bill wished to pursue. "I can't remember not wanting to be an actor," he says, citing such early role models as Laurence Olivier, John Mills, Paul Scofield, and John Gielgud. "Those actors did both theatre and film," he recalls. "Television was not around then."

Treacher's upward mobility began with a series of Albert Square-type jobs. "I worked on the railways as a lad," he says. "I was a porter, the one saying 'Mind the doors, please!'" He later served in Royal Air Force, "and then I went to sea as a ship's steward for four years."

The earnings from those efforts paid his way through acting school at the Webber-Douglas Academy in Kensington. There, ironically, he worked very hard to lose his East End accent. "Strangely enough," Treacher observes, "a number of people in the *EastEnders* cast attended Webber-Douglas: Ross Kemp, Den and Angie (Leslie Grantham and Anita Dobson)." He agrees that the institution has been to the adults of Walford what the teleseries *Grange Hill* (about a comprehensive school) has been to such younger actors as Todd Carty (Mark Fowler), Susan Tully (Michelle Fowler), and Letitia Dean (Sharon Watts).

Treacher's pre-*EastEnders* career included several periods of long-term employment.

"I've done a lot of plays in the West End," he reports. The longest-running play was *Let Sleeping Wives Lie*, a comedy that ran for two years at Garrick Theatre during the 1960s. "I'd like to do more comedy," he says, adding that the [then-] thrice-weekly Albert Square schedule makes outside work these days a difficult proposition.

As a young actor, he also acted in a radio soap opera called *Mrs Dale's Diary*, which had already enjoyed a long run before Treacher took on the regular role of a milkman. He was still there four years later when the programme was cancelled. Summing up the experience, he laughs and says, "I closed it."

The role that brought him to the attention of Julia Smith was that of a bank robber in a multipart episode of *Z Cars*, the popular police show Smith was then producing. "That's Zed Cars!" Treacher corrects the American editor's pronunciation, in mock anger. "I can't see you as a bank robber," says the editor. "That's because you've been brainwashed by *EastEnders*. I once played a murderer in Agatha Christie," the actor responds.

Treacher says in ten years he only once went to complain about script developments in the saga of Arthur Fowler. He recalls being delighted by what many considered the most radical departure from the public's perception of Arthur: his extramarital affair with Christine Hewitt. "I went to our producer, Leonard Lewis, and he told me 'This Christmas, you're going to be found in bed together'." What he liked best about the idea is that "it gave Arthur a spring in his step. Liz Power, who portrayed Christine, is a very nice person to work with."

Treacher speaks of an emotional closeness emerging between him and the actors who portray his on-camera family. "Let's face it, the Fowlers have been through a lot."

He admits there has been a bit of intra-family bickering. "Of course, we have a go at each other occasionally. But if anyone slags us off, we close ranks." The shooting schedule, he adds, allows "no time for nonsense." Constant contact with his on-camera wife (Wendy Richard) and offspring (Carty and Tully) has taken a toll on his personal life. As Treacher puts it, "I see more of that family (the Fowlers) than my own."

The problem of living several hours' drive from Elstree was solved early on, when he rented a flat near the studio. The alternative would have been to uproot his wife and then young children. The routine turned him into something of a weekend family man, travelling home from Borehamwood and arriving back Monday morning.

Subsequently he's watched very little telly. The only free time he has is early mornings when he's usually learning his scripts. "I'm often up at 4 a.m., studying. I might as well work – the mind is receptive at that hour."

He has been spending far more time with his son Jamie, who has become Treacher's flatmate at the apartment near the studio. "Jamie is now studying at Middlesex University in Performing Arts; I suppose he will go into the business. My daughter Sophie will start at university in the next couple of years. When I ask her what she will study, she holds her tongue. I think she has the same idea as Jamie, but she won't let on."

Asked what advice he has for young people who wished to pursue an acting career, Treacher forthrightly states, "I'd say don't!" For those who choose not to follow this sage advice, he has a bit more to offer before we end this interview. "If you are determined and single-minded enough, you will make it as an actor. But there is an awful lot of disappointment to get through."

–Dan Abramson

Susan Tully (Michelle Fowler), 1994

"My ego demands that I try to make Michelle as sympathetic as possible."

I really can't tell you whether I interviewed Susan Tully or Michelle Fowler. It was probably just another instance of the actress revealing certain aspects of herself through the prism of That Fowler Kid. But Tully gave her usual excellent performance, which I'll share with you after I indulge myself in some heavy verbiage....

To me, the most fascinating aspect of *EastEnders* has been the evolution of the characters who have been present since the beginning. This practice of each actor spending a decade perfecting his or her on-screen persona reminds me of those ancient Chinese craftsmen who would devote twenty years to carving a single Tree of Jade. The Walford Jade Trees that most intrigue me are Sharon, Ian, and Michelle – whom we met at the awkward, ugly-duckling stage of adolescence and have now travelled along with on the Road to Swandom.

All three of these performances have benefited from scripts of marvellous, on-the-money accuracy about the realities of Becoming a Person. This is particularly appealing in a medium that usually bollixes up its portrayal of the teenage years even worse than it does the Other Ages of Man. With all due respect to the fine work done by Letitia Dean and Adam Woodyatt, neither possesses the dramatic range of Susan Tully.

This real-life East Ender was an on-air TV personality at age nine, hosting a live children's programme entitled *Our Show*. She went on to a prime-time drama, *Grange Hill*, which was set in a working-class secondary school. After four years of *Grange Hill* matriculation, Tully was already an accomplished actress at 17, when she began playing the 15-year-old Michelle Fowler.

Her portrayal of 'Chelle has often approached a state of virtual reality, providing viewers with flashback/insights into their own teen experiences. Let's face it, even happy adults look back on adolescence in blind terror. Michelle's survival of the outrageous slings and arrows had an uplifting, heroic quality – sort of like an Icelandic Saga with lipstick.

I am not alone with this assessment of Tully-as-brilliant-artiste. One member of the *EastEnders* creative team (who asks to remain anonymous) told me, "Many of us are hoping that Sue Tully never figures out just how talented she really is because we'd all love to go exploiting her for at least another decade."

Furthermore, as I've said before in this august journal, I am more than somewhat in love with the fictitious 'Chelle. In any case, I wished I had possessed the courage, humour, and work ethic of Tully's Fowler back during my years as a teenager.

I was therefore quite happy when Tully's press agent tells me that her client is interested in being interviewed by the *Walford Gazette*. We agreed on a time and I was given Tully's home phone number. This surprised me a bit, as I had just seen the episodes in which Michelle had received the threatening phone calls from Jack the College Lad. (Incidentally, I can prove with mathematical logic that the scripts dreamed up "Jack" long before they ever heard of me.)

Tully answers the phone herself, then asked me to wait a minute "while I get the kettle." This comes as a double shock. I mean, anyone who had been starring in American prime-time television for more than a decade would probably have had one servant to answer the phone and another one to fetch the tea. I had heard that *EastEnders* doesn't pay anything like American prime-time wages, but this was the first time that point totally got through to me.

On returning with her "cuppa," Tully mentions she read the first three issues of the *Walford Gazette* from cover to cover with great appreciation. (I was embarrassed to realise that I had neglected to send her issue #4.) She then disarms me completely by saying, "I've been nervous about this interview. You've said such nice things about me that I hope I can live up to expectations."

From this point on, Tully takes control of the conversation. Any hope I might have had of being an incisive, Mike Wallace-sort of interviewer goes straight out the window. I revert instead to carrying on like a tongue-tied schoolboy talking to his favourite TV star. Luckily for me, I had prepared a list of questions.

Walford Gazette: In America, we've had a long line of TV performers who were convincing as teenagers but then lost touch with reality in their twenties. How have you managed to remain so convincing as Michelle?

Susan Tully: I was at Mum and Dad's last night and we talked about this sort of thing. The two areas responsible for maintaining my sanity are family and friends. My family still lives on the same council estate where I grew up, and the friends I have picked up along the way. I have given strict instructions to my nearest and dearest to slap me down severely if I'm not behaving. I am also still in touch with Anna Scher, whose school I used to pay 50p (pence) per lesson to study acting. She advises me. It's very difficult to be objective about your own behaviour.

WG: You're not the only *Grange Hill* alumnus to appear on *EastEnders*. Has *Grange Hill* become the *EastEnders* "junior" team?

ST: It's not a natural stepping stone. It just happened that way.

WG: Will Vicky go to school at *Grange Hill*?

ST: Hasn't been decided yet. I saw Samantha last night.

WG: Samantha Leigh Martin, who plays Vicky?

ST: Yes. She's so brilliant and natural, and such a lovely kid. It makes life so easy. Her background is not in theatre and her parents are down-to-earth with no pretensions. Samantha does take her acting seriously and knows where the cameras and boom mikes are. But you can't force kids to act. You have to make a game of it or they'd be like little robots.

WG: What does Michelle write about in her college term papers?

ST: I don't know. What matters is that she wants to be a teacher, and the quickest route to that is the study of sociology and English.

WG: But college changed her. For example, Michelle stopped using the term "me mum" and began referring to "my mum."

ST (amused): You really do pay attention to *EastEnders,* don't you, Dan?

WG: Well, you see, I never had a little sister of my own, and I always wanted one. (*Appreciative laughter flowed west across the Atlantic, in lieu of an answer.*) **Okay, you don't keep track of Michelle's papers. Could you tell us Michelle's favourite singer or movie star?**

ST: I couldn't tell you that. There's a serious Method involved here. I've been doing this for nine years and on average, 'Chelle appears in seventy or eighty shows a year.... If I had some sort of written, character breakdown of what Michelle is all about that would put her in a corner and prevent further growth. There would be no challenge left. That doesn't make for drama. I mean who cares who's her favourite actor?

WG: Okay then. Who's Susan Tully's favourite actor?

ST: Beryl Reid. She's one of the great British actors, mostly in TV and radio.

WG: Do you admire any American actors?

ST: Yes, the naturalists, like Pacino and De Niro.

WG: Would you call *EastEnders* a valid feminist statement?

ST: That's stretching a point. I get asked quite often if *EastEnders* is a true reflection of real life in London's East End. And I say that everyone has their own definition of real life. Obviously, a show this popular has a responsibility to try to reflect real life in a balanced and responsible way – while also trying to be entertaining – because it goes out in the early evenings on the BBC. I have to say though that the female characters are very strong. They are not portrayed as victims or stereotypes.

WG: Your performance includes many small gestures and vocal inflections. Who invents those?

ST: I do. And my ego demands that I try to make Michelle as sympathetic as possible.

WG: Have you ever objected to any scenes or subplots in the scripts given you?

ST: Fortunately, that has never happened. I've never had to go up and protest anything.

WG: How does the creative process work with the other actors?

ST: You never know how they're going to do a scene. And I can assure you, that's not boring. I've been in so many scenarios with Bill (Treacher) and Wendy (Richard). They've had much more experience in the business than I have, and they've brought new things to many situations. We've had to talk a lot about our scenes in the time we're given. Let's say a three or four-page scene. We may have five or ten minutes per page to rehearse it two or three times before we start to shoot. And the retakes we do are usually for technical problems, not performance problems. So there's a bit of pressure. It's only on the floor, in front of the camera, that these scenes come to life.

WG: I understand you've taken time out from *EastEnders* to do some stage acting.

ST: That was at Theatre Royal Stratford East – in the East End.

WG: How do you compare TV acting to working on the stage?

ST: It's a completely different experience. I have to say it was not the best performance I've ever given. People in the back rows couldn't pick up my voice. But it was something new, and I would like to do it again.

WG: Do you have any ambitions in film?

ST: Yes. Yes. Yes. I'd be a fool not to have that ambition. My leaning is towards camera work, and I think what I do can be most accurately done on film.

WG: Over the years, have you kept in touch with Leslie Grantham (Dirty Den)?

ST: Since he left the show I've seen him perhaps a half dozen times. But I do keep in touch through the grapevine. You know, mutual friends.

WG: Speaking of Den, during the first year of *EastEnders* you hosted a very well-received documentary called *Too Young to Be Pregnant*.

ST: You *really* did research this article. I remember that show as very topical at the time. And it made the point that it's silly to get pregnant at that age.

WG: Outside of *EastEnders,* what television shows do you watch and respect?

ST: Less and less. But I'm a big fan of *Cheers.* And I enjoy comic satire, *Monty Python*-type shows like *Have I Got News for You!* I also watch *Coronation Street* and *Brookside,* just to see what the competition's up to.

–Dan Abramson

Gillian Taylforth (Kathy Mitchell), 1995

"I still joke to this day that I only got the job on EastEnders because I slipped in through the back gate."

Gillian Taylforth is an interviewer's dream for many reasons: she's wonderfully friendly, extremely funny, and (HALLELUJAH!!!) she loves to talk. In fact, the afternoon that I spent chatting with her was an absolute joy.

I met with Ms. Taylforth in Elstree....

Walford Gazette: What were you doing just before you were hired for *EastEnders*?

Gillian Taylforth: I was working as a secretary for a travel agency. I had been on television quite a few times in various shows, but I always ended up behind a typewriter. I worked in the BBC photo department for a while, too. I always tried to get away from the little cubicle I worked in to another area in the office that had a bit of sunlight and more open space. I still joke to this day that I only got the job on *EastEnders* because I slipped in through the back gate.

My first audition was for the part of Sue Osman, Ali's wife. But Julia Smith and Tony Holland, who created the show, had other ideas apparently, because they called me back for another audition, and this time it was for Kathy. They whipped out a calculator and kept punching in numbers. "We're trying to work out if you could be old enough to be Ian's mum," they said.

WG: What did you tell them?

GT: I said, I *can* look older. I'll put my hair up... we'll scrape it back... I'll have a few late nights and I *promise* I'll look old enough to be Ian's mum. My acting coach rang me up a few weeks later and sang "CONGRATULATIONS" into the phone, and I had no idea what she was on about. I couldn't believe I got that part. I showed up later at my mum and dad's house and I told them I had incredible news – I had got the role!

WG: How did they react?

GT: My mum's face fell and she said, "But I thought you were going to tell us you'd got engaged." My Dad knew how to get one-liners off as well. The show had been on a while, and I would come over to watch it with my mum and dad. I'd be saying "Oooooh, that's terrible! Look at my mouth! Why did I say the line that way? Look at my face – what was I thinking?" And Dad would turn to me and say, "If you can't sit there quietly, go *home* and watch it." Good old Dad.

WG: *Kathy and Me* [Gillian's autobiography] must contain more than a few stories about your parents, your brother, and your three sisters.

GT: Oh yeah. We're very close. When my dad died a few years ago, well, that was a very rough patch for us. But Jessie – my daughter – coming along has helped us through... kids are great for that, aren't they?

WG: What was it like, growing up with three sisters? Was it something out of *Little Women*?

GT: It was great…. I'm the second eldest. Deborah, who's the eldest, wrote this brilliant play that we all saw together…. We were really proud of her. Kim and I were actresses together… she was even up for a part in *EastEnders*. She became a policewoman but she's on disability now and is starting to do a bit of acting again. She just got a part on a series called *London's Burning*.

WG: It was once mentioned on *EastEnders* that Kathy had a long-lost sister named Stephanie. Maybe your real-life sister could play her….

GT: That would be terrific! (giggling) We could be the show's female version of the Mitchell Brothers.

WG: I understand that your youngest sister, Janice, practises the Mormon faith.

GT: The funny thing about that is that she only became interested in it initially because she was mad about Donny Osmond and the Osmonds and wanted to find a way to get close to them! She grew to become quite serious about the faith and, in fact, even married a Mormon. Not Donny Osmond, though. Someone not in showbiz.

WG: Whatever happened to that really cool, blue-and-white baseball jacket that Kathy wore?

GT: It's still around somewhere in the BBC wardrobe department, but I really don't wear it anymore. Don't know why. I'll tell you one thing though. That great leather jacket I wore for a long time on the show got nicked…. I loved that old thing! I wish I'd nicked it before someone else had the chance. Why couldn't whomever it was have taken that rotten blue woollen bobble hat instead?

WG: On to more serious subjects. When Kathy was raped, how did you react to the mail you received from viewers?

GT: Well, I tried answering as much as I could, but it was tough. One very young girl wrote to tell me she'd been raped and nobody else knew and asked me what she should do. I was in a bit of a dilemma there because I'm not a trained counsellor or anything like that. I felt a very strong responsibility towards this girl who was obviously deeply affected by Kathy's story. All I could do was write back and ask that she tell her parents and take it on from there. And I wasn't even sure that was the right advice. I wanted to handle all the mail responsibly, but I had to realise that – since I wasn't trained professionally to give out advice – I should only extend sympathy to them. Those people were in so much pain, the last thing I wanted to do was to make it worse.

WG: How did you personally react when they told you Kathy would be raped by Willmott-Brown?

GT: I didn't think it was a great idea at first. That Kathy was being raped for the second time in her life bothered me. And second, I didn't think Willmott-Brown was a very likely rapist. I also loved working with William Boyd, and his longevity on the show didn't look good to me if he was a rapist. But he played it brilliantly, I thought. And it was his idea to step up Willmott-Brown's drinking in order for the rape to make some sense.

WG: Personally, I thought Willmott-Brown was the perfect candidate to commit rape. Because he seemed to me so tightly wound up that he even looked constipated sometimes.

GT: Right. That's also true. I hadn't really thought of it that way. Anyway, the story was meant to do two things. It was meant to be a way to finally bust up Pete and Kathy – and it was a way to send Den to jail, and then off the show. A lot would be different if that rape hadn't happened.

WG: Are you happy for Kathy now she's finally found love with Phil Mitchell?

GT: Oh yeah. It's about time, don't you think? Steve McFadden and I get along great so that's very helpful. When the news came out that Kathy was going to get involved with Phil, Adam Woodyatt (Ian) kept teasing him and asking, "Contract up soon, is it?" Kathy does seem to land the kiss of death on whoever gets remotely interested in her. Think about it.... Eddie got killed. Laurie disappeared. Donna died from an overdose. Pete got run off the road by gangsters... need I go on? But I do think Phil stands a better chance than the others.

WG: Does this mean there's a possible marriage in the offing for the latest star-crossed Walford lovebirds? (*Ms. Taylforth offered no reply to that question. She did, however, grin politely.*)

WG: Did you get along well with Peter Dean (Pete Beale)?

GT: Yes, basically. We had problems now and then, but he was such an important part of my life with the show that it was really hard when he left. I prefer to think of the early days when we mucked in together to make the show as special as we knew it could be. Pete's death really was the end of an era for *EastEnders*. And Peter did contribute a lot to it. (chuckling) Well, I'm not laughing because he was killed off, but it just reminded me about the day we taped his funeral. I was dressed all in black and feeling incredibly tearful. I looked over at the television monitor and saw that it was black... nothing was on it. I turned to Ross Kemp (Grant Mitchell) and asked what was going on. He said, "Don't you know, Gilly? They're shooting it from Pete's point of view!" That did it! I spent the rest of the taping of Pete's funeral trying to keep from bursting out in giggles.

WG: There's a blonde lady on one American soap who is currently being possessed by an Evil Spirit. Is there any chance of Pete coming back in that manner?

GT (laughing): Oh, right! They could bring Duncan the Curate back to exorcise Kathy, and she could spit pea soup at him. That would most definitely be an acting challenge!

WG: Or... Kathy could be possessed by the spirit of Donna Ludlow, her daughter.

GT: Oh no. That wouldn't be as much fun. Donna was a very dark character.

WG: Speaking of Donna, what did you think of the writers' decision that Kathy should resolutely refuse to accept her daughter?

GT (thinking for a moment): I didn't agree at first. After all, Kathy was one of the Samaritans and rather sympathetic towards people. But this was a very different situation. Donna – simply by her presence – reminded Kathy of the trauma of the earlier rape. I did get people coming up to me on the street and accusing me of being mean to Donna and telling me to give her a break! But playing through the Willmott-Brown storyline helped me see that Kathy – in her mind – could never have a normal relationship with Donna. Seeing her would bring the old trauma back in some way every time.

WG: Personally, I thought that the rejection of Donna was, psychologically, the more realistic choice.

GT: Well, God knows the show has tried to be as realistic as it could over the years….

WG: Incidentally, I saw Adam Woodyatt on that game show [*That's Show Business!*] the other day. He seemed like a very nice guy.

GT: Oh, he's lovely. Really lovely. Everyone's watched him grow up on this show, like they have with Susan Tully (Michelle) and Letitia Dean (Sharon). One of the most emotional moments in our time together was when Adam told me he was going to be a dad in real life. I was feeling particularly down that day, and that was just the news I needed to send me into floods of tears – I was so happy for him! He said, "That means you're going to be a granny." I was so thrilled – it was if my own son was telling me this.

WG: Are you still close with Anita Dobson (Angie)?

GT: Absolutely. She's the godmother of my daughter. We still see each other when we can. I love 'Nita. She's a great lady. I always enjoyed being with her. I used to go out sometimes with Anita, Letitia Dean, Susan Tully, and Sandy Ratcliff (Sue Osman) – we had a great time together.

WG: How did you take the news that Letitia Dean and Susan Tully were leaving *EastEnders*?

GT (frowning a bit): Well, I'll miss not seeing Sue and Tish on the set terribly. But they are doing what's best for them, and that's great. They're heading out to see what might be out there for them besides *EastEnders*. They need new experiences. I'm sure they'll be fine no matter what happens, because they're both great girls who have a lot going for them in every department. We all want the very best for them.

WG (with trepidation): You're not moving on as well, are you?

GT: I'm still enjoying the show too much. Adam is the same. He said to me – after it was made official that Bill Treacher (Arthur Fowler) was quitting too – "I guess it'll just be you and me at the end, Mum." It's very unsettling that the girls and Bill and leaving. But it's also quite exciting because it makes you wonder where the producer and writers are going to take *EastEnders* next. With those characters not in the Square, the show is going to have to focus on other people… everyone thinks it's going to be a most interesting time.

At this point, Gillian looked at her watch and apologised, saying it was time to pick up Jessica at the *EastEnders'* in-studio day-care centre. Could she drive me to the railway station? I nodded gratefully, gathered up my recording material, and followed her into her spiffy BMW. She drove a few miles out of her way to take me to the Elstree & Borehamwood station. By that time, I felt as though this was just a typical day in the life, chatting in a car with a very good friend.

–Tim Wilson

Todd Carty (Mark Fowler), 1994

"My first concern was that they would sensationalise the story of how [Mark] got the disease through no fault of his own."

While *EastEnders* aficionados are known to disagree, few fans will argue with the notion that Todd Carty's portrayal of Mark Fowler serves as the heart and soul of Albert Square, its pillar of humanity. Who else would reach out to the likes of Mandy?

Of course, Mark's illness has been a catalyst for dramatic conflict within the Fowler household, as we have seen how each family member deals with his dreaded disease. The knowledge that his HIV status could turn into full-blown AIDS at any moment (e.g., Gill's sudden decline) might also explain why Mark seems to have become nicer in recent years (e.g., polite to his elders, standing up to bullies on behalf of the meek, etc.), having lost the chip on his shoulder that was so apparent when he returned to Walford after spending several years "up North."

Carty, who was born in Ireland, has been honing his acting skills since he began his career at age four, launching an impressive résumé of work in commercials, radio, theatre, television, and film.

Prior to *EastEnders*, Carty was best known in the U.K. for his five-year role as Tucker in a BBC series called *Grange Hill* about a London secondary school. The show also spawned other *EastEnders* alumni, including Fowler sibling Susan Tully. Decked out in a leather jacket, Tucker's swagger à la James Dean suggested a younger version of Mark Fowler. Carty later starred in his own *Grange Hill* spin-off series, *Tucker's Luck*.

When Carty answers his telephone in his dressing room between scenes at the Elstree studio, he sounds nothing like Mark. During the course of a short interview made from *Inside Soap*'s office, where this interviewer was a guest that day, Carty confesses to knowing nothing about the British pop singer Morrissey, much to my disappointment. (To wit, both gents have – or appear to have – lived through the world's miseries. Both are often misunderstood, moody, and morose, and turn away adoring women.)

But Todd lifts my spirits with his endorsement of the *Walford Gazette*, which he calls "a great idea. We don't have that sort of thing here."

Walford Gazette: How do you approach playing Mark Fowler?

Todd Carty: The character already had been established. There was a certain precedent. But as an actor you develop your style.

WG: What was your reaction when you found out that Mark was diagnosed as HIV-positive?

TC: HIV never had been done in the soaps on a long-term basis. My first concern was that they would sensationalise the story of how he got the disease through no fault of his own. People can live with the HIV virus for five to ten years. Mark is still going strong.

WG: Do you have any favourite *EastEnders* episodes?

TC: I really enjoyed the scenes with Gill [before she died]. To prepare, we were away from the studio for ten to twelve days. There was a real feeling of camaraderie.

WG: To what extent was your acting persona influenced by the likes of Marlon Brando and James Dean?

TC: I was very much influenced by American movies. We had *Saturday Matinee Pictures* here in the U.K. My favourites include James Cagney, the Marx Brothers, Laurel and Hardy, but I especially loved Marlon Brando and the surly quality of James Dean. They had a lot of similarities in the early days.

WG: Do you ride motorcycles for real?

TC: I have been driving motorcycles since I was 14 or 15. I used to go down to the local dump riding around with my mates. I've been seriously riding since I was 16.

WG: Did you encounter Susan Tully at all on the set of *Grange Hill*?

TC: I started on *Grange Hill* in 1977 three years before she did. I was a fifth-former by the time she joined. Fifth-formers don't really mix with second-formers. But I do remember one scene involving a school meeting, in which the entire cast was on the set, and we might have met each for a fleeting moment.

WG: My favourite scenes of yours deal with your relationship with Ian. You both behave the way cousins really do, especially that scene several years ago when you were playing a football game, the same game you played as kids, and Ian bragged how he always won. And you said, "I let you win because you would cry if I didn't."

TC: Well I suppose we do. That's exactly right. It's a mirror of our childhoods.

–Larry Jaffee

Gretchen Franklin (Ethel Skinner), 1994

"A woman stopped me in the street and said, 'When [Willy] knew he wasn't wanted on that programme no more, he was so upset he just turned over and died'."

In 1994, during one of my visits to London, Gretchen's long-time agent, Barry Burnett, told me that Gretchen would be very happy to reminisce with me about her Albert Square experiences at her home on a mid-May morning, and he gave me her phone number. I called her, and was amazed how much she sounded like Ethel, who was part of the original cast from the very first episode in February 1985.

It's the first of many interviews to follow over the next 11 years at her modest home in Barnes, on the outskirts of London. Gretchen's flabbergasted to learn that I've been "banned" from the set. Gretchen immediately calls the *EastEnders* executive producer to register a protest, vouching for my good intentions to help publicise the show, but couldn't get him to change his mind.

Hanging up, Gretchen winks and says, "It's too bad that I'm not working this week because you could have come with me as my dog minder. They wouldn't have any say in that!" That rebellious streak was evident in her portrayal of Ethel, right up to the character's last breath.

"I can play the comedy scenes or the tearjerkers. The directors and producers have realised that," says Gretchen, who has often made viewers both laugh and cry.

Gretchen has done everything in show business, except the circus and opera. She lives alone with her tiny dog Urney, a Chinese Crested (a rare breed). Practically inseparable from her TV lapdog Willy, Ethel wouldn't give up her pet even for a man (Benny Bloom). A dog lover throughout her life, Gretchen grew attached to Willy off-screen as well.

"Willy never had a day of training," she explains. "He was a very mild dog. Of course, I worked with him so long, he was very attached to me. He would do whatever I wanted. He would follow me, cross the set. Roly [the poodle] couldn't do as much. The owner of Roly (*EastEnders* original producer Julia Smith) took him out of the series because he never liked it. He wasn't a strong dog. Willy, on the other hand, was tough; he would put up with everything. Sometimes they would have marvellous scenes together. Once I was supposed to be knitting and I left the wool on the stool in the bar. They got a hold of it and absolutely tore it apart. That was a very funny scene."

Another favourite scene involved her giving Willy a bath. "He had to run around the set. It wasn't a big set. We were chasing him, so of course he loved it." Gretchen agrees that perhaps Ethel's most poignant scene on *EastEnders* was when she decided to put Willy to sleep, particularly the moment when she explains how her devoted pet, lying on Dr. Legg's table, "looked just like a puppy." Having lost several of her dogs over the years, Gretchen cried real tears for those scenes, which always confounded her. "I never knew why they wrote that scene.... Willy's last scene was on a Friday. A fortnight later, I promised his dog handler that I would attend some bazaar, and they wanted Willy, Roly, and Urney. The dog handler said, 'I don't think you'll be very happy with Willy this morning. He's quite without any life and he doesn't look too good'. It was a very hot day. When I saw him, he got under a table. He wouldn't have anything to eat, and that was unheard of."

Two weeks and two days after being written out, Willy died. "It was extraordinary in a way. A woman stopped me in the street and said, 'It was like him committing suicide. When he knew he wasn't wanted on that programme no more, he was so upset he just turned over and died.' And that was the end of Willy."

Gretchen's regular appearances ended on *EastEnders* about two years before this first interview. Since she left the series as a main cast member, her attempts to secure other acting work at times have become a series of misadventures that often lead to almost comical impromptu reunions with former colleagues. "I saw Anna Wing (Lou Beale) the other day. Some casting director was holding auditions for a commercial – a mother and daughter thing – in the middle of Oxford Street at lunchtime. You can imagine what a hired car cost. I wish I hadn't gone. The whole thing was a waste. But I knew everybody there. Before I left I asked the director, 'You wouldn't have Edna Dore (Mo Butcher) coming in today?' He said, 'Yes.' Practically the whole [*EastEnders*] cast was there, I met Edna at the vet's the next day, and we both agreed that we should have not gone to that." To add insult to injury, neither Franklin nor Wing nor Dore won the part.

"It's terrible that actors are so poorly paid that we have to do jobs like this," Gretchen adds. She recalls another time her agent asked her to go down to a pub called the Queen Victoria in the real East End "to have a chat with a morning television show presenter." She was led to believe that it was for a charity. It wasn't. "It was dreadful. [The punters] said they were told 'The *EastEnders* were going to be there.' It was Anna, myself and some other old bag they could find," Gretchen laughs.

These days her *EastEnders* appearances are infrequent, partly due to two real-life injuries that incapacitated the 83-year-old Franklin for almost a year. (A mechanical lift helps her get up and down the stairs of her two-floor home. Her broken foot gave the producers a convenient excuse to pack Ethel off to "sheltered housing," what Americans call "assisted living."

"I've been off [*EastEnders*] for ages. About twenty months ago I broke my knee. Three months later I broke my foot on the same leg. Well, I didn't do it; somebody else did [stepped on her foot]. I couldn't work. I had to be wheeled about. I loathed it. After you've been active, you're embarrassed all the while. I had to go hospital for eleven days. I had been in what's called an 'elderly assessment ward.' I said it's actually the 'geriatric ward.' The food was atrocious." Being recognised in hospital was a "ghastly" experience. "After I had been there for a day, I phoned up the administration and told them if people wanted to know which ward I was in, 'Please don't send anyone down to see me.' They were very nice about that. They do understand. The nurses used to come and stare. Two porters, very dressed up in their best suits, once asked 'Are you in *EastEnders*?'" One of the chaps told Gretchen he could see himself being on telly.

A gracious host, Gretchen offers me a whisky, even though it's about 11:30 a.m. She tells me about her three trips to the U.S.; how she didn't care for the dirtiness of New York, and how she still has many American friends. "I'll be quite honest with you. Most of them were American servicemen," she laughs.

Her first trip to America in 1967 involved going to Hollywood to appear on *This Is Your Life*. "I was treated very well by Ralph Edwards [the show's host]," she remembers. Heading back east, she was offered a part in a Broadway play, but declined because the show wasn't scheduled to open for several months. Of the experience she remembers, "I got a job on the [Broadway] stage, of course. It was June and the show didn't start until October. The weather was balmy hot, and in those days they didn't allow you to take much money when you travelled. I went home.

"The last time I was in New York [in the 1960s] it seemed so dirty and rundown. Some of the shops in the buildings are magnificent. It was such a mixture. Terribly cheap shops for jeans. It's the same thing here. Sometimes when I go into town, I can't believe what I'm seeing at all. I never go to the West End unless I really have to. I really dread going to a show now."

Royalties from American and other foreign broadcasts of *EastEnders* are a nice bonus for her hard work. "It adds up very nicely. At my age, one isn't buying new fur coats and diamonds. If you get that extra lot four times a year, you can be a bit more generous to other people or favourite charities. My charities are all for animals or old people."

Even before she became a fixture on *EastEnders,* it took Gretchen three years to get the BBC to send a car to take her to the Elstree set, which is 17 miles away from her home, so she wouldn't have to deal with the Tube and British Rail. "Typically, I'd go back and forth three days a week: two days work, one day on the lot."

She cites recently deceased *EastEnders* scriptwriter Colin Humphreys as "someone who wrote very well for me. We sort of understood each other. We appreciated each other. He was a big loss to the Company." Besides her fun times with Willy, Gretchen's favourite *EastEnders* scenes are the periodic "two-handers" featuring only Dot and Ethel about the ways things used to be around Albert Square. "We had some good scenes. Sometimes you think, 'This is a lovely script.' But it'll probably go all wrong for you."

These days, Gretchen watches *EastEnders* only occasionally. "I'm not a big soap fan. I can't believe it all," admits the actress, whose favourite television show is *Yes, Prime Minister.* "It's really a good programme, isn't it?"

It doesn't bother her that more and more of the original cast members have left *EastEnders.* She attributes the attrition to the natural progression of any long-running series. However, she'll turn the show on "if I know some good storyline is going to be on or there's a bit of fighting, something they always have on *EastEnders.*"

Gretchen's appearances on *EastEnders* for the ensuing decade had become a lot more infrequent, but our subsequent nearly annual visits always yielded new titbits. It had been some time since Ethel had been at the centre of any plots, and when she did return to the Square from her "home for the aged," it was usually for a special occasion like a wedding or funeral to add a few witty lines while having a drink with old mates like Dot and Pauline in the Queen Vic.

Following 9/11, Gretchen tells me tales of World War II, of how the German Blitz forced Londoners underground down in the Tube for several years to avoid the bombs. Not surprisingly, she was fond of American servicemen during the war (perhaps not unlike Ethel).

She reminisces of happy times when she was on the stage in the West End, and how sometimes would be jealous of shows that were doing better business next door or across the street.

She tells me details of her personal life, such as how her husband died fairly young and was a writer, Caswell Garth. With a sly wink, she mentions that she could have remarried many times and had plenty of offers, but preferred living alone.

A few months before turning 89 on 7 July, Gretchen was getting ready to return to Albert Square to tape some scenes after a few years of absence. The decision to have Ethel return came from then-new executive producer John Yorke, who explains to me separately that he thought it was a good idea to bring back some familiar faces.

I hustle across London's Hammersmith Bridge to her home in Barnes around 7 p.m. to give us a half hour before *EastEnders'* start. Indeed, there are a few *EastEnders* scripts scattered on her coffee table. Gretchen agrees when I ask if she would grant me the pleasure of watching *EastEnders* with her – the first time she did during our friendship.

On my arrival, Gretchen requests that I open a bottle of champagne for her – a tradition of our meetings. She agrees that watching with me would be almost like doing her homework, enabling her to become more familiar with some of the current storylines and her new colleagues. *EastEnders* shoots about six weeks in advance. Gretchen, of course, is as witty as only Ethel could be about her observations of the episode we watched, but some things shall remain private.

Gretchen shares some new stories with me about working on *EastEnders*. For example, she speaks fondly of Ross Kemp (Grant) and Steve McFadden (Phil), whom she refers to as "those boys," and commends them for their professionalism. "They came to work prepared, knew their lines, were on time."

I remind her that Grant danced with Ethel in the Mitchell Brothers' first episode on *EastEnders*, swinging her around, as Dot looked on with horror. Ethel meanwhile appeared to be having a grand time. Dot comes on the screen we're watching, and Gretchen tells me about June Brown's daughters.

Kemp once saw Gretchen struggling to keep her dressing-room door open to get some air on a particularly sweltering day, and asked if he could help. He promptly returned with a long steel pipe, which kept the door ajar. She's still grateful.

A few months before her 90th birthday, I had the privilege to visit with Gretchen again. The previous autumn Yorke, still in charge, had talked her into coming back for the storyline in which Gretchen enlists Dot's help in helping her die peacefully.

Gretchen tells me that it involved five weeks of work and that the experience was "very satisfactory from both a personal and professional perspective." She has especially kind words for Yorke, and also for June Brown, with whom she's enjoyed so many terrific scenes over the years. She didn't mind that the plot involved Ethel's dying, which I think is extraordinary given her advanced age.

On finishing her scenes, the *EastEnders'* production team presented Gretchen with a glass vase. That reminded her of a gift that the series presented to the cast members when the show was first starting: an *EastEnders* shirt, which Gretchen thought was cheap-looking. "Anna Wing (Lou Beale) asked me what I was going to do with mine. I told her I couldn't think what it was good for. Anna Wing replied, laughingly, 'around the house.'"

Our conversation moves to Martine McCutcheon (Tiffany), who was then starring in *My Fair Lady* in the West End. Gretchen notes that when Julie Andrews played Eliza Doolittle in the West End in the late 1950s, Gretchen was starring in an Agatha Christie play in an adjacent theatre. "Our show was a bomb. We used to enviously look out the window at the long lines [for *My Fair Lady*]."

Gretchen says she's not surprised that McCutcheon ended up landing such a plum role because once on *EastEnders* Martine had the opportunity to sing, and Gretchen thought she had a nice voice.

She also thinks Lucy Speed (Natalie) is very talented and could be doing things other than *EastEnders*.

The naughty side of Gretchen comes out as shares gossip she had just read in the tabloids about the personal lives of *EastEnders* actors and their occasional transgressions. "I'm glad I'm a cracking bore," she quips, as if to suggest that she'd hate the attention from the tabloids.

When my local public TV station, WLIW, threatened to cancel *EastEnders* in January 2005, one of my first thoughts was that I might not get to see Ethel die, since I didn't yet have digital cable when those episodes first aired on BBC America and in the U.K. on BBC-1 nearly five years ago. New York-area fans privately raised $35,000 to keep the show on, and eerily Gretchen died only a few weeks after public TV viewers in the U.S. watched Ethel's last moments of life – it was as if she had held on for our benefit.

I last saw Gretchen in June 2004 when I visited her at Queen Mary's Hospital, where she was recovering from a fall. I said, "I guess there won't be any alcohol." She winked and said, "Don't be so sure. I can nick one of those bottles from the nurse's station."

She was the British gran I never had.

–Larry Jaffee

Leonard Fenton (Dr. Legg), 1996

"Lorry drivers go past me at fifty miles an hour and yell, 'Hi, Doc!' I think it's the eyebrows."

Leonard Fenton prescribes more appearances by Ethel Skinner and Dr. Legg to cure what ails *EastEnders*. The recent rash of youth-obsessed subplots has, in Fenton's opinion, been bad for the programme's health.

"We've lost Dot Cotton and Lou Beale," he believes. "And Gretchen (Franklin) and I only show up on odd occasions." While the ranks of Walford's middle-aged residents are still full, the Good Doctor sees a holistic need for more senior citizens on-camera. "It is necessary to have a cross-section of the population," says Fenton in measured, Legg-like tones. "Even younger people can appreciate that."

In the meantime, Fenton has been keeping busy with his preferred medium – the stage. He recently appeared in a one-act play by Wolf Mankowitz, entitled *The Irish Hebrew Lesson*, "which we performed in a small fringe theatre attached to a pub." Set in Cork during the 1920s, the play casts Fenton as a Jewish refugee from Lithuania who has established a synagogue on the roof of a house. The old man has learned Gaelic in order to earn his living as a market trader. When a fugitive IRA gunman breaks in, the Hebrew makes friends with the Rebel.

"I did this play seventeen years ago," says the 69-year-old Fenton, "at a place called The Almost Free Theatre." Customers at that venue, he recalls, were encouraged to show up and pay as much or as little as they wanted for an evening's entertainment. "This play made a great deal of money that way."

Fenton has also appeared in Mankowitz's one-act stage adaptation of Gogol's short story *The Bespoke Overcoat* and says, "I plan to revive both as one evening of theatre." He says the game plan calls for this to take place "hopefully next year in Hampstead. I eventually want to bring it to America."

Fenton is, in fact, American on his mother's side. She had reversed the usual Atlantic crossing and emigrated from Newark, New Jersey, to Stepney in the real-life East End of London. Fenton's father was a tailor in Stepney.

Leonard himself likes to brag about the other superior brains that emerged from what was then a heavily Jewish borough. "Harold Pinter came from Hackney, to the north, where there were a large number of Jewish families living in tenements. Arnold Wesker and Bernard Cox are both well-known Jewish authors from Stepney who are slightly younger than I."

Fenton says he would rather have been a musician or a painter than a thespian. He had acted as a child and had come to the conclusion that it did not suit his ego. "An author has written the words and the director would tell you what to do and, in my conceited way, I thought, "What's in it for me?'"

Seeking to act like an adult, Fenton matriculated at King's College, London, getting his degree in engineering. This was shortly after World War Two, and he soon became Second Lieutenant Fenton of The Royal Engineers. The postings included Belgium, Holland, and Germany.

But all roads led to Walford as Fenton responded to his muse by way of "a fortnightly repertory company in Sheffield, Yorkshire." There, the company followed a two-week cycle of performing one play at night, rehearsing the next production by day, and reading the play scheduled after that whenever time permitted.

Fenton then graduated to a weekly company in Aberdeen. This meant that, instead of keeping three plays on his mind every two weeks, the schedule was now three per week. Young Leonard's journey through apprenticeship continued with a rep company in Morecambe, Lancashire.

"I prefer the stage to film and television," he comments, "because of the feedback and also because the nature of a play changes every night. This is especially true of comedy. If they laugh, it spurs you on to greater efforts."

During his long career as primarily a stage actor, Fenton was often cast in Shakespeare as comic relief – which indicates there may be more to Dr. Legg than meets the eye. Paul Bradley (Nigel Bates) was also cast in such bardic comic roles during his early stage years. It would be interesting to see the two – on consecutive nights – play Dogberry or Falstaff. In the latter role, Fenton successfully toured Northern Ireland in 1967.

"I'm very good at fat men," he says, with a mild laugh. "The secret is to think fat!"

Acting, he elucidates, is "all a matter of suggestion." He recalls having appeared later in a West End production of *The Seagull*, as the estate manager, and having friends visit him backstage who asked the question, "How do you make your hands fat?"

A few years before his Ulster Falstaffian tour, Fenton had played Bardolph to the better-publicised Falstaff of Orson Welles. "That was a career high spot," says Fenton, "because Welles was so interesting to work with… not difficult at all. He was very kind to me."

Fenton has worked with other famous names. The aforementioned production of *The Seagull*, for example, starred Joan Plowright under the direction of Lindsay Anderson.

Then there was a fellow named Samuel Beckett, who wrote and directed a two-character play for Billie Whitelaw and Fenton in 1979, entitled *Happy Days*. Fenton has subsequently read from Beckett's work at festivals and is scheduled to do so again next year at Bath.

A few years after the Beckett/Whitelaw experience, Fenton had what he describes as "a very happy season" at the National Theatre. The works included Molière's *Don Juan*, translated by the novelist John Fowles. This was followed by Turgenev's *A Month in the Country*, adapted by "the scholar/philosopher Sir Isaiah Berlin." Then it was on to John Arden's *Sergeant Musgrave's Dance*, "which I consider a classic."

That year, Fenton also portrayed Verges, one of the comic characters in *Much Ado About Nothing*. Lest anyone get the impression that he only plays humorous roles in Shakespeare, it should be pointed out that the collection of Fentonian press cuttings contains excellent reviews for his work as Polonius in Hamlet and Polixenes in *The Winter's Tale*.

He also played King Lear at age 26, "which required a great deal of imagination," he recalled.

Between the National Theatre and Albert Square, Fenton gave a very interesting performance in a series called *Shine On Harvey Moon*. This dealt with survivors of World War Two coping with peacetime. Fenton's portrayal of a German Jewish baker who had escaped the Holocaust was memorable.

How different from his next triumph as Legg! Fenton says he had great expectations for *EastEnders* in the artistic sense, but did not anticipate either its popularity or the manner in which this soap of soaps has become wired into the British national subconscious. In that regard, he tells of a medical friend, a general practitioner, who had a woman patient tell him, "I saw a wonderful doctor on TV last night."

The GP replied, "He's a friend of mine." The woman then asked for Dr. Legg's office address and telephone number. On being informed that the *EastEnders* – including Legg – are fictional characters, the lady took offence.

Asked what it is like to play a saint, Fenton chuckles and says that Legg has character flaws just like everyone else. On the other hand, he reports, "I have seen an article written by another real-life GP, which stated, 'No doctor could work as many hours as Legg does.' So, in that sense, he is mythical!"

The truly delightful side of all this is the fact that, "At my age, I have become a household name – or at least Legg has!" Fenton adds, "Lorry drivers go past me at fifty miles an hour and yell, 'Hi, Doc!' I think it's the eyebrows."

And this engineer from Stepney can offer a pretty good comeback. "Someone recently came up to me at a party and said, 'You're familiar!' So I said, 'I'm not trying to be familiar!' which I thought was worthy of Groucho."

When you get down to it, those are Groucho-type brows. Fenton adds that sometimes he deals with fans by running away, "like Fernando Rey fleeing Gene Hackman at the end of *The French Connection*."

But this does not always prove feasible. The Fentons maintain a vacation home in the Spanish province of Catalonia, where *EastEnders* appears, dubbed into Catalan. This led to a farcical situation where Leonard was visiting a mediaeval Moorish castle and found himself walking through an enclosed passageway as a Spanish woman walked by in the opposite direction. The woman, according to Fenton, was dressed in traditional Spanish garb and looked as if she also might have been from the Middle Ages. She looked at Fenton, searched her brain to remember where she had seen him before, and yelled out, "*Aieeee! El Médico!*"

Unfortunately, Fenton has not received the same sort of recognition at Elstree, where "the last three years I've been doing one episode every two or three months." For quite a while, he said, no more than one script was sent to him at a time.

He thinks, however, that the new executive producer, Corinne Hollingsworth, shares his belief in the need to show more Legg. "This week," he said, "two scripts showed up instead of one."

Which is a good vital sign.

–Dan Abramson

Ross Davidson (Andy O'Brien), 1994
"I made the mistake of telling off Julia Smith."

The story of why Ross Davidson stopped portraying male nurse Andy O'Brien has been told so often in England that Davidson himself has become bored with it. But we cajoled him into repeating the tale one more time for the sake of North America's *EastEnders* fans.

"What happened was that we did an *EastEnders* LP of cockney songs," said Davidson, who sounds on the telephone like a cross between Andy O'Brien and Errol Flynn-as-Don Juan. "The producer of that LP thought it would be a great idea if Shirley and me did a record of our own."

That would be Shirley Cheriton, who played Andy O'Brien's live-in lover Debbie Wilkins during Walford's first year. Since Davidson and Cheriton were having a not-so-secret love affair of their own at the time, the record producer thought that an album of their love songs might do nicely on the open market.

"Shirley did not want to do the record, but I did," recalls Davidson. "Unfortunately, I took the producer as my manager. BBC Records heard about it, and this manager chap insulted the head of BBC Records." This, in turn, led to a confrontation between Davidson and *EastEnders* producer Julia Smith, who had never been too thrilled by the public's knowledge of the affair between Davidson and Cheriton.

"I made the mistake of telling off Julia Smith," says Davidson. "She was a bit rude to me and I unfortunately reacted like a Celt." The argument progressed to the point where Smith threatened to write Andy out of the show. Davidson remembers his reply as being something along the lines of "If you're going to write me out, you'd better kill me off." Soon afterwards, the fictional Andy perished in a traffic accident.

Davidson is philosophical about this, admitting that the money from *EastEnders* was nice but adding that he never intended to be a permanent resident of Walford. "I would have liked to stay another six months to a year, but like a lot of their characters, it was time to move on."

This led to some major changes in the plans for Walford in the late 1980s, according to Davidson.

"They wanted Andy to marry Angie – which would have been the wedding of the year – and then leave the nursing profession to run the Dagmar pub." Instead, of course, Willmott-Brown took over the Dagmar and Angie left Walford, and then... oh heck, you know the rest.

Davidson was left with the interesting need to rebuild his career just as his name was becoming well known in Britain.

"I tried to get as far away as possible from the character on *EastEnders*." His subsequent work has mainly been in theatre, although there have been excursions back into cathode rays. Davidson spent one year on the satellite channel Sky Television, presenting "what was supposed to be a chat show but turned into a shopping channel-type show." He later hosted a BBC One chat show "for celebrities and music groups called *Pebble Mill One*."

There was also a children's programme on England's Channel 4 entitled POB, which was "sort of an educational show with puppets." Davidson defines POB as "one of the most wonderful things I've done – the people were lovely."

On-stage, his post-Andy performances have ranged all the way from the chief villain in *Wait Until Dark* to Jack Absolute in the classic Sheridan play *The Rivals*, on tour throughout Britain, plus the role of Bassanio in a London production of *The Merchant of Venice*. Davidson was also involved with *The Butterfly Children*, "a musical we hoped would get to the West End, but didn't quite make it."

When Shirley Cheriton left *EastEnders*, she teamed with Davidson in a two-character play called *The Monkey Walk*. "We were engaged in real life, but ended it two years ago," says Davidson. He added that it was "my doing, I wanted to keep my freedom."

Asked if he still watches *EastEnders*, Davidson replies that he does so only on rare occasions when he has turned it on by accident. "It had more humour when I was in it. For a period of time, *EastEnders* got very depressing. I tend to watch other soaps which are lighter. I also watch some American shows, like *Cheers, NYPD Blue,* and *Roseanne.*"

Professionally, Davidson has also kept busy with a just-completed, six-episode appearance on the Scottish soap opera *Take the High Road*. "They're revamping that as *High Road*, and I've been asked to come back as a regular. That's great, because now I'll have the means of paying my mortgage."

First, however, Davidson plans to make the rounds of casting offices in New York and Hollywood, to see if there's any demand for a medium-sized Celt with hundreds of hours of on-camera TV experience.

"I'd love to have a try in America," he says chuckling. "My ambition is to work with Nicollette [*Knots Landing*] Sheridan."

–Dan Abramson

Judith Jacob (Carmel Jackson), 2006

"People couldn't understand how a professional woman can stay with someone who beats her. That shows the durability of the character."

In the early days of *EastEnders* there was a pretty black health visitor named Carmel Jackson, who tended to various woes of Albert Square's residents. Think back to the time of the traumatic cot death of Hassan, the baby of Ali and Sue Osman, or when young, single mum Punk Mary was in need of some serious professional help.

Carmel fit the bill, but she had a domestic problem of her own: a violent white boyfriend named Matthew, who sometimes beat her. He later became her husband.

"It was a great part to play," says the London-based Jacob, in a hastily arranged transatlantic telephone call. "People couldn't understand how a professional woman can stay with someone who beats her. That shows the durability of the character," she says.

She looks back on her three years as an *EastEnders* cast member (from 5 June 1986 to 25 July 1989) only with delight, especially because a year into her work on the series, her young daughter became a member of the cast as well.

"They needed a two-year-old to play my niece," says Jacob, who initially resisted the casting idea, which came from *EastEnders* creator Julia Smith. "Children on the set can be so horrible," Jacob said, noting the awkwardness inherent in disciplining someone else's child in the workplace.

But Jacob found it hard to turn down Smith, with whom she had worked earlier in her career on another TV series, *Angels,* which Smith produced with *EastEnders* co-creator Tony Holland.

Midway through *EastEnders'* second year, when the time came to cast Carmel, Smith recruited Jacob, who a year later realised that she'd get to spend more time with her daughter if she also was working on *EastEnders.*

Aisha is now 20 years old, studying drama in college, following in her mum's footsteps. "She's aware of the reality of acting. You can earn money and you also can be not working," said Jacob.

In recent years, she has made appearances on episodes of the British television series *My Family* (whose cast features *EastEnders* alumna Daniela Denby-Ashe a/k/a Sarah Hills), *Black Books, Doctors,* and *Holby City.*

Following her stint on *EastEnders* in the early 1990s, she was a regular cast member on a comedy sketch show, co-starring with Sanjeev Bhaskar and Meera Syal, whom both went on to *The Kumars at No. 42.* At the end of every episode, the cast would spoof *EastEnders,* and Jacob once got to play Bianca Jackson, which was a lot of fun.

Like many of the first wave of younger *EastEnders* cast members, Jacob attended London's Anna Scher acting school. Among her classmates were Susan Tully (Michelle Fowler) and Phil Daniels, who later joined *EastEnders* and is best known for playing Jimmy in the film version of Pete Townshend's rock opera *Quadrophenia* (in which John Altman also had a role).

It was Jacob's decision to leave *EastEnders,* and she doesn't appear to have any regrets about doing so. It seemed like the right thing to do at the time. "They didn't want me to leave, and made me a couple of offers to stay," she said.

Before landing the *EastEnders* job, Jacob was a co-founder of Black Theatre Co-op (BTC), a London theatre group of black actresses, who hadn't worked together in a show in ten years, until late March. It was a warm reunion. "We've [individually] been through so much. We've had children. People lost people. A few of them are working in the U.S. One of the girls died four years ago."

Asked why BTC was formed, Jacob doesn't hesitate: "It was about control – actors don't have any. It gave us the chance to produce the things that we wanted to do."

Jacob doesn't buy into the occasional criticism *EastEnders* sometimes receives that it only pays token lip service to blacks and minorities, who are usually depicted stereotypically.

"*EastEnders* was the only show to [regularly employ] black actors. *Coronation Street* just recently started bringing in black characters. There has always been a good flow of people in *EastEnders.*"

When informed that she is listed on the show business website imdb.com as having done in 1990 a short film called *Fruits of Fear* with Tilda Swinton (who has gone on to Hollywood success), Jacob says she vaguely remembers making it but has never seen the film. She adds that she would have remembered if her co-star was Swinton.

Paul Medford (Calvin Carpenter) is the only *EastEnders* actor with whom she is still in contact. Medford in the early 1990s attracted some attention as one of the leads in the West End musical *Five Guys Named Moe.* "Paul can sing and dance. I can dance, and I can sing… in the bathroom – not anything people would pay for," she laughs.

When asked if there are any humorous anecdotes about her days on *EastEnders,* Jacob recalled the scene when Carmel was getting married and they were drinking champagne. "A little voice came from behind, 'Mummy, can I have champagne too?'" – even though Aisha's character was not Carmel's daughter.

"They left it in. I couldn't believe it when I watched," Jacob laughed. When the *Walford Gazette* suggests that little Aisha understood the fine acting art of "ad-libbing" at such an early age, Jacob laughs. "That's funny, I'm going to tell her that."

–Larry Jaffee

Nejdet Salih (Ali Osman), 1995

"My agent told them, 'I have a wonderful Turkish actor who was born in England'."

Nejdet Salih lives in Hollywood these days, trying to recapture the celebrity he once took for granted in Walford. "Nej," of course, used to play Ali Osman, who owned the café and cab service on Bridge Street, and was married to Sue until their world fell apart with the cot death of their infant son Hassan.

Salih, who believes in the concept of reincarnation, counts Ali Osman among his less spiritual personas. He practises a psychological technique called rebirthing, whereby "there comes a certain point in life where you accept certain things about what has happened to you – including things that happened in past lives, five hundred years ago, things like that."

In contrast to the devil-may-care Ali of Walford, Nej looks back on his past lives and says, "I believe I have been a priest quite a few times."

This is an interesting point, especially since Nej adds that, in his current lifetime, he had no religious upbringing of any sort.

He did, however, get to observe many differences between lifestyles in a childhood that began in north London in 1960, and then quickly moved to his grandparents' farm on the island of Cyprus.

It was a wonderful childhood," says Salih, sounding not at all like a major character from *EastEnders*. "We had a farm that included a beach and I could run from the fields and into the sea. I loved it."

This was near the town of Limassol, in the Greek half of Cyprus. Nej's people are of Turkish-Cypriot ancestry, but he was a child in Cyprus before the partition of the island along racial lines. He remembers absolutely no hostility.

Nor does he recall problems in moving back to London at age six and a half, except for the mild difficulty of English as a second language. "I don't think it took long, though. Just three or four months and then it just clicked! I suddenly realised that I was fluent in English."

There were two younger brothers and a sister in Nej's family. As a schoolboy, he says: "I was very clever, but a prankster – setting off alarm bells and that sort of thing. Because I was clever, I got away with murder."

The chief cultural influences on young Nejdet included the Arsenal Football Club, James Cagney, and Elvis Presley. Of Cagney, Mej explains, "I liked gangster movies and always wanted to be an explosive kind of actor."

In regard to Presley: "I discovered Elvis when I was 12 or 13 and used to imitate him in front of my bedroom mirror. I would dance around and sing like Elvis, using my hairbrush as a microphone." It didn't matter which songs were being sung into the hairbrush. "I just loved the sound of his voice."

In what might have been a good plot for an Elvis movie, Nej's dad tried to discourage the acting impulse. Salih Senior did not, however, object when Nej and his younger brother began "dancing like Zorba the Greek on tables as entertainment at my parents' restaurant."

Ironically, it was his father's death at 44 that provide Nejdet with the inspiration to forgo the legal career the elder Salih would have preferred for him. He attributed his dad's early death in part to his having sublimated all artistic ambitions to a businessman's life. "There were so many things dad would have liked to do," Nej recalls. "He sang and wrote poems. At weddings, he was the first one to get up and encourage everyone to dance." His son decided not to suppress the same impulses. Nej's effort to get into MountView Theatre School had its amusing side, at least in retrospect.

"I walked into the principal's office and said that I wanted to be an actor." The principal asked if Nejdet knew of Shakespeare. When Nej replied in the affirmative, the principal asked if he knew of Wilde. "Wild Who?" Nej asked.

Apparently impressed by young Salih's flair for comedy, the educator offered him a chance to audition for MountView. So Nej politely asked, "What's an audition?"

In spite of that exchange, Nej eventually attended the school, becoming more acquainted with Shakespeare as Puck in *A Midsummer Night's Dream* and Mercutio in *Romeo and Juliet*. Of the latter role, Salih describes himself as "a good duellist," although the skill never proved that valuable offstage.

Salih's student course work also included key roles in *The Madwoman of Chaillot* and *Look Back in Anger*, before he advanced into the cold, cruel reality of British show business.

"I had no big credits before *EastEnders*," he says. "Just *Minder* and *Doctor Who* when it starred Jon Pertwee." Other telly appearances included *The Brief* ("about an attorney in the army") plus the comedy, *Auf Wiedersehen, Pet*.

The latter production was a bit prophetic, since its fictional construction site in Germany was filmed at Elstree. As Salih confirms, the unfinished buildings left over from the final year of *Auf Wiedersehen* were used as the basis for the finished buildings that became Albert Square. "It's absolutely the same set."

When he returned to Elstree for his audition as an *EastEnder*, Salih was up for a key role in *Death Wish 3,* which was shot in the docklands of the East End. He was to have portrayed "one of the good guys. The role went to a Mexican actor."

Ali Osman was originally conceived as either Indian or Greek, according to Salih. When he was called for an audition, the show was not yet in production, but over fifty scripts had been written, and the future "Ali" was labeled "Chris" in those scripts.

As Nej recalls it, "My agent told them, 'I have a wonderful Turkish actor who was born in England.'" Initially, *EastEnders* creators Julia Smith and Tony Holland said no, "but they called back twenty minutes later and said 'Bring him to Elstree. We plan to expand the family and maybe he can play the brother'."

This did not immediately result in an audition, just an interview. Smith informed Salih that they were looking for someone "rather like Tom Selleck."

"Since she could see I had no moustache," Nej recalls, "I figured it was a game. This was leading to something. So I replied, 'The only thing is, I don't have a hairy chest.'" At which point, says Salih, Smith "melted – and became friendly."

Salih told Smith of his father's life as a restaurateur with artistic yearnings. This seemed to interest Smith, but she told Salih that the character of "Chris" had already been created. Three weeks later, Salih was called back for an audition. Once there, he was kept waiting an hour by the late arrival of Sandy Ratcliff, who would soon be portraying Sue Osman.

Before the screen test began, Nej remembers, "Julia said, 'Sorry we kept you late, Nej – but blame it on Sandy'." So Nej turned to Sandy and spoke in the manner of Ali to Sue Osman. "Don't do that to me again!" he yelled. He looks back on that ad-lib as a key to his being cast as Ali.

Laughing, Nej recalls that, when told he had been offered an 18-month contract in Walford, his immediate response to his agent was, "Great, but what happened to *Death Wish 3*?"

Like most of the original cast, Nej says he had no idea how successful *EastEnders* would become. In fact, the anticipation of post-Walford unemployment caused him to build up a side career, "singing in pubs and acting with different theatre companies. I did music hall and travelled around the country." This turned out to have been a good career move because, when he left *EastEnders* after five years, Salih found himself typecast as "the guy who played the Turk." He had expected the show to be the equivalent of the time that most ambitious actors spend in "rep" – with some regional repertory company before going on to bigger and better things. Instead, most of Nej's post-Bridge Street career has been in the legitimate theatre, playing "Hindus, Jews, and Italians" as part of an ongoing effort to break that Walford/Turkish stereotypecasting.

On-screen, Salih had a nice supporting role in *Carry On Columbus*. This was an attempt to update the *Carry On...* films of the sixties and seventies with a Marx Brothers-like assault on the Age of Discovery. According to Nej, this was both work and fun. "I never laughed so much in my life."

Otherwise, he has spent the last year in Hollywood, acting in theatre and "rebirthing" himself psychologically. He also took time out recently to view early episodes of *EastEnders* acquired on videocassette from the *Walford Gazette* contributor Mackenzie Jones-Currey.

"It was the cot death episode. I sat there saying to myself, 'I could have done that better'."

But who knows what the next career rebirth may bring?

–Dan Abramson

Nick Berry (Simon Wicks), 1993

"They were very nice about leaving it open, not killing off Wicksy. There's nice security in that."

"Can you get eggs Benedict in America?" asks Nick Berry, the deeply uncomplicated bloke who played Simon Wicks for five years, while on holiday in New York with his brother.

At the time of this interview, Berry has recently completed his starring role in the second mini-series of *Heartbeat,* set in Yorkshire, England, during the mid-1960s.

The line between Berry and Wicksy gets even further blurred as a well-dressed waiter reassures him that eggs Benedict, indeed, have been heard of in the colonies and that an order is on its way. With delight in life's simple pleasures, Berry's face crinkles into a Wicksy-like smile and he utters a Beatles-ish "Y-e-a-h-h-h" that goes on for what seems like twenty seconds.

He is clearly enjoying himself, and that emotion is pushed to the sixth power by word that there are a wide range of Americans who consider *EastEnders* an intellectual masterpiece.

Berry was an *EastEnders* fanatic himself when the show went on the air. Six months later, he was the first significant new cast member. "I auditioned on a Wednesday and then on Friday I arrived in Albert Square and began shooting my first scenes with Dirty Den, whom I had enjoyed watching on the box for some time," says Berry. "For my first few episodes, I walked around with a big smile on my face, grinning at everyone. It was funny."

As with most amusing matters, this had its roots in tragedy. David Scarboro, the original Mark Fowler, left the show due to a variety of reasons "especially tabloid harassment."

The complex plotting of life among Albert Square's teenagers demanded a replacement for Mark Fowler, "And so my character, a distant cousin – kind of a bastard child – was written in because somebody had to be the oldest adolescent."

It also put Berry in the same crossfire of tabloid harassment that had proved so detrimental to Scarboro (who committed suicide some time before Todd Carty took over the Mark role). But Berry proved better to able to cope with than Scarboro had.

"I was a bit older," Berry recalls, "and it was just a matter of people can deal with that and some can't. I'm very lucky to have come from a close family."

The tabloid journalists, Berry recalls, subjected him to "just a constant invasion of privacy. They never stop hounding you, following you around, hiding outside your house behind trees. At first, I didn't know how to deal with that, but then I decided it was fun. So I was able to just ignore them and go off to spend time with my family."

The mega-publicity created by those tabloids did, however, provide numerous career opportunities. While he did not follow Leslie Grantham's lead of making personal appearances in neighbourhood pubs, Berry did accept offers from music halls.

"Variety was dying in England," he recalls. "So, suddenly, instead of having acts, they would get an *EastEnders* actor to come down – and basically – just wave," he laughs. "You didn't give a performance, you just sort of go 'Hi!' and then the crowd would scream and go mad. Then you sort of throw out a few autographs and go home."

More important, Simon Wicks' pub-singing helped launch Berry as a top English singing star. In addition to "Every Loser Wins," which debuted on *EastEnders*, Berry scored another hit with "Heartbeat," the Buddy Holly classic that is the theme for his new series.

"Wicksy would sing in the pub," grins Berry, "but we would have another boy sitting on the other side of the studio playing the piano. You never saw my hands on the keys."

His professional training goes back to primary school when "I was part of a performing troupe called The Young 'Uns. We performed to make money for the local parent/teacher association, so they could build a swimming pool, that sort of thing.

"Then I toured in *Oliver!* as one of the ten or so boys. I didn't have any lines, just sang 'Consider Yourself' and the other songs."

That was a decade or so before he landed the role of Wicksy. During the interim, he auditioned, taking whatever job came along. "I found villains are a lot more fun than heroes. Just look at Dirty Den. I think the audience identifies more strongly with you in roles like that."

His reason for quitting the distinctly non-villainous Wicksy had to do with the fear of becoming typecast.

"Five years is a long time in one role," he says. Berry described Wicksy as "sort of the boy next door" in his original incarnation. "But then they changed it. Dirty Den had left the show and they chose Wicksy as the new romantic lead. I resisted that change because I never really saw Wicksy like that and you have to be consistent with these characters."

Berry's favourite scene from *EastEnders* was one of his earliest, with Anna Wing (Lou Beale). "There was some terrible storyline about Wicksy being with loan sharks and owing money.... I loved the emotions going on in that scene about Wicksy and his feelings towards his grandmother. I think most people can identify with the sort of thing."

Asked how closely Wing resembles Lou, Berry chuckles. "They're exact opposites. Anna is a wonderful comic and does very funny impersonations. Not at all like Lou Beale."

Having left the safety of Wicksy, it is perhaps significant that Berry describes his character on *Heartbeat* as "basically, a fascist. When they arrive in Yorkshire, at first his wife doesn't have a job. She's just a housewife and everything is all right for a while. Then she starts her career, and he has problems with that."

Berry's character is a London policeman who has transferred to Yorkshire in the mid-1960s, seeking to escape the anarchy of Swingin' London and immerse himself in a more traditional lifestyle, definitely not a move that Wicksy would have made.

Heartbeat was produced by Yorkshire Television, one of several independent companies Berry has worked for since leaving *EastEnders*. "The good thing about those companies is that once you develop a reputation as a reliable actor, you're in." Berry's search for variety and more career challenges means that he probably will not be back as Wicksy. "They were very nice about leaving it open, not killing off Wicksy. There's nice security in that."

–Dan Abramson

Michelle Collins (Cindy Beale), 1995

"I like playing Cindy. But I don't particularly like Cindy."

Michelle Collins's days are filled with personal appearances and efforts to find backers for a proposed feature film, along with her full-time job portraying would-be lady of leisure Cindy Beale. There is, to put it mildly, a contrast between the character of this actress and that of her Walford persona. "I like playing Cindy," says Michelle. "But I don't particularly like Cindy."

Asked to analyse the chief differences, Michelle focuses on matters of self-sufficiency. She defines Cindy as "more of a man's woman" than her real-life self. "I'm a lot more independent than she is," says the actress. "I have girlfriends and financial independence where Cindy does not. Also, I have a sense of humour and I don't think she does, really."

Finally, "I think I'm a lot more sensible than she is. Cindy is ruled by her emotions."

When we began our interview, Michelle says that she originally found the whole concept of this *Walford Gazette* – and a North American cult following for *EastEnders* – somewhat surprising. That is because, as a child, she considered British television rather boring in comparison with the programmes imported from America. Her favourite was *Hawaii Five-O*. "I had a big crush on Steve McGarrett."

Michelle, born in Islington, north London in 1963, graduated from Highbury Hill High School at age 16 and took a two-year drama course at Kingsway Princeton College. The future Phil Mitchell, Steve McFadden, was at Kingsway at the same time. "But Steve doesn't like for me to talk about that," says Michelle, "so let's not."

One interesting college experience that Michelle does wish to talk about is her audition for Bow Wow Wow, the New Wave group then being formed by Malcolm McLaren, manager of the Sex Pistols. She did not get the job, but enjoyed trying out. "I was seventeen, young and naive, and did not even know that I was auditioning for Malcolm McLaren. When you're that young you have a lot more bottle and confidence. You just go for things."

Another character-building rejection occurred the following year, when Michelle sought entry into the Royal Academy of Dramatic Art. "They said I was too young," recalls the older-and-wiser Michelle. "I never did go back." With a laugh, she editorializes about her career by singing a few Sinatra-like bars of "My Way."

Her first break was membership in a doo-wop group, Mari Wilson and the Wilsations. They enjoyed some success, and the beehive hairdo Michelle wore as a Wilsation brought her into the lucrative world of television commercials. Her first such advert was for the Bradford & Bingley Building Society, which was just then starting a series of 1960s nostalgia spots. Michelle portrayed a secretary with a beehive, thereby proving that there is no such thing as wasted experience.

"I later did commercials for British Telecom, the Halifax Building Society, Daily Box chocolates, the Trustee Savings Bank, KFC, and loads more. That's what kept me financially okay as an actress."

Michelle also seems to have done quite well for herself between commercials. Her first post-Wilsation gig was in HMV, described as "a musical about the music business." She later appeared in the film *Personal Services* as a waitress and in *Empire State*, which she describes as "pretty awful."

Her telly credits include episodes of *The Good Neighbours, Albion Market, Going to Work, Pressures, Morgan's Boy, Marjorie and Men*, and *Gone to the Dogs*. Her favourite part, though, was that of "a handbag-snatcher on *Bergerac*. They still show that occasionally."

More steady employment came from a regular role on *Gems*, a soap about the world of fashion models. Ironically, "while I had done some photo modelling before *Gems*, at five foot five I was never tall enough for big-money fashion shoots."

She also appeared as support for Ray Brooks in twenty-four episodes of a sitcom called *Running Wild*, in which Brooks played a man suffering through his midlife crisis, with Michelle as his grown-up daughter Stephanie.

The first time round, in the spring of 1988, Michelle contracted to appear on *EastEnders* for eleven episodes. She stayed there for two and a half years after moving very quickly to centre stage of an important plotline. This gives some indication of how much the British fans of Walford enjoyed seeing Michelle in the role of a twenty-something bitch-goddess. On her return after a two-year absence, Cindy's character had mellowed a bit (school of hard knocks and all that), yet she again fitted marvellously well into the show's warp and woof.

"I left because I thought I'd had enough," she reflects. "I got itchy feet." As for her return to Walford, "I got a good offer." Clearly, she does not approach the role of Cindy Beale with any kind of religious fervour.

During her Albert Square hiatus, Michelle appeared in twenty episodes of a comedy entitled *Where Is Don Day?* for a series called *The Krypton Factor*. She also co-hosted nine episodes of a youth-oriented, showbiz documentary series called *The Word* and toured onstage in two comedies with Nick Berry (Wicksy).

Michelle enjoys playing comedy and drama about equally, but says, "You have to work a bit harder at drama." Before her Walford redux, she appeared at the Liverpool Playhouse in a comedy called *Raving Beauties* and then toured the U.K. in a farce entitled *Anybody for Murder?*

The renewed popularity of Cindy has enabled Michelle to engage in the aforementioned career-building efforts. After our interview, in fact, she was "heading off to Glasgow to do a children's show called *What's Up Doc?*" She says she does "quite a lot of public appearances, as my schedule permits." Along with the occasional kids' show, she also does a fair number of adult chat shows – "the less tacky ones, like *That's Show Business*." Following her trip to Glasgow, Michelle planned to take part in a bike ride for Friends of the Earth.

With her manager, she took a trip to the U.S. last spring, concentrating mainly on the northeast. Michelle had spent a year in late adolescence living with a boyfriend in Venice, California while he attended film classes at UCLA. So she thought she knew America.

But New York City had some surprises for her in the shape of an English pub and then a fish 'n' chips shop offering free copies of the *Walford Gazette*, which included a cast photo with her in it. "That," says Michelle, "was quite funny."

As for her film project, she reports that the title is *Bad Medicine*, "a quite serious drama about urban culture in south London," which has heavy racial overtones. Gary Kemp (co-star of *The Krays* and *The Bodyguard*) is mentioned as co-star. "My character is a bit of a femme fatale," says Michelle. "She's a bit of a gangster, as well." Which, when you get down to it, is not all that far from Cindy.

–Dan Abramson

Tom Watt (Lofty Holloway), 1996

"A train derailed. The story about the train crash was on page two or three of this tabloid. The front headline was LOFTY WED IN MENTAL HOSPITAL."

Remember Nigel's recent pathetic attempts at organising a Queen Vic football team at the behest of Mrs. Mitchell. Little did he know, at one time there was a ringer right there in the pub. No, I'm not talking about the dearly departed Aidan from a few seasons ago, purportedly the Walford soccer team's rising young Irish star, who suffered a career-ending (life-ending?) injury before he ever played in a real game.

Rather I'm talking about that meek, asthma-ridden Queen Vic bartender known as Lofty, an original *EastEnders* cast member, whose alter ego, actor Tom Watt, is one of Britain's leading football journalists.

Just my luck I chose to come to London in late May the day before Watt's one-man, fringe-theatre play, *Fever Pitch*, is closing.

The play was adapted from the book of the same name written by Nick Hornby, who chronicles his obsession with the Arsenal football team (which also counts among its ardent fans Susan Tully (Michelle Fowler), Watt's erstwhile on-screen wife).

When Watt and I finally make contact on the telephone to set a time and place for our interview I realise that my timing couldn't have been worse since the Euro Cup competition was just starting and he was busy trying to firm up his press credentials for the opening ceremonies at Wembley Stadium. In addition to his acting career, Watt writes a regular column on football for *The Observer* newspaper, and has authored two acclaimed books (*The End* and *A Passion for the Game*) about the sport, which he also covers for BBC Radio and a London cable television station.

We end up meeting late afternoon in the lobby of Broadcasting House, the BBC's headquarters, where Watt is taping a session. A car is waiting for Watt, who apologises for the abrupt introductions and invites me to take a ride with him to north London, near where he lives and grew up. It's not easy interviewing someone in a car, but I'm willing to give it a shot, considering I might not get any other chance.

It's apparent that *EastEnders* was nearly a lifetime ago for Watt, considering he left the show nearly nine years ago. Yet the often-derided Lofty made Watt a recognisable face with the British public, which is not necessarily a bad thing for an actor.

I ask him if he's surprised that a publication like the *Walford Gazette* exists. Watt replies that he's not and remembers participating in a 1988 public television junket to America, in which he and several other cast members met *EastEnders'* fervent New York fans at a downtown pub for a WNYC fund-raiser.

Walford Gazette: *EastEnders* must be ancient history for you.

Tom Watt: It was quite a long time ago.

WG: Do people still associate you with Lofty?

TW: Yeah, there is that association.

WG: Has that been a hindrance to your career?

TW: No, a great help. I haven't been out of work for nine years. Know what I mean? How many actors can say that? It's been great. [*EastEnders*] opened a lot of doors. It was a great time. I worked with a lot of great people. It was a fantastic part. It was interesting. *EastEnders* changed how soap operas were looked at. Half of the [British] population was watching some of those early episodes.

WG: Does anything in particular stick out about your experience?

TW: For the three years I was in it, *EastEnders* was mad, wasn't it? It was on the front page of the newspapers. I remember one day, there had been some big train crash down in south London. People were hurt, somebody maybe even got killed. The train derailed. The story about the train crash was on page two or three of this tabloid. The front headline was LOFTY WED IN MENTAL HOSPITAL. It was insane and got completely out of hand. It's obviously more interesting being involved in it than it would be on the outside looking in sort of thing.

WG: Were you ever victimized by the tabloid press?

TW: No, what would be the point of victimizing the person who played the character that I played? There was no mileage in it. There were no newspapers to be sold. The only chance I got to be slagged off was things like a big trade union dispute that got very ugly and violent down in Wapping when Rupert Murdoch took over *The Sun* and Times Newspapers and sacked a lot of people. Basically, the idea was to break the unions. I felt quite strongly about that. There weren't a lot of people prepared to put up their hands and say, "I support the sacked workers." So I went down to Wapping a few times. Obviously, *The Sun* slagged me off. They printed a picture of me with the director-general of the print workers' union; we looked like the couple from heaven.

WG: Are you involved in any political issues now?

TW: No, I'm not involved in party politics at all. But if there's something that seems important to me, like that Wapping dispute, the miners' dispute, the Nicaragua Solidarity campaign, if I'm asked, I'll do something.

WG: What kind of acting jobs have you had in recent years?

TW: For the last three or four years, I've just seemed to go from one theatre job to another. I've also done the odd [television programme] episode and pilots for things. I did a few episodes of series for the BBC called *South of the Border*, a south London detective show. I did a film in 1990 for ITV called *And the Nightingale Sang*, which has been shown more than once in the States on PBS's *Masterpiece Theatre*. It was a love story set during the war. And I've done yards and yards of presenting stuff for Channel 4, Radio 1, Radio 3, Radio 5, and cable TV. I do features for a programme on Radio 4 called *Afternoon Shift* that aren't necessarily about football. I'm producing this summer a new television series for Channel 4 – a kids' sports show called *Rookies*. It's my idea; I'm producing it, directing it, and presenting it. It's the first time in a long time that I've done a long run in TV for a while. It starts in the middle of July and goes until Christmas. Ten half-hour episodes. We're looking at sports in an unusual way. We have kids doing a lot of the presenting and interviewing. Our experts will be kids, not adults.

WG: Weren't you in *Patriot Games*, the movie starring Harrison Ford?

TW: Four minutes. I was excited because I had never done a Hollywood movie before. I was in the only scene in the film that somebody doesn't get shot. The thing about TV and film, you need to be around, meeting people, give it time for things to happen. To be honest, I'm never around because I make a great living doing theatre.

WG: Do you prefer one medium over another?

TW: Obviously for the fun of it, stage work is in a different class. That's live. You can't compare it. If the right theatre job comes along I'll always say yes to it. I have a show scheduled in the West End in November.

WG: What do you write for *The Observer*?

TW: Match reports and features on football. The newspaper saw my two books about football and asked me if I wanted to write for them.

WG: I was already familiar with Nick Hornby through his second book, *High Fidelity*. I'm a huge record collector and could relate to someone who's completely obsessed with his records.

TW: Every time I go to America I come home with loads of tapes and records because they're so much more expensive here. The music I listen to is American music. I like blues, R&B, soul and hip-hop. I'm an American passport holder; my mum's an American. She's lived here for 30 years.

WG: A sales clerk from Virgin Megastore in London a couple of years ago told me you recorded a single of Bob Dylan's "Subterranean Homesick Blues." Were you serious about a music career too?

TW: No, that was just a good laugh really. Most people in soap operas have more money than sense, and I was no exception. I had these mates in Manchester who had a band and I worked with them ages ago just messing about doing comedy routines and theatre stuff. They had this idea for a record and this idea that I might like to pay for the studio time. Yeah, that went to No. 67 with a bullet, that one.

WG: Have any copies survived?

TW: Yeah, they do survive, but you can't get one in a music shop. I think they might be up in my mum's attic. It was a good record, an "electro'" version of "Homesick Blues." Great video. New Order was on the video. The only time they were ever seen smiling. It was just a good crack, you know what I mean. It wasn't the kind of record that people in soap operas are supposed to put out, a money-making exercise.

WG: Being a big fan of Arsenal, when you read Hornby's *Fever Pitch* did you say to yourself that this book was written for you?

TW: No, I'm nothing like the guy. I've known Nick for some time and in fact he contributed to the first book I wrote (*The End*, which was also about Arsenal). I don't particularly see eye to eye with him about football or even Arsenal. But I did see it as a really great piece of writing. There was a lot in it that's true about the game and about how people feel about the game. To be honest, when I was asked to do the show [*Fever Pitch*], my first reaction was to say no simply because it was a bit obvious. But I've never done a one-man show and the money was good. You know, bollocks, "When do we start?"

WG: What was the experience like doing a one-man show?

TW: It was fantastic. I really enjoyed it. You learn to concentrate. You can't afford to have an off night. When you're in a show with other people, you're doing your best every night, but there are nights when you're on and nights when you're off, when you let other people carry you, or people have a bad night and you're carrying them. But in a one-man show, you're in your jacks. It's just you. You've got to be on the case every night. And that's a great feeling. Every night is a good night because of that.

At Watt's request, the driver drops us off at an outdoor cafe, not far from where Watt grew up in Finsbury Park. He mentions to me that he still stays in contact with Susan Tully, who he calls a "great actress and a great lady." Watt notes that Tully lately has been very active in actors' union affairs.

We're about to enjoy our drinks, when a motorist waiting at the traffic light on the corner interrupts, honks his horn and yells towards Watt, "YEAH, ARSENAL!!!" It's always nice being recognised, offers an embarrassed Watt.

–Larry Jaffee

Michael Cashman (Colin Russell), 1996

"Dot, God bless her, didn't find out for months. She put two and two together when Barry was doing the washing in the laundrette, and she said, 'Oh! There's only one set of sheets'."

Strong, admirable, eloquent, and gay are just four of the adjectives that describe both actor Michael Cashman and Colin Russell, whom he portrayed on *EastEnders* in its early days. In fact, "East Ender" qualifies as a fifth word that describes both men. Cashman was born and brought up in the real-life East End, the son of a cleaning woman and a dock worker. These days he resides in Canary Wharf, one of the upscale housing developments built on what were formerly the slums and docklands of east London.

I met with Cashman at teatime in his spacious flat, where he lives with his longtime companion, Paul Cottingham. Cashman's home is every bit as spotlessly clean as the fastidious Colin Russell would have wanted. Our conversation begins with my asking Cashman if the flat has just been cleaned up for my arrival, or if he really is like Colin in that regard.

Michael Cashman: I think Colin was more than a little all right, so I don't mind being compared to him. To directly answer your question: Paul and I like to keep a nice home. There you go.

Walford Gazette: In an essay I wrote for the *Gazette,* I listed Colin as one of the characters I would most like to see return to Walford. Is there any chance of that happening?

MC: First of all, thanks for your support. That's very nice. I was approached by the show quite soon after I left, when I was appearing in *Bent (Editor's note: the acclaimed play by Martin Sherman, dealing with Hitler's persecution of homosexuals)* in London. And I gave them the indication that I was not interested at the time.

I really don't know. There are certain characters that it would be very attractive to work with again, like Pat or Dot. I suppose if I'm absolutely honest I have to say that there isn't much of a chance. I left for career reasons, because I wanted to do other things. In my opinion, going back would be like sending a signal to the industry that there's nothing else for me, that there is no other option. I've always considered myself a character actor, so that as I grow older and my talent grows into its better years, I hope to get my chops into the best material.

WG: I'm sure you will. You also write professionally. Please tell us about that.

MC: I was just going to follow up on that point. If *EastEnders* approached me about writing for the show, I'd say yes. I have an intrinsic knowledge of the subject matter. I was born in the East End. I live in the East End. I think I'd bring the show an authenticity that has been... diminishing.

WG: In what way has *EastEnders'* authenticity diminished over the years?

MC: In the beginning, it was realistic in media terms. When the show first came on, it was a slightly romanticised idea of the East End. But it was beautifully written and it certainly had a realistic element to it. I think what's changed in the show is that very strong feeling of community and what happens when secrets are exposed to that community. The show did it beautifully in the early days – material and information was seeped out. It wasn't on a conveyor belt that hit at all the community immediately.

The only thing these characters have in common is the community in which they live. And there have to be minor explosions going off that cause interaction between characters who wouldn't normally interact. I don't think that happens much these days.

WG: I've sensed that, these days, the show has been veering towards a more middle-class feel. Do you agree?

MC: Yes, very much so. If you watch the early episodes, you'll notice that many of the characters looked dowdy. Their hair was unkempt. They didn't wear make-up.

WG: Anita Dobson as Angie was the big exception, of course.

MC: Of course. Julia Smith, our producer, was famous for following the actresses into the make-up department and saying: "Get that stuff off your face. You're playing a working-class character, not a middle-class actress!" The show needs to be brought back to its grittiness and its integrity – which it's in danger of losing if everything is viewed from a middle-class value. *EastEnders* works because it's about a bit of culture that is fast disappearing.

WG: You live in the East End. Isn't gentrification taking place rather quickly?

MC: Gentrification was well under way by the time *EastEnders* began. Colin was considered part of that when he moved in.

WG: I guess he was meant to fill the gap left when Andy died and Debs moved away.

MC: He was. My 90-year-old nan said to me a little while back, "I hear you moved to Free Trade Wharf." And I said, "Yes." And she said, "But I used to clean the steps there." And I said: "But Nan, it's not the same place. They pulled the old building down." And she said, "I bet they had to, the way I cleaned the steps." That's an example of what I mean. The show is becoming too character-led, rather than community-led.

WG: I think the show would do very well to have you writing for it.

MC: Last time I tried to work as a writer, they told me I didn't have enough experience. I told them: "That's funny. I've had plays produced before. And as an actor I was certainly trusted when it came to helping with scripts that needed improving on taping days."

WG: It appears you haven't been considered fairly in comparison with the other aspiring scriptwriters.

MC: That's probably true. Someone told me they think the attitude is, "Well, if we let him write for us then maybe Adam Woodyatt (Ian) and other actors will want to write, too." That doesn't make much sense, does it? First of all, I doubt that Adam has any desire to write for *EastEnders*.

WG: Sounds like unnecessary paranoia to me.

MC: I'll tell you something at the risk of blowing my own horn too much. I'm pretty sure that, if I did write for the show, June Brown (Dot Cotton) might be interested.

WG: That alone should be the reason for hiring you! What kind of a story would you write for Dot?

MC: Oh, I'd love to see Nick Cotton winning the National Lottery – a few hundred thousand quid – and buying a house in Walford to rub a few noses in.

WG: It would all have to end in tears.

MC: Absolutely. To get back to the discussion we were having a bit earlier about minor explosions seeping through the community: The revelation about Colin being gay was a prime example.

WG: That's right. I forget, who found out first? Was it Dot?

MC: No. Dot was, in fact, the last to find out. Angie was the first. The "reveal" scene was in the Vic. Angie leaned over to Colin at closing time and said, "Problems?" and Colin said, "Yeah." And Angie said, "Men, huh?" And he went, "Yeah, you're right!" And then he tried to cover up, but she said, "It's all right, darlin'. I understand." There must have been this collective whoop all over the country when everyone who thought Colin was gay had it confirmed! Of course, one of the tabloids, *The Sun*, had already leaked it out that Colin was going to be gay when I arrived. The headline read: EASTBENDERS. On the show, Pat was the next to know. She tried to bed Colin, remember?

WG: I do. I think it was one of the show's finest moments. Pat thought that all Colin needed was the love of a good woman. Or a bad woman, in Pat's case – at that time.

MC: That's right. Colin's relationship with Pat really brought out the different sides to her character. If Colin was introduced into the show today, within two episodes everyone would know he was gay! Dot, God bless her, didn't find out for months. She put two and two together when Barry was doing the washing in the laundrette, and she said, "Oh! There's only one set of sheets." And then the shock-horror set in. I love the scene where Dot is going on about HIV and AIDS and how it was God's curse on homosexuals and all that. And Barry said: "But how about lesbians? They don't seem to be becoming infected." And Dot, of course, clinging to her faith, said, "Well, I suppose he's saving up something special for them." I think a lot of the audience felt the same way. But, as Dot made a sort of educational process with it, the audience did as well. I really think that's true. And that's how powerful and valuable *EastEnders* can be as popular drama.

WG: She wasn't homophobic. She was just ignorant, wasn't she?

MC: Yes. She liked Colin. She was a lonely person, and he looked after her a bit and tried to sort out her problems. He had time for her. Unlike her son and everybody else who would disappear around the corner as soon as they saw her coming.

WG: When you were being considered for the role, did your being gay become an issue?

MC: It's a generalisation, but it's probably true that a lot of gay actors won't play gay characters in high-profile work. The spotlight inevitably gets thrown onto them and the Inquisition begins. Julia Smith and Tony Holland [creators of *EastEnders*] told me they wanted me for this part. They showed me two years of storylines and they told me he was gay. They said: "It would be easier to cast a heterosexual actor, because he wouldn't have problems with the press. But we only see you in this part. Please say you'll do it."

I said: "I can't right now. I have to go home first and discuss this with Paul, because he'll be affected. And I've got to talk to my family as well. I need their backing." They said: "Fine. We'll wait to hear from you." I got complete backing from Paul and my family. I had many responsibilities to take on when I took this role. One was that if I was playing a member of a minority, I mustn't do anything in my public life that undermines the integrity of what I'm doing on-screen.

I did have a falling-out with the actor who played Guido – Colin's second lover on the show – because I said, "I'm leaving, and the baton of responsibility gets passed on to you." And he said, "There's no responsibility." Well, I feel that if you're playing a member of a persecuted, misrepresented minority, there is a responsibility that is incumbent upon you. And if you don't take it on, then you are undermining the rights and reinforcing the deprivation of that minority.

WG: Doesn't Colin still own that flat in Albert Square, the one now occupied by Ian and Cindy?

MC: Yes, I think it's still technically his.

WG: I hope he'll show up one day to get back his CD/stereo stack-up equipment, which is still sitting there. He never took it with him.

MC: And what about all that rent? Cindy and Ian owe thousands!

WG: I particularly admired the way you played the scene where Colin finds out he has multiple sclerosis. Dr. Legg tells him, and this prompts his departure from the series.

MC: I'm so glad that not only did we inform the public about multiple sclerosis, but we broke the stereotype about a gay man getting AIDS. At first, Barry was going to be the character who developed MS, and Colin would be the one to look after him. But stories have a way of changing on these shows.

WG: Off to a wildly different topic. You've been to America many times. What are your opinions?

MC: I love New York… the Upper West Side, Chelsea, the Village. I love the American energy… I love the American challenge. Americans don't take (expletive deleted)!!! They go: "What? Why!!!!" Over here in Britain, they go, "Oh, all right…" and then they whine about it to themselves.

WG: Tracey Ullman once said, "The biggest British export is envy."

MC: I've heard that and I'm afraid I agree. I blame the tabloids that proclaim that somebody is successful, and Brits go: "They've got it! Why have they got it?!!" The Americans' attitude is: "They've got it I can do the same!" I think it's to do with the fact that we're an island race. We're frightened of anything that will make us feel small. Small in the world, small in our communities, small in our intellect.

WG: Don't hold anything back, Michael.

MC: I'm not known for my shy and retiring side.

WG: What do you think when you constantly see *EastEnders'* younger generation mentioned in the tabloids?

MC: You really want to know? Those kids love to see their pictures in the papers, and they think it heightens their credibility. They're young. Maybe some day they'll learn that, in fact, media exposure reduces their credibility. And the tabloids here are the cruellest type of media anywhere in the world. They're vile. They sent a young man to my door once so they could get a picture of us together to "prove" that I was cheating on Paul.

WG: I see perched on your telly there is a photo of you with Paul and Pam St. Clement (Pat) and Letitia Dean (Sharon). Who were you close with from the cast of *EastEnders*?

MC: June Brown, Pam, and I were very close indeed. We'd sit in the canteen and we formed quite a clique. Wendy Richard was with us a lot. So were Letitia and Sue Tully (Michelle). And Leslie Grantham (Den) and I were quite good friends. We got on terribly well – we'd love to get in little digs at each other. Leslie and I were both frustrated about stories being leaked to the press by someone on the show. I was one of Leslie's trusted few, I'm pleased to say.

WG: I vaguely remember reading that you wrote a novel about soaps. What happened to it?

MC: Yes, I did. How did you hear about that? It was called *Bloody Soap*. I wrote this murder mystery about the soap world, three drafts' worth. The publishers were really only interested in a thinly veiled kiss-and-tell book about *EastEnders*, which I wasn't interested in writing for many reasons.

WG: That darned integrity popping up again!

MC: I didn't want to compromise with it. It will be finished and it will be published because the characters and the situations have great potential. All I can say is that it is about a soap that has Greater London as its setting.

WG: I wish I could have seen you last Christmas, when you starred as Herbie in *Gypsy*, when it played the North of England.

MC: It would have been a schlep for you, wouldn't it? I loved doing it. Herbie's a great character. The man drives himself against his will, and, hence, to ulcers.

WG: Didn't Colin have ulcers?

MC: He should have, with Barry around. Barry drove Colin almost to murder, but not ulcers. Wasn't the man tortured enough?

WG: Did you meet the actor who played Barry during his audition?

MC: No. In fact I said to Julia Smith just before I was introduced to him on the set, "I feel like a bartered bride." I did feel rather that I'd been hoodwinked into an arranged marriage. I like Gary Hailes, who played Barry. Although he was heterosexual, he was quite relaxed about playing a homosexual. But he was not prepared for the public reaction. He took a lot of crap, on the one side from the people who were homophobic, and on the other side from people who did not like the way he was treating Colin! One lady hit him with a canteloupe or something in a supermarket.

WG: Barry was always spilling stuff on Colin's computer.

MC: Yes, chocolate sauce. I remember the chocolate sauce. Very sticky. He always left his dirty socks lying around, too. That would do me in.

WG: Please tell us a little about your political work.

MC: I was chairman of the Stonewall Organization for seven years – that's a gay civil rights group. I helped found it, along with Sir Ian McKellen. We'd lobby and campaign through the major institutions like Parliament. There were amazing developments, and I'm proud of my work there. My main strength was political lobbying. I recently resigned from that chair because I had to let it go and move on. But I'm still actively involved. It would be like cutting off my right leg to leave completely.... I've still got a lot to do with my life!

–Tim Wilson

Pam St. Clement (Pat Butcher, later Evans), 1995

"I remember saying to Julia Smith, 'How can this character be watchable long-term? She's so full of venom that she hates everyone except Angie, and maybe Roly'."

As far as I'm concerned, Pat Butcher is the "diva" of *EastEnders*. She doesn't stroll, she formidably struts her way through Albert Square, sometimes leaving grown men and women quivering in her wake. Pam St. Clement, who portrays La Butcher, is a woman of operatic proportions – and I am not just referring to her ample figure. Pat's emotions are large – and anyone who dares cross her should bloody well expect a tidal wave of recriminatory bile to flow his or her way. Hey, they don't call it soap opera for nothing!

So I therefore assumed that Pam St. Clement was herself a lady of Pat Butcher-style emotions and habits. This turned out to be extremely far from the mark. I learned the error of my assumptions when Pat invited me to her dressing room, backstage at Elstree. She greeted me at the door with a warm smile, a sweet peck on the cheek, and a respectful handshake. Not your basic prima donna greetings.

Furthermore, it turned out that, while I was on my way out to Elstree, a BBC Arts programme had decided to interview Pam at the same time she had agreed to see me. Now, a true diva would have gone for the BBC interview, leaving the *Walford Gazette* guy in the lurch. Pam, instead, honoured her commitment to me. When I expressed surprise, she whispered to me in a reassuring tone: "It's all right. I think I'm going to enjoy this a lot more." Which is a nice way to start an interview....

Walford Gazette: Was Pat originally brought in as a long-term or short-term character?

Pam St. Clement: She was brought in short-term to begin with, although she was mentioned in the early "books" as being part of the history of Albert Square. She was Pete Beale's ex-wife, as well as the mother of his child, David. Early on, Pat's biography was changed quite heavily by one particular script editor, who shall remain nameless. I think this was done to make her more consumer-friendly, to blend her into the community and help the audience root for her relationship with Frank. I did not want Pat to lose her rough edges that quickly.

WG: What about Frank? Was he intended as a long-term character? Were you interested in Pat being happily married? How did that happen?

PSC (smiling): Hold on. You're asking a lot of questions at the same time, aren't you?

WG (trying to get a grip): I didn't want you to be late for your interview with the BBC.

PSC: Don't worry. I shall tell them when I'm ready for them.

WG: Thank you.

PSC (laughs): All right, where were we? Right. There was all this tweaking of Pat's initial biography, which made me very angry. Because I realised that all the new writers who would join thereafter would see Pat as a different character. I thought it was terribly important for Pat to retain those roots. But, actually, it's been put back on track again the last couple of years.

Pat has had to change anyway, for a variety of reasons. But, back to your original question: I really had to think long and hard about coming onto this show to play this sort of character. I was initially brought in short-term but obviously the powers that be felt the character worked, that there was a place for her, and so I was asked back.

I knew this job would literally change my life – my career and my personal life. This is such a high-profile show in every respect. Every one of us is subject to press attention sooner or later, and it is not always pleasant. But it's worth it, because the show is good, and it is satisfying to be on it. I had never before wanted to work on a show beyond six or nine months. But this time it was different.

WG: Have you had the time to do other acting jobs since you joined *EastEnders*?

PSC: Gosh, no! It's impossible now that we're on a roller coaster of an hour and a half screen time a week. This show is very bold in terms of shooting. We do a lot of location work – the schedule is tough. Right now, Pat is involved in a lot of different areas, different sets, such as the pub and the car business, as well as the laundrette. I'm working scenes in the cafe these days because the show is developing a strong friendship between Pat and Kathy. All that plus the family scenes with Janine and David. I'm all over the place! I'd like to flesh out your earlier question, Tim. Pat was first brought onto the show to act as a sort of dramatic catalyst with Pete and Wicksy – and to give Angie a drinking buddy. Pat was brought on to make waves and wreak havoc for three episodes, and then she went back to Guildford or something like that.

WG: Not Mudchute [the East End borough]?

PSC: No, not Mudchute! Somewhere a bit more suburban, like Guildford. Pat went off in a taxi with a few bob she got from Wicksy and Angie, and that seemed to be it. Julia Smith, the show's producer, liked the character and wanted her back. I remember saying to her: "But Julia, how can this character be watchable long-term? She's so full of venom that she hates everyone except Angie, and maybe Roly." And Julia said: "Ah, but there's quite a way for us to go to find out about this character's defence mechanisms and how she's survived on the edge all these years. Once we start to get to know her – peel off the layers of onion to find out why the fists go up before the brain engages – that's what will draw in the audience...." And that's exactly the challenge I was given, which was very smashing. Pat's attitudes about men, how she was determined to use them before they used her – that defensiveness. All of that has been used over the years. Most of that onion has now been peeled away.

WG: What about those episodes in Clacton? Did you feel these were even more insightful about Pat's history as a bad mother to David and Wicksy?

PSC: Not really. I think those episodes were more concerned with David's point of view – his resentment. They did accentuate the extraordinary love/hate relationship between Pat and David, though. After all, he did not come back to Albert Square to make it up with his mummy. Albert Square was his last refuge.

WG: *EastEnders* seemed to bring in David carefully, with great calculation, as a buffer for Frank's eventual departure.

PSC: Well, I had been agitating about David for years. Every so often, I'd bring up David's existence to the script department and tell them, "Don't forget about David." I felt strongly that when Nick Berry left the show he had left a very large and particular slot open for a young and very good-looking male actor.

Sid Owen, who plays Ricky, is certainly very attractive – and he certainly appeals to the young audience – but he didn't really fit that slot. I think that too many publications have unfairly labelled Ricky as being stupid. I think of him as a bit naive and certainly ingenuous. As a result, many females want to mother him, as well as the other thing.

Anyway, no one had yet filled that sort of easy-come-easy-go, laid-back, Wicksy slot. The show brought on David, who does fill that slot. I always knew he was a card we had up our sleeves that we just had to use, some day. And I was right.

WG: In my opinion, the casting of Michael French as your son and Nick Berry's brother is something of a miracle – you look so much alike!

PSC: It's true. The writer Hilary Kingsley said that even our hair curls the same way. And it does!

WG: Changing the subject... during the early 1980s, you appeared in two films about Hitler's Germany called *SS* and *The Bunker*. Could this be described as your Nazi period?

PSC: Yes, I guess it was. In *SS*, I was a Bavarian wench. And in *The Bunker*, with Anthony Hopkins as Hitler, I was Hitler's cook, who loyally died in the bunker with everybody else. Maybe my character really poisoned the bratwurst and thereby ended the war in Europe! I did not play your stereotypical, dyed-in-the-wool Nazi. Those were the days when I was doing television everywhere in Europe, except England.

WG: Meanwhile, back in Walford... why did they replace Rebecca Michael, that beautiful little girl who played Janine? Was she too much like her character?

PSC: No. Rebecca got to the stage where she wanted to do other things with her out-of-school time. She made a conscious choice not to be an actress, at least for now. She told her parents, and they asked the show to release her, and that was that, at least for now.... She's a lovely child... and she had this wonderful pouting quality, which was perfectly natural.

WG: Have there been any storylines with which you disagreed?

PSC: I wasn't thrilled when Pat and Frank left the Queen Vic. I don't really know to this day why they did that. Because they replaced us with Eddie Royle, and he didn't last two years. Maybe they weren't happy with a family living at the Vic with a small child. But it's very hard working on that Vic stage set all the time. Both Mike Reid and I had dodgy backs. So maybe it was a blessing in disguise.

WG: I would love to see a two-hander episode between Frank and Pat when he does come back.

PSC: I think that would be very interesting. But I don't know about Mike Reid, if he's coming back to play Frank. I hope he's back here some day. But I know that he's happy right now, doing other work, enjoying his family, and taking it easy.

WG: Do you see Pat as the "diva" of *EastEnders*?

PSC: Yes, to an extent. She's a proud woman, and she has suffered. In that respect, I suppose you might call her a diva. But she is hopefully never superficial, which the term "diva" suggests. In the months following Frank's abandonment, you get to see the final "jam" on the "bread and butter" of her development. She is not relying on anybody. Pat is entirely on her own this time. In my opinion, that sort of story, of a woman doing, is the core of what ongoing drama – or soap opera, if you must use the term – is all about!

–Tim Wilson

Caricature of Dot Cotton drawn by June Brown's daughter Louise Arnold

John Altman checks out the Walford Gazette at an Irish pub in New York's Greenwich Village
(PHOTO: DANA GORDON)

Anita Dobson playing bartender at a Florida pub (PHOTO: MELISSA BERRY)

Leslie Grantham, 2005 (PHOTO: JULIE GRANT)

Walford Gazette co-founder Dan Abramson meets Nick Berry on Central Park South in New York, 1992

Bill Treacher and Tom Morrell, who recorded the tribute song "Free Arthur Fowler"

Wendy Richard, terrier Shirley Brahms, and Larry Jaffee, London, 2003

Wendy Richard and John Burns, London, April 2008

Pam St. Clement signs an autograph for Esta Asteroff at WLIW-TV
in-studio fund-raiser (PHOTO: GENEVIEVE RAFTER-KEDDY)

Michelle Collins, Greenwich Village, New York, January 2005
(PHOTO: DAN CALLISTER)

Russell Floyd and fan Amy Stoller, WLIW studio fund-raiser, 1999

Michael Greco, WLIW's Luanne Miller, and Larry Jaffee, Greenwich Village benefit, 2002 (PHOTO: DANA GORDON)

Shaun Williamson and Lucy Speed, Elstree Centre

Nadia Sawalha and Larry Jaffee, Granada Television, Manchester, 2000

Leila Birch and Larry Jaffee, Covent Garden, London, 2003

Perry Fenwick in his Elstree dressing room, 2003

Hannah Waterman in an EastEnders meeting room, 2003

Nick Bailey, Jake Jaffee and Larry Jaffee, New York, 2003

Derek Martin, Kensington, London, 2008

John Bardon meets American soap star Eileen Fulton at Friars Club,
New York, 2005 (PHOTO: SUE COLFIN)

John Altman.
18th August, 2004.
'Old Jersey',
Ch. Islands.

Dear Larry,
Thanks for the copy of 'The Gazette.' Glad you enjoyed your trip round South-west london. It was good to see you.
I am on Jersey in the Channel Islands, in another 'American' musical. Having a ball. Hope All is well with you.

All The Best
from

Handwritten note from John Altman

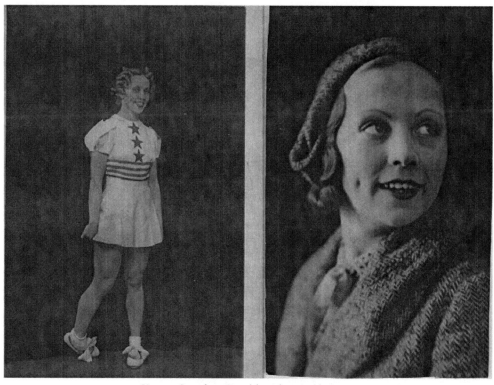

Letter from Gretchen Franklin

Young Gretchen Franklin, dates unknown

Barbara Windsor (Peggy Mitchell), 1998

"Anybody who raised Phil, Grant, and Samantha must be a mad cow!"

I now believe in second chances, and it's all because of Barbara Windsor. Why? Because she gave me a second chance, you see. I suppose I'd better explain. Two years ago, a pesky IRA security alert prevented me from reaching the *EastEnders* studios at Elstree where I was to interview Ms. Windsor. Unfortunately, I had to be on a plane back to New York four hours later, leaving no time for us to meet. She was not at all amused with the situation, especially since she'd failed to receive my message of apologies from the actor who was our go-between.

I quite rationally thought I'd blown my chance forever, but put in for another interview request this past January and, miracles of miracles, she said okay! Ms. Windsor informed me in a non-B.S. sort of way that she wasn't too thrilled at having been stood up and that I'd better not even contemplate a repeat performance. (I think I could literally hear her eyebrows raise over the phone.) After my emphatic assurances had reached their conclusion, we agreed on a time to meet the following day. I showed up at Elstree that next morning 20 minutes early with a bouquet of roses, which I hoped would be accepted as a token of my apologies.

Barbara Windsor, to my relief and delight, was a great gal. She was tremendously energetic, articulate, and an awful lot of fun to be around. We sat in the actors' lounge next to the make-up and hair room, accompanied by a charming and lovely publicity representative named Sarah Burke.

I silently resolved to make the most of the second chance that I was given by this wonderful lady.

Walford Gazette: Thank you for talking to the *Walford Gazette*.

Barbara Windsor: That's right, darlin'. You showed up early, with roses yet! Thank you, they're lovely. I'm very happy to do this actually because I realise your readers don't know anything about me except that I'm on *EastEnders*, and I thought they might like to learn a bit about why I am. Peggy [Mitchell] can be quite a piece of work at times, and I hoped that maybe American viewers can grasp from this interview that I'm not so bad.

WG: I'll make you sound like Mother Teresa.

BW: You don't need to go overboard. Let's just do an honest interview, and let 'em make up their own minds.

WG: It's a deal. Why don't I break Americans' image of you by revealing that you once had plans to be a nun.

BW: Oh, okay, yes, I did receive a scholarship to Our Lady's Convent School but that obviously wasn't my calling, was it? I loved performing from a very early age and I suppose singing in a choir just wouldn't do it for me.

WG: Was it also true that you were born Barbara Ann Deeks in Shoreditch, east London, that you were evacuated to Blackpool when you were a very small child and that you later joined classes at a dancing school with the improbable moniker of Madame Behenna's Juvenile Jollities?

BW: That moniker may sound improbable, but it's all true, sweetheart, believe it or not. It's all there in my autobiography, which I've promised to update to include what's gone on in my life since *EastEnders*. Maybe I'll get around to it this year.

WG: Well, we at the *Gazette* would love make it available to our readers when it's published. I, for one, cannot wait to read about Madame Behenna.

BW: I can trace a note of sarcasm from you, but I'll let it pass.

WG: I'm actually serious.

BW: Oh, you New York types. I've been over there quite a lot over the years and I've got you lot figured out, you know (laughs).

WG: Both Tony Caunter (Roy) and Dilys Laye (Nigel's mum-in-law Maxine) told me in interviews that they came over to the U.S. to work on Broadway. You did too, didn't you?

BW: I was on Broadway in *Oh, What a Lovely War*. I actually first visited New York in 1963 for the premiere of a film I appeared in called *Sparrows Can't Sing*. I know you shouldn't talk about your reviews, but these were fantastic. It was this cockney film that opened at some little artsy cinema and caused quite a buzz.

WG: I read somewhere that it had subtitles.

BW (nods): Isn't that something? *EastEnders* doesn't have subtitles over there, does it? *Sparrows* somehow captured people's imaginations. I was flown over for the opening, put up at the Plaza Hotel and before I knew what hit me I was booked to appear on TV shows like *What's My Line?* and *The Tonight Show* with Johnny Carson. I was really feted and it was a marvellous experience all the way round.

WG: You must have been the toast of the town.

BW: It was amazing. Even Judith Crist, who was a very influential, tough critic at the time, likened me to Judy Holliday. And to me Judy Holliday was the best. *Born Yesterday* is one of my favourite films.

WG: *Sparrows Can't Sing* was your first big break, then?

BW: No, my first real break was a musical called *Fings Ain't Wot They Used T'Be*, and yes, it was a cockney show. So I went from a cockney musical to a cockney movie and eventually to a cockney telly programme. Well, I'm a cockney lady and damn proud of it. Anyway, back to your Broadway question. David Merrick was an enormously powerful Broadway producer who put on *Hello, Dolly!* and all sorts of top shows, and he decided that he wanted to bring me over to New York to do *Oh, What a Lovely War*, which already had been running in London, without me in it! He apparently told the show's director, Joan Littlewood, that he wanted her to get that "little girl from *Fings Ain't Wot They Used T'Be*." By then I already had gathered quite a bit of steam from *Sparrows* and a TV sitcom called *The Rag Trade*. The papers were beginning to do write-ups on me, and I was sort of, you know, commercial. It was lovely that Mr. Merrick requested that I be hired for Broadway on the basis of my work. Living in the States, he wasn't aware of the hype beginning to build around me.

WG: I guess that was good preparation for joining the cast of *EastEnders*.

BW: I was prepared, but nothing can really prepare anyone for that kind of press attention. It's crazy being on *EastEnders,* darlin', crazy time.

WG: Being on Broadway in the 1960s must have been a crazy time.

BW: It was an experience I wouldn't trade for anything. Our show was on at the Broadhurst Theatre, which was directly across the street from Sardi's restaurant, the Broadway hangout. I'd sit in there with Barbra Streisand, who was doing *Funny Girl* around the corner, and Sammy Davis, Jr., who was doing *Golden Boy* down the road, and we'd all have tea together between the matinee and evening performances. People like Paul Newman and Warren Beatty and Cesar Romero came to our opening night. My dressing room faced the street. and I could hear couples walk by after failing to get in to see *Oliver!* or *Funny Girl*, and they'd say things like (*Babs in her best Noo York accent*), "Oh, Harry, what's this? So we can't see *Funny Girl*. Let's see this *Lovely War* thing." Most of the time the audience didn't have a clue as to what the show was about. We'd be singing our guts out onstage, and there'd be this ticker tape sort of thing behind us that would announce stuff like 15 GASSED AT LE MANS, 200 BLINDED AT TOULOUSE because it was set during World War I, and I'd look out and see some very confused faces. It was all very funny. Well, what the hell, at least Paul Newman got it. In fact, he said it was one of the best bits of theatre he'd ever seen. But he's not the norm, is he? While I was over there, I was asked to audition for the lead to musicals like *On a Clear Day You Can See Forever*. And get this, I was asked to go to California to audition for this new TV show called *Laugh-In*.

WG: You could have been the "Sock-It-To-Me" girl.

BW: Judy Carne was a girlfriend of mine. I was more than happy that she went out there for *Laugh-In,* and became a success. Quite frankly, I wanted to go back to London and be a star on my home turf. It's just what I wanted to do. I wanted to make my mark here (England) and get married here and all that sort of thing. I know I made the right decision; no regrets. I still come over to New York to see shows and visit friends every two or three years. I'd actually like to come over a lot more often these days because as I get older beach holidays don't lure me at all any more, darlin' [laughs]. The sun doesn't quite hit me right anymore, d'you know what I mean? I enjoy New York tremendously, so I'll just have to get on the old plane and get over there!

WG: An interview with you would not be complete without mention of your *Carry On* films. How many did you do?

BW: Eight, well nine if you count a compilation. They were all simply brilliant to work on, and before you ask I have to say my favourite was *Carry On, Henry* because it was a period piece and I love anything to do with another period of time. It was set during the reign of Henry VIII and I got to wear one of these wonderful frocks, which was also used in the film *Anne of a Thousand Days*. Some critics thought that our film was better. I agreed with 'em.

WG: Is it true that you weren't allowed to show your belly button in the *Carry Ons*?

BW: Absolutely true, and isn't that silly?

WG: Well, I guess *Carry On, Hawaiian* wouldn't have ever been considered.

BW: (laughing) With the budgets we had we'd only get as far as Blackpool. Those films were always dismissed as rubbish but they were obviously loved by the public and constantly get shown on telly nowadays.

WG: Belly button or no belly button, the *Carry On* films established you as something of a sex bomb, didn't they?

BW: Yes, but more in the style of Goldie Hawn, who I was often compared to. People started referring to me as "Bubbly Babs." My mum was a bit annoyed at the way I was being perceived and would tell people, "My daughter's been trained to be a proper actress. Not the boobs and bottoms type, you know?" (laughs) The *Carry On* films absolutely solidified my name value, and because of them I got to work with Sid James, Kenneth Williams, and Hattie Jacques, great comic actors in England at the time. I got to do an enormous amount of theatre all over Britain on the strength of my marquee-value name, in large part thanks to the *Carry Ons*.

WG: You were actually the biggest name that *EastEnders* had ever added to its cast.

BW: Wendy Richard certainly had name value but I suppose it was regarded differently because she was part of the original cast. When I was brought on the press made such a big deal. They made it seem like I was brought on to "save" *EastEnders* or something, which was ridiculous.

WG: Well, I believe it was the worst creative period the show has ever had.

BW: I won't totally disagree with you there. At least the show decided to move into the "Sharongate" storyline, which gave it an enormous push, creatively and ratings-wise. Peggy was brought on as an extension of the Sharongate story because she was Phil and Grant's mum. I understand why the show was uneasy about bringing on any really well-known actors because they want the audience believe in and identify with the character without having any of the actor's baggage in their heads, you know what I mean?

Before *EastEnders,* I was actually thinking about becoming an actors' agent. I'd been touring all over Britain doing shows like *Guys and Dolls* and *Entertaining Mr. Sloane* and I was so tired. In *Guys and Dolls* I was playing a character much younger than myself. I could get away with it onstage, but all the energy expended took a lot more out of me [than it did to] those chippies in the cast. I was literally days away from sending out letters to various agencies saying something like: "Ageing ex-sex symbol who knows a lot about the business and has a keen eye for talent seeks new vocation," when I got the call from my agent's office about *EastEnders.*

WG: Wasn't it practically by public mandate that you would play Peggy Mitchell?

BW: Chris Evans, a very popular chat show host over here, turned to the camera one day and said: "*EastEnders* really has lost it. I wonder what can be done about it. I know! Babs behind the bar! I want you to fax or phone the show and let them know that you want to see Babs behind the bar!" And they did. Little did Chris and the viewers know that I was already in negotiations with the show. Spooky coincidence, eh? June Deitch, the *EastEnders* casting director, had been to see me in a London show to prove that I was not the bubblehead from the *Carry Ons*. She apparently saw me in a new light. We met backstage after the show, and I casually mentioned that I'd like to play my own age for a change. I suppose that fixed something in her mind. At the time, the show was thinking about bringing back Peggy. I was thrilled. I could rest my tired bones working on a marvellous television show that I deeply respected. I was very excited about the possibility of playing this feisty lady who would come in and shake up her two boys' lives.

WG: Did you know any of the cast members already?

BW: I had already met Ross Kemp (Grant) at a charity function and he was lovely to me. He was crazy about the *Carry On* films. I had also met Steve McFadden (Phil) at the odd function, and we got on well.

WG: What was it like to join the cast?

BW: The first weeks on the show were very odd in so many ways. I'd really thought I'd known the score about television, but for God's sake, 27 million people watched that first episode I appeared in! I'm essentially a theatre lady and I couldn't think of an audience in terms of millions at a go. I was thrilled to be on the show, but I'd be lying if I didn't admit that a few things weren't quite right about Peggy at the beginning. On a purely superficial level, the wig didn't fit right. And the clothes weren't right either. They appeared too downmarket. I was particularly worried about how the character was viewed by the producer and writers. I saw her as much ballsier than they did. I think they envisioned Peggy as this rather sad, vulnerable lady who spent all her time worrying about her children.

WG: Sounds like they saw her as another Dot Cotton?

BW: Exactly, which I really didn't want to do. Luckily, Corinne Hollingworth came back to produce the show very soon after I came on and agreed with me that anybody who raised Phil, Grant, and Samantha must be a mad cow! She was great. I remember she capped our first big meeting with "And, by the way, Peggy's going to run the Queen Vic. She's not going to be allowed to just sit in some flat polishing her nails." It was like a dream. She let me go out with the costume designer and choose Peggy's wardrobe, which needed to be a lot more flash and upmarket. Corinne and I worked on getting Peggy right, and I finally began to believe that this was ready for the West End!

WG: What was it like when you did get behind the bar?

BW: I was very, very nervous. I still get nervous. Even today! I'm about to do my first scene with Ross [Kemp] after our two-week holiday break, and she has a go at him, and I'm all anxious about it. (laughs) I take my work very seriously even though I can have a laugh about things.

WG: Surely Peggy's more than a mad cow?

BW: Of course she's more than a mad cow. She's from the old school, the generation, which doesn't put up with rubbish from anybody. She always loved Eric, her first husband, who fathered the three kids, even though he would occasionally get drunk and row with her. He made a widow out of her, didn't he? She can get through practically anything because she's tough, tough, tough.

WG: What can you tell me about your first day on the set?

BW: I was so petrified I was literally ill. I was being driven up by my boyfriend, and we had to stop because I needed some fresh air. We were in a town called Henman, and I was standing in some sort of gutter inhaling the air, and I looked up and the first thing I saw was the flat I shared 20 years ago with my ex-husband Ronnie Knight. That story goes in my book, that's for certain.

WG: What's your book called?

BW: *The Laughter and Tears of a Cockney Sparrow.* Read it and weep! And hopefully laugh a bit.

WG: A friend sent me a tape of the National Television Awards and I watched you accept the award for Best Soap on behalf of the *EastEnders* cast. You seemed so proud.

BW: I am proud, I really am. I think the show goes from strength to strength. We not only won the National Television Awards last year, but we won the BAFTA [the British Academy Awards]! That was absolutely remarkable because the show never had been nominated before and we won over a brilliant series called *This Life.* The BAFTA was shocking enough but winning our second National Television Award in a row was a big surprise. I really thought it might be *Coronation Street*'s turn. We did have a gangbuster year.

WG: Without giving away details so we don't spoil anything for American fans, what's in store for Peggy?

BW: Her first love interest. It took them long enough! Yes, poor Peggy's going to go through an awful lot. Her sons will continue to give her to no end of grief and there's a big health scare right around the corner.

WG: Is there any other character on *EastEnders* you would have liked to play?

BW: That's an easy one – Angie. I'm really great friends with Anita Dobson, and once I turned to her and said, "So how 'bout it, 'Nita? Come back to the show even if it's only for a few weeks?" Her reply was, "I've had my time on the show already, darling. Anyway, they have you now. You're behind the bar now and you're great." I thought that was a very kind and generous thing to say. She's a wonderful, wonderful lady and I adored her as Angie. She went vastly O.T.T. [over the top] but it worked, my God, it worked. She got to do her own make-up and pick her own wardrobe, just as I was allowed to do.

WG: Angie and Peggy were in-laws for a while, weren't they? I dream that one day Sharon will return, remarry Grant, and it'll all end with a big catfight between Peggy and Angie at the wedding reception in the Vic.

BW (laughs): Yes, like Krystle and Alexis in *Dynasty*. Dream on, kid, dream on!

WG: And Den could show up and seduce Peggy.

BW: Now you'll get me dreaming. Stop this at once!

WG: When is Peggy going to sing in the Queen Vic? You've got a sensational voice, I gather.

BW: Peggy doesn't have any talent except for meddling in other people's lives and running a pub. I did sing at my 60th birthday party last August. I sang "You Made Me Love You" in A flat! I hope to record an album this year in addition to updating my autobiography; when I'll find the time I do not know.

WG: You must be quite a role model for the younger actors on the show.

BW: It's lovely that it's now my turn to lead newcomers of all ages around by the hand and introduce them to the Queen Vic set, which Ross and Steve were so kind to do for me. You might notice that when a new actor does his or her first scene in the Vic that their hands are most likely shaking. I could usually tell this by the way the beer in the glass moved from side to side. They are understandably freaked out, as I was. But I do what I can to help them believe that they'll be fine. If they show up on time and are fairly serious about their work they'll have no problems with me!

WG: They're very lucky to work with you. I certainly feel very lucky to interview you.

BW: Oh darlin', that's all right. Now let's find this bouquet some water. It must be gasping.

Postscript: Barbara Windsor writes that North American public TV viewers should stay tuned (in about two years) for a two-hander episode featuring her and Pam St. Clement (Pat).

–Tim Wilson

Steve McFadden (Phil Mitchell), 1993

"Me and Ross [Kemp] have the same hairdresser, and she says that I have much more hair than he does... I really do have more hair."

I was having an extremely stroppy Monday when my answering machine recorded the first phone call I've ever received from a citizen of Walford. "Hello, Dan," said a familiar voice on tape. "This is Steve McFadden. I'm an actor in *EastEnders*."

That last sentence was not necessary. I had already identified the voice of Phil Mitchell – that noted east London family man, entrepreneur, and street thug. Steve McFadden and Phil Mitchell speak in the same non-dulcet tones. "I just was interested in your publication," said McFadden, "and I was going to ask you a couple of questions about it...."

Abramson's cry of delight could probably have been heard in Britain without a telephone. It drowned out the rest of McFadden's message. You see, I had been trying unsuccessfully to get through to authentic East Enders for several months.

When I rewound the tape, I heard McFadden provide his phone number and the best time to call him on the set at Elstree Centre in Borehamwood, Hertsfordshire. "Okay," he said in closing. "Hope to hear from you. All the best. Bye now." My heart sang. I'm not sure exactly what tune it was singing. But Nick Berry's "Every Loser Wins" does come readily to mind.

Two days and half a dozen phone calls later, I get through to McFadden just as he was leaving the Queen Vic. I start by telling him that I had recently seen the "three-hander" episode with Sharon, Grant, and Phil, adding, "You make a marvellous drunk."

"Thank you," he responds, with becoming sobriety. I follow with, "Have you had much experience?" McFadden quips, "Loads," then proceeds to ask me several questions about this *Gazette* and the methods by which we distribute it. The main reason for his call, he says, was to compliment me and Larry Jaffee on the quality of our publication.

"Most fan newspapers are cawling," he says. "But yours concentrates on humour instead." The transatlantic connection was not all that good. I couldn't figure out what "cawling" meant. Was this some new cockney slang term to include in our glossary? "Not 'cawling,'" he yells, in a chief mechanic's angry voice. "Crawling! You don't crawl or act sycophantic. I like that." I like it, too. Hearing Phil Mitchell of the East End tell me that he likes my style is a big moment for me. The week had become a lot less stroppy.

Unfortunately, I then ruin things by acting progressively more sycophantic through the rest of the conversation. But McFadden is understanding about that for the first few minutes. In any case, some degree of sycophancy was called for, as I had two favours to ask of him. The first was, would he distribute copies of this *Gazette* to his fellow backstage Walfordites?

"I'll do that," says McFadden. "But we already have it slipped under our dressing-room doors. It's very popular here on the set." My heart began singing again. This time it was definitely the "Victory" theme from *Chariots of Fire*. I then ask McFadden for an interview. "I don't usually do interviews," he replies. "I've had some bad experiences with English newspapers. I really just called to tell you that I like your paper."

Somehow I get him to change his mind, but only on condition I fax him the interview in advance of publication for his approval.

It immediately occurs to me that this is how Phil Mitchell would have responded to a similar request. I mean, let's fantasise for a moment: If I were to ask Frank Butcher for an interview, he probably would take me to lunch and tell me more of his life story than I would care to know. By contrast, Grant Mitchell would say "No f-----g way!" in a tone that implied violence.

But Phil Mitchell would carefully weigh the odds and demand to see the interview before it went into print. There is obviously a great deal of Steve McFadden in Phil Mitchell and vice versa.

"The trouble with interviews," he says, "is that implicitly you lie." "Isn't that equally true of acting?" I ask. "Yes, but at least you get to read a script." I then mention Hilary Kingsley's *EastEnders Handbook*, which states that McFadden and Ross Kemp (who plays Grant Mitchell) regularly have portions of their heads shaved to create identical male-pattern baldness, so they will look like brothers.

McFadden laughs at that in a tone of friendly sibling rivalry. "Me and Ross have the same hairdresser," he explains, "and she says that I have much more hair than he does. She didn't say that just because she likes me better than Ross. I really do have more hair."

Walford Gazette: What do you like best about *EastEnders*?

Steve McFadden: Its realism. Tough guys in the movies and on other shows just act tough. But, on *EastEnders*, they also show the softer side of Phil, the whole 360 degrees. After a robbery, you see him go home, head for the loo and do some washing-up.

WG: When you were younger, which actors were your role models?

SM: Anthony Hopkins, Maggie Smith, Maggie Steed, and, of course, Brando.

WG: Is there any element of Brando in your portrayal of Phil Mitchell?

SM: I think more Fred Astaire.

WG: Who are Phil Mitchell's favourite actors?

SM: The comedy star, George Coe, plus Phil is a big fan of Liz Taylor.

WG: Were you given a "biography" of Phil to work from when you started on *EastEnders*?

SM: Yes, and it was quite interesting. It said that Phil's politics are to the left of the Socialist Worker's Party and to the right of the National Front. That sort of left me playing an anarchist.

WG: Does the work schedule on *EastEnders* leave you time for any other acting jobs?

SM: No time at all.

WG: How do you feel about the increased workload of three episodes per week, rather than two?

SM: Ours is not to reason why, ours just to do or die....

At this point, McFadden starts a conversation with someone else in his dressing room, and asks if we could finish the interview. My natural sympathy then got out of hand. The glossary calls this "Giving him the old flannel."

"Listen," I say, "thanks for the interview.... I can't speak for my readers, but there's a lot of people in North America who consider *EastEnders* a terrific programme...."

"Yeah, yeah, yeah..." replies McFadden, in a tone that sounded more annoyed than Beatle-ish. "Have a nice week, Dan, and fax me the copy." Oh well. I guess I didn't do very well on my first test of Walford Macho. Then again, it has often taken me a while to get the hang of certain skills. Bicycle riding, for example. (Several other analogies also come to mind.) But I intend to work on this and be less sycophantic in future conversations with Walfordites. In fact, if Ross Kemp ever grants me an interview I'll verbally knock him into a cocked hat!

–Dan Abramson

Danniella Westbrook (Sam Mitchell), 1996

"I was making too much money at a very young age and I let things get way out of hand. What I've hated the most is that my mum doesn't deserve the stick she's got in the press for my problems."

Individual cast members from *EastEnders* have in many cases been good to me – granting interviews for this paper and taking me to lunch at assorted Elstree restaurants. But Danniella Westbrook is the only one of that company of players who managed to get me onto the set of Albert Square. This was an exquisite experience for which I shall always be grateful.

So grateful, in fact, that – out of respect – I'm now going to type up the Westbrook interview before I start writing about what it was like to stand on Albert Square and walk in the footsteps of Dirty Den, Angie, Pauline, Arthur, Rachel Kominski, Mark, Michelle, Ruth, et al. The interview began with my welcoming Danniella back to the show (*Editor's note: the first time*) and asking her if she had missed *EastEnders* during her years away from Walford Borough.

Danniella Westbrook: Oh yeah. Very much. I particularly missed Gilly, Ross, and Steve (Kathy, Grant, and Phil). We were very close when we were working together. I'm also good mates with Michelle Gayle, who played Hattie Tavernier. She's a pop star now. I'm so proud of her. Sid Owen is great as well. It's wonderful to be back with him again. He ain't thick like Ricky! I suppose I missed the security bit of *EastEnders*. They were a second family, and it was tough leaving them in the first place. But hey!!! It's great to be back!!!! I'm with my second family again and I'm getting paid more this time!

Walford Gazette: In professional terms, what were you doing during your years away?

DW: I did some "panto," and some stupid chat shows, and a series with Timothy Spall called *Frank Stubbs Promotes*. I played the title character's niece. It was fun to do and it was a nice part. But it didn't give me as much satisfaction as *EastEnders*. The money was brilliant, though. And that made up for a certain lack of creative stimulation. You know what I mean?

WG: Is there any truth to the rumour that BBC actually stands for Bloody Bad Cash?

DW: Huh? Where'd you hear that rubbish? Oh, the money's not bad, although you don't see any of us coming to work here in a limo. We certainly do all right. Don't get me in problems with my bosses. I've got enough troubles.

WG: I wouldn't dream of it. You initially got your start on *EastEnders* as an extra, didn't you?

DW: Yeah. I whizzed past Den and Angie on roller skates. They were the greats, the legends, weren't they? My dad had actually known Leslie Grantham (Den). They'd been mates. Not from acting. They mixed socially.

WG: Then, a few years later, you came back to the show as one of the main characters.

DW: Yup. I read for the producers five times. Four hundred girls were up for the part, and I beat 'em all to it. Lucky, lucky me!

WG: I can see why they auditioned so many girls. Sam was, after all, slated to be Ricky's first love interest.

DW: And the Mitchell Brothers' sister. Very important to get that right.

WG: Did you meet Sid Owen while you were auditioning?

DW: Sort of. He was hanging around the reception area to check out each auditioning girl as they walked in and out. I guess he was concerned about which of the girls he'd have to be snogging with in a few months' time. He and the receptionist must have compared scores. I remember walking past Sid and saying, "Hello, Sid. I'm Danniella. It's good to get a look at you in person, even if I don't get the part."

WG: That sounds like a very good strategic move for a first audition.

DW: Hey, I was just being friendly! I never flirt. Ha ha ha. Anyway, I thought I didn't get it. I went away with my family on holiday in Florida. When I came back, the first call I got was from the wardrobe people, who said, "Where've you been?! You start work tomorrow! What's your size?" My agent called two minutes later to make it official. Surprise!

WG: Which of the episodes in the first few years were your favourites?

DW: The episodes where Ricky and Sam eloped to Gretna Green. Loved those.

WG: They weren't actually done in Scotland, were they?

DW: Are you kidding? They were done in bloody St. Albans. *(Editor's note: The historic town of St. Albans is just a short distance from* EastEnders' *home base at Elstree.)*

WG: But you did go to Spain to tape Sam's re-entry into *EastEnders*.

DW: That's true. And I only had to work for about an hour on-camera. I spent the rest of the week lying on the beach, working on me tan and sipping pina coladas. If everybody else got jealous, tough!

WG: Nice work if you can get it. (At this point I nod towards her dressing-room wall.) Do you have a fixation on Leonardo DiCaprio? He's plastered all over your wall.

DW: No, not a fixation. I'm just deeply in love. I think he's the most brilliant actor around, and also the most gorgeous. I used to be mad for Rob Lowe, but I've gone off him. I now touch one of Leo's photos before I go off to the set to work.

WG: Lucky Mr. DiCaprio. Who is your favourite actress?

DW: Jodie Foster, without a doubt. Everything she's done since she was real young –*Taxi Driver* and *Bugsy Malone* – to the latest stuff like *Nell*…. She's so great! And she can direct, too. I'd love to meet her someday. If Dustin Hoffman and Laurence Olivier can visit the set of *Coronation Street*, why can't Jodie and Leo come here?

WG: What did you think of DiCaprio's performance in *The Basketball Diaries*?

DW: Ooooh!!! Aren't you clever! I know where you're going with this. You really mean to ask what I thought of the drug storyline in that movie, considering I've had first-hand experience myself. You clever boy!!!!

WG: Sorry. I hope you're not offended.

DW: No. Okay, first of all, he was amazing in that film. Second, yeah, it's no great secret that I had a very bad problem with drugs and alcohol over a two-year period. But thank God the worst of that is over – I hope. I spent probably about a hundred thousand pounds over those two years on cocaine and booze. I was involved in a rotten relationship with a pop star. He didn't want me to have a career, so he could be the famous one in the household. In a moment of clear-headedness I dumped him a week before we were supposed to get married. I spent a bit of time drying out in a drugs-and-alcohol clinic and then moved back home with my mum and dad. That was the best thing I ever did.

WG: It sounds as if your life was a soap opera in overdrive.

DW: What else can I say? I was making too much money at a very young age and I let things get way out of hand. What I've hated the most is that my mum doesn't deserve the stick she's got in the press for my problems. I was uncontrollable. She did everything she could but I had to hit bottom alone.

WG: The tabloids were a bit uncontrollable themselves in their coverage of your problems. How has the public reacted to you?

DW: Mostly okay. It didn't help that Sam had behaved like an immature bitch and walked out on Ricky. Some people would yell things to me in the street or in a shop. One bloke must have been wound up by something he saw about me in the paper. He walked up to me in a club, called me something unprintable, and smashed a glass in my face. I've got the scars to prove it. I've experienced so much for a 22-year-old. It's unreal. But I'm not going to say I regret it, because I've learned a lot and I would rather have made my mistakes now than in ten years' time. From now on, I'd like to reserve all the drama for my work, not for my private life.

WG: Before our interview officially began I heard you talking on the phone to your mum about giving your cousin five hundred pounds to help get him out of his dodgy neighbourhood. Do you worry about him getting into drugs?

DW: Sure. But that's not the whole problem. He's in an area where there are these gangs of really rough lads hanging about. I hope he does use the money to move to Bristol. That'd be the best five hundred pounds' worth I'd ever get.

WG: That's the type of story the tabloids should cover.

DW: I don't care. They'd still wind up getting in a dig about the amount of money that went up my nose.

WG: I see a certain tabloid headline you've got pasted on your mirror. WHAM, BAM, THANK YOU SAM.... Charming.

DW: Oh, come on. It's a laugh! I don't care if they harp on the sex thing. That can be fun. They're always at it with Martine (McCutcheon) and Patsy (Palmer) as well. They never give us a break.

WG: Have there been any good catfight stories involving the three of you?

DW: No. Sorry, we get along just fine, thank you. We even hang out together when we have time. And Dean [Gaffney, who plays Robbie Jackson] is like our mascot. He's our little friend, we love him.

WG: The Bitches of Walford… that could be a great one-off special at the very least.

DW: It would work, dammit! We could be great in one of those. Our three characters are each bitches in their own right. Tiffany's the clever one, very streetwise. Bianca's spoiled. She's really been spoiled by her family and by David in every possible way. Sam is manipulative. But she ain't no gold-digger like Bianca or Tiff. Sam is massively thick. She thinks her brothers can bail her out of any difficulty. Well, she's in for a rude awakening some day.

WG: Does she still love Ricky?

DW: I think that was really a puppy love kind of thing. She really gets her kicks by teasing and tormenting him. Sam's out for a good time, while Ricky likes TV and the pub. Sam also likes a bit of rough, a bit of sleaze. A moth to the flame, she is. Like I used to be, ha, ha.

WG: Where do you think she'll be on New Year's Eve, 1999?

DW: Lying on a beach on the Costa del Sol in Spain, sipping a pina colada and snogging her latest boy toy. By then, she wouldn't be caught dead in Albert Square.

WG: Is she a Peggy-in-training?

DW: No. Peggy is stronger and smarter. As I said earlier, Sam is massively thick. She better hang on to her looks for as long as she can is all I can say. And, unlike me, she doesn't have any talent to fall back on. Let me say for the record that it is so brilliant having Barbara Windsor playing my mum. She's fantastic. Did you know that Ross Kemp had a huge crush on her when he was ten? And now she's playing his mum.

WG: I think most viewers have noticed that there's an Oedipal subtext in that relationship between Grant and his mum.

DW: Speaking of mums, mine is picking me up in a few minutes. Let's go off to the green room.

Whereupon I follow Danniella to the "green room," which at Elstree is not green at all, just a designated meeting place for actors to unwind. The room is equipped with a TV and VCR, and Danniella tunes in to a British version of the old American series, *This Is Your Life*. On-screen, a soccer star is being gushed over by the show's host. When I look over at Danniella, I am surprised to see tears in her eyes. "This show always gets me choked up," she explains. "And I don't even like that bloke!"

And I thought she was a tough chick! At this point, her mum, Sue, and 14-year-old brother, Jay, walk in. Sue Westbrook is a youthfully attractive blonde with a blazing smile, who would not be out of place herself in the cast of a soap opera. This is apparently Jay's first visit to the studio. When his elder sister asks if we would like to stroll through Albert Square, we both breathlessly say yes. I then politely mention to Ms. Westbrook that, in the past, the Elstree security forces have seen to it that reporters from the *Walford Gazette* were almost always kept away from the sacred environs of Albert Square.

Danniella's reply is worthy of Sam Mitchell. "Well, Jay hasn't seen it yet and I'm showing him around. I could give a toss if the Elstree people don't like it.... C'mon!" And so, footloose and fancy-free, I accompany the Westbrook siblings onto the outdoor stage set at Elstree. The show is shutting down after that day's taping, and there doesn't seem to be anyone about. Danniella quickly shepherds us onto the lot, past George Street and Nigel's video shop, and then past Phil's auto repair garage "underneath the arches."

Whereupon I look up and see Albert Square in living colour, with the park and the Vic and the Fowlers' exactly where they are supposed to be.

I've been looking at the brightly lit vision for perhaps thirty seconds before a distant voice yells "Lights out!" and the lights in fact do go out, providing an equally exquisite view of Albert Square at nightfall.

I smile at Jay Westbrook, who smiles back. My feelings at this moment are very hard to describe. But, if you've ever been on a long voyage and then suddenly realise that you've made it "home...." Well, anyway, that's the general idea.

–Tim Wilson

Kim Medcalf (Sam Mitchell), 2000

"When I first started getting the scripts I used to hear the lines first in my head with her (Danniella Westbrook's) voice saying them!"

When I was a kid my much-missed Uncle Bob from Tennessee once said to me, "It takes a big man to own up to a big ol' crush." I will always be grateful for all his well-meaning yet vaguely incoherent words of advice and encouragement regarding matters of the heart. So O.K., I'm owning up to having a crush on someone right now. It developed one day in mid-January when I met Kim Medcalf (a/k/a Samantha Mitchell Butcher No. 2) in the green room at the BBC Elstree Television Centre, where the *EastEnders* actors sit and relax between shooting scenes.

Ms. Medcalf arrives decked out in typical Sam gear – tight jeans and a halter top – *Charlie's Angels Gone Walford*, if you will. I'm immediately entranced. Actually I've developed many a crush on nearly all of the *EE* actresses I've met over the years, ranging from simple admiration to unbridled (and hopefully concealed) lust. Sorry, I won't elaborate on which one inspired which stirrings!

Kim strikes a particular chord with me. I surmise she reminds me of someone I had a big crush on in my distant youth: Samantha on the ABC-TV series *Bewitched* as played by the truly lovely Elizabeth Montgomery! I certainly wasn't the only guy who adored Samantha/Elizabeth, believe me (*Editor's note: Me too*). Those of us, young and old, who desperately yearned to be in Darren's shoes must have numbered in the millions. That's who the truly lovely blonde enchantress now sitting before me reminds me of, and I am enough of a fool to use that to help break the ice for the interview.

Kim Medcalf: *Bewitched*? Yes, I've heard of that series, but I've never seen it. I think it was a big hit over here in its day, as it was in the States but they don't show reruns of it, do they? Maybe on digital or satellite?

Walford Gazette: Oh, that's right, you guys don't have the same TV as we do, where sitcoms can be shown endlessly on local channels and TV Land, especially late at night.

KM: At least we can buy or rent videos and DVDs of TV shows now. I'll see if there are any of *Bewitched* out! Funny that her name is Samantha, as well.

WG: I'd love to see you play that Samantha. I gather that Nicole Kidman will be playing her in a big-screen version with Jim Carrey as Darren.

KM: That sounds great! But man, she always gets the best parts! (laughs) I wish she'd leave some for the rest of us.

WG: But let's talk about YOUR Samantha role on *EastEnders*. First of all, I have to tell you that I saw your debut on the show about two months before the nation did.

KM (confused): Oh yeah? Really?

WG: I was spending a weekend at the story consultant/script writer Tony Jordan's house, and he sat me down with an advance copy of the *EE* episodes set in Spain.

KM (laughs): Wow, lucky you!

WG: I was mostly interested in seeing them because I was very curious about what the new Sam would look like and how she'd be reintroduced to the viewers.

KM: And?

WG: And I turned to Tony, who'd been in the kitchen making the Sunday roast for him, his family and myself, and said that the *EE* team did a great job in selecting a new Sam and her reintroduction was one of the better aspects of the episodes! He already knew I wasn't very fond of plotlines involving capers of any kind.

KM: Oh, right, it had Peggy and Frank running around Spain chased by bad guys out to get back their money. Well I'm glad you liked *me*! (laughs)

WG: You and Barbara Windsor – I think that's the most comical stuff she's ever had to play as Peggy. She was wonderful in those first scenes when she found out Frank was alive after all.

KM: Yep, you're right on that one. She was very funny. She got to dip into her comic resources from those days when she was such a big star in those *Carry On* films.

WG: I was pretty impressed that they chose an actress who somewhat physically resembled Danniella [Westbrook, the original actress to play Sam] and not someone so different-looking as to jar the viewers.

KM: Yes, I see what you mean. It also helped that Danniella wasn't out on the Friday show and I was in on the Monday show, d'you know what I mean? She'd been off-screen for about two years by then, I think.

WG: That helped, too! Sam and Mark Fowler are really two of the biggest recasts the show has had to do thus far. I don't really count Scarlett Johnson as Vicki because the original Vicki was a little girl when she was last seen leaving Walford with her mother Michelle.

KM (proudly): Oh, I love Scarlett, she a lovely young girl. I'm her on-set mentor, you know.

WG: Oh? I just heard about that from Lucy Speed (Natalie).

KM: It's a fairly new system where someone from the cast is assigned to more or less help them get used to the schedule and such. I think it makes a lot of sense.

WG: Me, too. All the soaps should do that. You were certainly a newcomer to TV when you got this job, right?

KM: I hadn't done *anything* on TV before – anything! Just theatre. I didn't even know what a "boom" [microphone] was. It used to just mean an exploding sound for me until I found out it's like a big Q-tip with hair which the sound crew use to record the show from an audio standpoint! (laughs) I dunno, in a way it was quite good that I didn't know anything at all about filming – I might have been more scared and nervous! Everyone was so kind to me as I learned on the job.

WG: Like Barbara?

KM: Definitely Barbara. She's a pro from the old school, which is the best sort, and she was very, very good to me. It really helped that my first scenes on the show were done on location in Spain and not on the sound stages over here. If my first bit had been to stride into the Queen Vic and shout, "Hello, Mum!" I would have been rather petrified!

WG: In an interview I just conducted with Lucy Speed, I included questions from fellow *EastEnders* viewers back in the U.S. and I thought I'd repeat the practice here. Irene Feldman from New Jersey sent me this question: How did you prepare to play a role once played by someone else? Did you watch tapes, for instance?

KM: Well, Irene from New Jersey, thanks for your question. Uhhh... I actually watched the show a bit when Danniella had been on so I had a distinct memory of her to work with. What I basically did was to read a prepared, detailed biography of the character which was provided by the production office. I did sit down to watch a five-minute clip of Danniella but I quickly realised I didn't want to carry on watching because I was afraid of falling into doing an imitation of her, d'you know what I mean?

WG: Absolutely.

KM: I'll tell you something weird: When I first started getting the scripts I used to hear the lines first in my head with *her* voice saying them! But that changed over time, thank God, as I hopefully made the character my own and I gave her *my* voice.

WG: And you have. Here's a question which might strike you as a bit unfair but I'll ask it anyway. In what way is your Sam different from Danniella's?

KM (laughs): Yes, it's a *lot* unfair but I'll answer it as best I can! O.K., let's see... I think much of it is down to the fact that I'm playing Sam at a different time in her life. Danniella played Sam from when she was around 16 years old! She played Sam, I think, as a little girl, sheltered by her over-protective brothers and mother and who never really grew up. I think I play her as a young woman trying to find her place both in a career and in relationships with the opposite sex.

WG: At least you didn't have to walk around the streets of London dressed as a wedge of cheese when poor Sam had that awful promotions job back in the early 1990s!

KM (laughs): Oh, I heard of that! Never saw it, though. Poor Sam, indeed –the silly cow probably thought it would lead to a modelling contract or something.

WG: Dana from NYC has this question: Any new older men to come in Sam's life?

KM: Well, Dana from NYC, I think perhaps there very well might be. Let's all hope he's attractive, eh?

WG: She did have her share of older men, didn't she? That's one thing she had in common with Bianca besides Ricky. David Wicks, Beppe di Marco, Trevor Morgan, that modelling agent guy. I'd love it if Michael French came back to the show as David and he could be Sam's boyfriend but would also get it on with Kat Slater in the PortaKabin when Sam wasn't around.

KM: Oh, how rude! (laughs) Michael French was *brilliant* as David. I'm afraid that's not likely to happen, unfortunately. He's moved on and is doing other things and is quite successful. He's a big TV star over here.

WG: Esta from Florida had this to ask: Who picks Sam's wardrobe? I realise East End barmaids do have a certain style but some of her behind the bar ensembles are a bit over the top.

KM: Gee, *thanks*, Esta from Florida! (laughs) Yeah, yeah, Sam has worn some questionable items from time to time but this year she's going to be looking more upmarket and businesslike since it looks like she'll get sucked into the Ian Beale empire this year.

WG: Dear God, what a revolting image.

KM (laughs): It'll be fun, though. I can't wait.

WG: I'm kidding. Actually I think it would be quite good. To be honest I think the writers haven't been sure of how to write for Sam for a while. This Ian/Sam partnership might bring her into focus a bit more.

KM: I agree. I'm quite excited about the storyline they have coming up for her.

WG: Esta's got another gem: Does Sam ever think about getting a proper job and *not* telling Phil about it until she starts? That way he can't go ahead and ruin it for her.

KM (laughs): Good one, Esta! Well obviously she won't find herself working for Ian with Phil's help! (laughs) Not unless he *really* wanted to punish her for something. I think in this case one of the reasons she takes the job is to punish *him*.

WG: Totally off the subject of Sam, is it true you're a singer as well as an actress?

KM: Yes, that's right. Before *EastEnders* I'd appeared in a production of the Kurt Weill musical *One Touch of Venus*. I played Venus! It was done at the King's Head in north London.

WG: I've been to the King's Head. It's a highly regarded theatre with a pub up front, and in the back there's a stage the size of a postage stamp.

KM: You've obviously been there! Well done. It was a wonderful experience, doing that show. I'm happy to say that the critics were very complimentary to the production as well as to myself. It was directed by an American named Timothy Childs. He's directed a lot of productions of *Annie*, including the revival that was on Broadway a few years ago.

WG: I absolutely believe you could have a future doing light comedy roles like the ghost Elvira in Noel Coward's play *Blithe Spirit*.

KM: That role is a few years off for me I think, but thank you very much. I hope to be doing things like that in the future. *One Touch of Venus* had light comedy and singing combined. I do love to sing and I hope I can show that off on telly some day. And I'd looooove to do a film musical like *Grease*. I really loved that movie when I was a little kid.

WG: Here's something I noticed that you haven't been showing off on telly as Samantha lately. That pout.

KM (laughs): Oh, what on earth are you referring to? When I began on the show I thought that was the sort of face a saucy barmaid like Sam would pull along with her punters' pints! My boyfriend finally told me I looked like a duck when I did that and would I please stop?

WG: Is he still your boyfriend?

KM: Yes, he is. We just came back from New York City where we saw the New Year in together. We had the best time. We stayed in a gorgeous hotel with a concierge and everything! (laughs) And we saw that incredible Broadway musical *The Producers*.

WG: Hey, you could play Ulla, the sexy Swedish secretary. Perhaps in the West End?

KM: The lady who I saw play Ulla was amazing. I gather she's been doing it since the very beginning. I would *love* to be in that show some day. I adored New York. I love the people a lot. And the shopping was fantastic, obviously.

WG: Did you get recognised in the stores when you were out shopping?

KM: Yes, by Brits but not by New Yorkers or other Americans – how disappointing! (laughs)

WG: Is it true you actually studied law for about three years before you decided to make the transition to performing?

KM (nods): Yes, I did study law for three years.

WG: What kind of law?

KM: Medical law, mostly. After three years I began to seriously question why I was pursuing a career in law when my gut was still urging me to be a performer. So I guess I was a bit of a late bloomer compared to other young actresses starting out. I was in my mid-twenties by the time I entered drama school. I went to the Central School of Speech and Drama, which is quite a good one to attend. I learned a lot there.

WG: We're nearing the end of this interview unfortunately since it's almost time for you to head back to the set. Who do you socialize with from the *EE* cast when you're not here at Elstree?

KM: Oh, let's see, there are a few of them I really enjoy spending time with off the set. Michelle Ryan (Zoe) is so lovely and a great person. Gary Beadle (Paul Trueman) – he's a right laugh. Charlie (Brooks, who plays Janine) is a sweetie and a good mate. And there's Nick Bailey (Anthony Trueman) – love him! If I didn't have a boyfriend I was so crazy about....

WG: He's a terrific guy. I just interviewed him – that should be in the next *Gazette*.

KM: I'm sure he was never at a loss for words, was he? (laughs)

WG: No, he wasn't, thank God.

KM: I hope this has been all right. I hope you've got what you needed.

WG: It's been great, thank you very much, Kim. Now go out there and make the barmaids of Britain proud!

KM: Uhhhh, excuse me, right now Sam is a club manager, thanks very much!

WG: Oops, sorry.

Before she ran off I ask her if she ever watches the American TV series *24*, of which I'm a huge admirer and which is a big hit in the U.K. She says she loves it so I give her two tapes containing the first seven episodes of the 2002–2003 season as thanks for giving such a terrific subject interview. She's thrilled to get them and says she can't wait to watch them with her boyfriend in their flat in Notting Hill. Her boyfriend – the Darren to her Samantha – is a lucky fella.

–Tim Wilson

Sid Owen (Ricky Butcher), 1998

"Let's move on to something else. That one's been done to death. Ricky Ain't Thicky!"

My fears of using the phrase "Thicky Ricky" around Sid Owen prove groundless. It's Sid, in fact, who first uses that label as we lunch at a pizza-and-pasta restaurant in London with the tape recorder playing. So I reply by pretending to have seen the "Thicky Ricky" designation in print once or twice, even though I know darned well that the British tabloids had been insulting Sid for most of the 1990s by interchangeably calling both the actor and his fictional character that unfortunate nickname. (In Britain, "thick" is a popular slang term for "stupid," which Sid, emphatically, is not.)

Walford Gazette: When exactly did that insult begin?

Sid Owen: Probably two or three years into my run with *EastEnders*. I don't know where it actually appeared first. I'd like to know. Because then I'd go over to the newspaper office and thump that so-called journalist. If it was a lady, I guess I'd just shout the "B" word at her in front of her colleagues and that would make me feel much better. But if it was a bloke, I'd definitely thump him one.

WG: I wouldn't blame you. The labelling of Ricky as "thick" reduces him to a one-dimensional character, doesn't it? I don't think Ricky's genuinely stupid, anyway.

SO (grinning sarcastically): Thanks for your support, Tim. I genuinely appreciate it. No, seriously. I can handle it when I see a photo of me in the paper accompanied by some crack about "Thicky Ricky." Guys used to think they could get away with shouting it at me in nightclubs. Let's say they know better now! Ricky is just a sort of lovable innocent, really. He's just bungling his way through life the best way he can. All right, so he'll never win any prizes for his brainpower. So what? He's a good bloke, a good mate to his friends and he can work miracles with motors.

WG: In an episode that ran in Britain last year, Ricky's sister Diane told Bianca that, when Ricky was a little boy, he was labelled "a bit slow, a bit thick" and that he'd started to believe it. Growing up, she said, he would sometimes use that label as an excuse for not trying harder to learn.

SO: And, in that same scene, Bianca told Diane that she'd heard on the Square that he couldn't tie his shoelaces until he was fourteen! Isn't that a bit far-fetched? I mean, c'mon... Maybe it's true of Robbie Jackson!

WG: Ricky's Dad, Frank, sometimes treated him like he was not very bright. Frank would roll his eyes in exasperation when Ricky was not being particularly quick on the uptake.

SO: Yes, he did. But Frank loves him and cares about him. So it was all right. It was sort of a comic relief for the show, wasn't it? Anyway, Frank obviously loves his kids even though they're not terribly clever. Diane got knocked up by some French guy before she even got to see the Eiffel Tower. Am I right?

WG: You are correct, sir!

SO: Janine's probably not going to be the Brain of Britain, either. Am I starting to sound defensive? Okay, let's move onto something else. That one's been done to death. Ricky Ain't Thicky!

WG: You started on *EastEnders* when you were about sixteen. Prior to that, you had appeared in an Al Pacino movie.

SO: Yes. It was called *Revolution*. I guess you could say it was not one of his more successful efforts.

WG: Among snide cinephiles, that film is known as *Duh British Are Coming*.

SO (politely but without laughter): Oh, that's funny. Hmmmm. I did that movie when I was fourteen, and it was a really brilliant experience. Al is a genuinely great guy, and we got on extremely well. I visited him a few years ago in New York and had a laugh together. I still have his home phone number, but I wouldn't just ring him out of the blue: "Hiya, Al Baby! It's Sid! How ya' doin'?" I don't think so. He's a big star.

WG: So are you, Sid.

SO: C'mon! I'm nowhere near as big as Pacino. He's an international movie star, for God's sake. Big difference!!! Anyway, he's really cool.

WG: What made you want to start acting in the first place?

SO (quietly): I was very young when my mum died and my home life was not very good. So I jumped into acting head first, doing the Anna Scher theatre workshops. Anna and the school became a second family, a good family. And *EastEnders* eventually became another family, a *great* family!

WG: I gathered from Edna Dore (Mo Butcher) that you all got on well.

SO: Absolutely. Mike (Frank) is great to work with. Pam (Pat) is great to work with. Edna was great, Sophie Lawrence (Diane) was great... even that little brat who first played Janine! We were close. Thank God we all liked each other.

WG: What about Danniella Westbrook, who played Sam?

SO: Sure, Danniella was a lot of fun. She's a wild girl. Very tough but also very sweet. We enjoyed working together. I wish she could have been on longer after they brought her back from Spain. That seemed a bit of a waste. She came back and then left so quickly. Anyway, Ricky's got Bianca to torture him, for the time being.

WG: Didn't you already know Patsy Palmer (Bianca) from your Anna Scher theatre days?

SO: We practically grew up together. We'd known each other for years. It was weird when she started on the show and we began playing the "Ricky and Bianca Get to Know Each Other" bit. I had already spent a lot of time with Patsy. I think we were both seven when we met.

WG: I'd like to backtrack to Ricky and Sam. Do you consider the episodes dealing with the break-up of their marriage to be some of your best work?

SO: Not at all. I think my best work has actually been done in the past ten months, because some absolutely brilliant stuff was written for Ricky and Bianca to play. Big problems to sort out and a very big, dramatic... tragedy I guess you'd call it. You Yanks won't see it for a really long time, I hear.

WG: Yes, by the time those episodes get here, I'm expecting to see the wedding of Ricky and Bianca done in either Virtual Reality or Three-D.

SO: And you'd get to throw rice at us and see it land in our hair! That'd be pretty funny.

WG: Wasn't Ricky a racist for about two minutes in 1989, after his Indian girlfriend's father forced them to break up?

SO: Yeah. He also smoked cigarettes for about two minutes. But he stopped doing that because the show didn't want him to set a bad example for the kids who watched. The racist thing was strange. He just stopped one day from seeming racist. The show didn't tell me anything beyond what I read in my scripts. I was a little relieved that he wasn't going to keep acting that way. John Altman (Nick Cotton) had gotten a lot of hassle from people on the street because his character was a racist. Being a recognisable TV celebrity is difficult to cope with.

WG: Who were Ricky's other love interests, besides Sam and Bianca? Let's see if we can dredge them up. Sometimes it seems as though Ricky has only been with Sam and Bianca.

SO: What about Natalie? How quickly you forget! I guess she really wasn't a love interest, though. He just shagged her, like he did Mandy, the street urchin. The Indian girl was his first love interest, I guess. I can't remember her name.

WG: Shireen.

SO: Right, Shireen. Then there was that hairdresser's assistant. And I definitely can't remember *her* name.

WG: Uh... Marie.

SO: Oh, right. Aren't you a source of useless information?!

WG: I know.... I frighten myself sometimes. But what about Tiffany? Wouldn't it be fun for Ricky and Tiff to get drunk and fall into bed?

SO: They'd have to get *real* drunk to get it on, wouldn't they? They're just like chalk and cheese.

WG: Let's get into some more personal stuff, Sid, which our readers do enjoy to a certain extent. Do you share Ricky's passion for autos?

SO: Well, let's see.... I've got a Mercedes and a Porsche in my garage. Does that answer your question?

WG: Ricky would have to win the national lottery to acquire those...

SO: ... or become an actor in a long-running television show!

WG: You live in a house in the countryside now, don't you?

SO: Yes. In Cambridgeshire. It's very nice, if I do say so myself.

WG: And I hear you have a beautiful girlfriend.

SO: God yes, she's lovely. Her name is Lucy Braybrook. (grins) She's a model.

WG: Oh. Big surprise!

SO: She's got brains as well, Tim. She's also sweet and funny and we enjoy a lot of the same stuff. Believe it or not, we both like to hunt for antique furniture. And we both like to cook.

WG: You're a stay-at-home kind of guy, then?

SO: These days, yes. I have gone wild in the past, clubbing and all that. These days, I like to pull out a bottle of wine and watch a video on my 43-inch TV screen. That's my idea of a good time.

WG: Do you plan on staying with *EastEnders* for a while?

SO: I don't know. I've currently got an offer for another TV series, which will be firmed up by the spring. I'll know by then. I'd leave the show, take a few months off and start working on the other show by the end of the year.

WG: Can you provide us with any details about that project? Perhaps Sid Owen: General Practitioner?

SO: I won't talk about that. What's a general practitioner? Is that a Yank occupation?

WG: Fuhgeddabout it. What does Patsy Palmer think about the possibility of your leaving? She was quoted in a magazine called *The Big Issue* as saying, "No. No! He can't go without me. Not my Rick-kay!"

SO: She's a very smart girl and she certainly understands this situation. All of us face it eventually, this need to go off and do other things. Gillian (who plays Kathy) is taking a six-month break to explore what's out there. Paul Bradley (Nigel) is leaving too.

WG: Back to Rick-kay. Do you believe those rumours which state that Ricky is a closet stamp collector?

SO: Don't make me gag on my pizza classico! I mean it. Ricky does actually develop a hobby which ties in with his job – and it ain't stamp collecting. Besides, Ricky's not a closet *anything*. What you see is what you get where he's concerned.

WG: You don't see the writers changing him in any radical way?

SO: No. Why should they? I don't think the audience wants him to change. They like the same old Ricky.

WG: What would you like to have the writers come up with for Ricky?

SO (smiling): I want him to shag every hot girl in sight, baby.

WG: That was an excellent *Austin Powers* impersonation.

SO: Thanks. Anyway, I know Ricky loves Bianca, but she can be such a domineering cow. He should be allowed to run wild for a while. Maybe become a Male Escort.

WG: Pam St. Clement told me that Ricky is doubly appealing, because women want to mother him, as well as "that other thing."

SO: Pam's a very smart lady, isn't she? Very perceptive.

WG: Thanks for the interview, Sid.

SO: No problem, Tim. Next time, let's go for the pasta, okay?

–Tim Wilson

Patsy Palmer (Bianca Jackson), 1995
"I didn't know I could pull them off because there were a million beats in each scene, emotionally."

As she speaks to me, Patsy Palmer is knackered, which is understandable for a single mum with a high-pressure job. We meet at Elstree during the Christmas holiday when *EastEnders* is not in production. Patsy has already put in an appearance at a children's hospital. For her second good deed of the day, she fetches me a mince pie (plus one for herself) from the studio canteen. This puts me in an extremely festive Yuletide mood.

Patsy's hair is every bit as vividly red as what you see on telly. We go back to her dressing room, where Patsy curls up on her couch. I seat myself on a nearby chair and read prepared questions from a steno pad while recording her answers for future analysis. I begin by complimenting her performance in an episode recently aired in Britain.

Walford Gazette: The episodes where Bianca found out that David was her father [a fact that the audience already knew] were absolutely brilliant. Were they difficult to do?

Patsy Palmer: Difficult to do doesn't begin to describe it! But Jo Johnson, the director, was fantastic. After those episodes were finished, Jo sent me a right lovely card. Have a look, will ya.... (Attached to her dressing-room mirror was Ms. Johnson's effusive praise for Patsy's performance.)

WG: Classy of her to do that.

PP: You're telling me. I was sooooo worried about those episodes. I didn't know I could pull them off because there were a million beats in each scene, emotionally. In one bit, Bianca's coming onto him, hoping he'll be her next Tricky Dicky and then he devastates her by telling her he's her dad! I was nervous before each filming day, but I always had Michael French (David) and Lindsey Coulson (Carol) to count on. They're fantastic actors and Lindsey and I get on particularly well. I usually come to her for advice before the big dramatic scenes. She's great.

WG: Have you watched those episodes recently?

PP: Not since they were screened.... Hmmmm.... I think I'll pull out the videos of them that I recorded and have another look. I've got some more rough stuff coming up and I could use some inspiration.

WG: What led to your job on *EastEnders*?

PP: I started working in theatre when I was six. I tagged along with my brother Harry to an audition for the Winchester Theatre production of *Joseph and the Amazing Technicolor Dreamcoat* and we both got in. I stayed with it for three years. I was in the children's chorus. Around that time I started at the Anna Scher Theatre School, which is a brilliant place for young people to learn about acting. Gillian Taylforth (Kathy) and Susan Tully (Michelle) began their careers there. Anna is a wonderful person and the school is an excellent place for kids to really use their emotions and imaginations. It doesn't push them into a career. In fact, the kids there are not allowed to do commercials until they are sixteen. Pretty good policy, I think. Commercials can make kids a bit too spoiled and rich before their time.

WG: I bet you did one the day you turned sixteen.

PP: Of course, I'm no fool. It was for Clearasil. I played the girl with a face full of spots who uses the tube of Clearasil and cleans up her complexion straight away.

WG: I think one episode of *EastEnders* should revolve around Bianca and a sudden skin eruption.

PP: It should have something to do with Ian's chippie. She gets a full-time job there, and her skin keeps breaking out because it's exposed to all that grease. So she leaves in a huff.

WG: She chooses clean skin over her job.

PP: Right, that's the essence of Bianca.

WG: How did you get cast on *EastEnders*?

PP: Well, Tony McHale, Barbara Emile, and Jane Deitch [one of the show's writers, producer and casting adviser, respectively] came over to the Anna Scher Theatre to have a look around. I don't think I'd been put up for the part initially because Bianca was supposed to be sixteen, and I was already twenty. Tony, it turned out, had been watching me having a laugh with a few of my mates, and he saw me later on in an acting exercise with the class. He thought I was right for Bianca. I showed up here at the studio the next day and read for the producers and the day after that I was cast.... Boom Boom Boom.... Amazing.

WG: What went through your mind when you found out you got the part?

PP: I was with some mates when I got the call. Earlier in the day my mum yelled out to some painters in the council flats that her daughter was up for a role on *EastEnders*. I was so embarrassed! Anna Scher rang up and said "Patsy – bad news I'm afraid. You've got the part!!!"

WG: Why did you change your name from Julie Harris to Patsy Palmer? Was it because the American actress with the same name was registered with British Equity?

PP: My real name is Julie Harris, and she got into British Equity years before I was born. My mum's name is Patsy Palmer and well, that is a great stage name – don't you think?

WG: I love it. The creative staff was wise to not throw you into the deep end of the pool. I liked the way they phased Bianca into the show gradually.

PP: I wasn't heavily experienced. I'd done television before, but Bianca was my first major role.

WG: How do you see yourself in comparison to Bianca?

PP: I think I'm a nicer person! I'm also a very different person in terms of responsibility, because I have a three-year-old son to raise.

WG: Bianca still has a lot of growing up to do....

PP: Absolutely. But I hope the writers keep her mean. Bianca is so much more interesting when she is a right evil little cow.

WG: What do you think Bianca will be doing on the night of December 31, 1999?

PP: Good question! I know that I'd love it if she got a job as a croupier in a casino. She'd be shaking around in a flashy frock – acting like the lady of the manor and being a total bitch to anybody who stands in her way.

WG: What do you think you will be doing in the future?

PP: I only hope she does not get written off with a bloke who lives in a more genteel neighbourhood far from Walford. My mum still says that Bianca is somehow different from the other characters. It's not that she doesn't fit in, she just seems different. I love *EastEnders* and the people here.

–Tim Wilson

Lindsey Coulson (Carol Jackson), 1995

"Soap, it's so fast-moving. You're not really sure who you are or what you're doing."

At a time when *EastEnders* appeared to have lost its way, when all traces of cinema-vérité had been replaced by pub shoot-ups and soap opera flash, the Jacksons arrived. And although 1994's episodes on U.S. public TV would get a lot worse before they got better, the show received a shot of realism it sorely needed in the form of Carol Jackson, played to perfection by actress Lindsey Coulson.

Here, in a fax interview, Coulson tells us a bit about herself and offers us a glimpse into the only character in Albert Square who could tell Michelle Fowler, "Yeah, you think you've had it tough!"

Walford Gazette: Was Carol Jackson your first major television role? Before *EastEnders*, were you primarily a stage or screen actress?

Lindsey Coulson: Yes, Carol Jackson was my first major television role. Before *EastEnders*, I had done mostly theatre and radio.

WG: Have you done much Shakespeare? If so, what roles did you play?

LC: No, I haven't done a great deal of Shakespeare, although I love it and would like to do a lot more. However, I have played Ophelia in *Hamlet* (pregnant I might add!!), small-scale tours, and workshops.

WG: Has it been a positive experience working with the people at Elstree? Was it easy for you to assimilate yourself into the cast? Were there any cast members who made you feel particularly welcome?

LC: Yes, it's certainly been an interesting and positive experience. Everybody was very welcoming.

WG: Were you given a prepared biography of Carol? What can you tell us about her that we may not already know? Since you are the person with the greatest insight into this very complex woman, have the writers taken any of your suggestions into account?

LC: Yes, I was given a biography of Carol, although it has changed since. What can I tell you about her that you don't already know? Obviously, she comes across as very fiery, loud, and determined, but I think shortly (hopefully) you will see a different side to her and be able to understand why she is the way she is. The writers have been brilliant for my character, giving me a lot of work to do.

WG: Why does Carol have so much trouble disciplining her children?

LC: I think a lot of mothers find their adolescent children hard work, and with four children, well, what more can I say? She's out working, trying to get money. She's always tired – it's hard being a mum.

WG: In what ways do you think the character has evolved since she first appeared?

LC: Maybe she's a little more approachable. It's difficult to find a level when you step into a soap, it's so fast-moving. You're not really sure who you are or what you're doing. I think as the actor relaxes, maybe the character softens a little. Everybody's trying to find their level.

WG: Do you have any idea why so many people have left the show in the last two years? By our count, it comes to 17 (including Roly the Poodle).

LC: I think people get tired and want to move on, try other things, new challenges.

WG: What kind of acting training have you had?

LC: I trained for two years at an acting school in London.

WG: After watching a scene between you and Wendy Richard in the cafe, it struck me that time and time again, Carol is the only one on the show that seems "real." Can you explain why this is? How do you entrench yourself so deeply in your character?

LC: That's difficult to answer, as I think everybody works well on this show. It's hard to sustain a performance for X amount of years. I think you have to listen to what is being said and act accordingly. Maybe you just have to *be*! I'm not sure, it's hard to write this one down. I think it's about different people's opinions.

WG: I understand you're a great supporter of Greenpeace. Do you feel that, because of your responsibilities to *EastEnders*, you can't do as much for the organization as you would like to do?

LC: I don't do as much for Greenpeace and other charities as I used to. Not only because of *EastEnders* commitments but because I like to spend as much of my spare time with my young daughter as I can. Yes, I would like to be more involved and I will be in the future. I think it's really important to have organizations like Greenpeace that play a vital role in protecting our environment.

WG: What is the best thing about being married to your agent? What is the hardest part?

LC: I suppose at least he knows me inside out, and knows exactly what I can and can't do. All the auditions he gets for me have been spot on!

–A. S. Berman

Natalie Cassidy (Sonia Jackson), 2001

"[Sonia] was always the sensible, reasonable one in that crazy, messed-up family – maybe the most sensible, reasonable one in Walford!"

Natalie Cassidy has literally been growing up on-screen thanks to her role as Sonia Jackson on *EastEnders*, but to her it's no big deal. Let me tell you, this is a young lady with a really good head on her shoulders. And it was my good fortune to have the opportunity to sit down with her at the *EastEnders* studios recently to discuss, oh, this and that.

Walford Gazette: Thanks so much for agreeing to do this, Natalie. I know all your schedules here at *EastEnders* have been going haywire since the show added a fourth episode in August, and things haven't quite settled down yet.

Natalie Cassidy: It's my pleasure. I like the *Gazette* – I've read it over here – in the make-up room!

WG: We're honoured. You've been doing the show for how long, then?

NC: Eight years, believe it or not. Started here in 1983. I was 10 – I'm 18 now. Legal! (laughs) I guess you could say I've grown up here. It's hard to believe at times, but it's great. I'm very lucky to have been given the chance to work here – I know there are worse places to grow up than a successful television show!

WG: I gather your getting cast in the first place wasn't courtesy of a standard audition process?

NC: No, it wasn't. It was through this school I went to – Anna Scher's.

WG: Oh, yes, Patsy Palmer (Bianca) and Sid Owen (Ricky) went there, too. An after-school acting school, of sorts.

NC: Yes, exactly. A lot of other actors on our show have gone there, too, like James Alexandrou, who plays Martin. Anna's so great. It was just an after-school activity, really. A neighbourhood thing as well because it was so near to where I lived, in Islington, in north London.

WG: Were you ever in the same class as Patsy and Sid?

NC (smiles): No, they're older than me so they were in the "grown-up" class! Going there was like taking up a hobby, like going to a youth club. I always enjoyed it and made lots of friends there.

WG: It seems to be a place where the kids aren't put under pressure to book jobs, unlike some other so-called "theatre schools."

NC: That's right. Anna Scher's kept your head on the floor! It's not a place which is concerned with making kids go out to an audition where they must put on a fake smile and say things like "Hi! I'm Natalie! Let me entertain you!"

WG: Like Baby June in the musical *Gypsy*?

NC (laughs): Yes. Ugggh. So the *EastEnders* people stopped in one day and saw us do some improvisations and theatre games. Tony McHale, who created the Jackson family, was there to have a look around. So was the casting adviser, Jane Deitch. They liked me, apparently! I got sent up here to Elstree for what we here call a "re-call," did my thing and got the part!

WG: There was no matching up of the Jackson family members?

NC: No, it was all decided without doing that. I don't think it particularly mattered that none of us kids looked much like each other because all our characters had different dads!

WG: Speaking of dads, I gather your dad is one of the reasons you became interested in acting?

NC: Absolutely. It all started with the fact that Dad was and is a *huge* Frank Sinatra fan. And so was I, from the time I was two years old. I developed a real passion for him and his singing. In fact, I'd stand in the middle of our living room and belt out all his great hits like "My Way" and "The Lady Is a Tramp"!

WG: Did they let you hold a glass of Scotch in one hand and a cigarette in the other?

NC (laughs): No, of course, not. They didn't want me to pick up his bad habits! I must have been two or three when I'd stomp into the kitchen or wherever and order them to put "Frank 'n' Arthur" on our stereo system. I didn't know that his last name was really Sinatra because I was so small! Frank 'n' Arthur – Frank Sinatra! (laughs) I really, really loved him. What a brilliant singer. He told a story when he sang, didn't he? He was unique – a poet. I know every word to each of his songs and every bit of the Nelson Riddle musical arrangements, too! I have a shrine to him of sorts in the hall of my small flat! I'll always love him. He's the man!

So my parents could tell from all my carrying-on in the living room that there was something there – that maybe I was interested in entertaining or becoming an actress. They never pushed me into it, which was good, but they always supported me through it, which makes a big difference, I think.

WG: Did you start off in school plays?

NC: Yes, we did fantastic shows because we had this great teacher named Mark Wardour who'd write original scripts and songs for us. They were such good shows, and I don't say that because I happened to play the lead in most of them!

WG: Ahhhh, so that's why you looked like you were having a lot of fun when Sonia participated in the community play.

NC (smiles): Yes, it took me back a bit to that time, yes. And I started after-school acting classes with Anna Scher, did bits and bobs and got cast in a production of *The Beggar's Opera* for the Royal Shakespeare Company when I was nine, which I loved doing.

WG: Well, lah-di-dah, the Royal Shakespeare Company.

NC (laughs): Yes, lah-di-dah.

WG: Wasn't it a bit scary, going from a school play almost directly to an RSC production on that massive stage at the Barbican Theatre?

115

NC: No, which was strange. I loved it all. I particularly loved being under the floorboards before my entrance and smelling that stuff they used to make smoke – dry ice! Yeah, I remember that smell very well. I had to creep up out of the floorboards and peer up and out at the audience in that show at every performance.

WG: You must have played one of the miserable, downtrodden, urchin types, huh? Like those kids in *Les Misérables*!

NC (laughs): Yeah, right! That finished up in July 1993, and as soon as the curtain came down I whimpered to my mum, "I only want to be an actress now, Mum!"

WG: Awwww....

NC: And in October I got *EastEnders*!

WG: The Jacksons were the major new family on the Square, that's for sure. And you were part of it!

NC: Yes, I'll always be thankful to Tony and Jane for seeing me as part of it. We all had very different personalities to bring to our parts – that's why it worked so well in my opinion. Everyone was distinctively different.

WG: It must have helped that you all started more or less at the same time.

NC: We grew into a family together. I'm glad they never had the idea of Sonia being a kid brought up by Carol's parents or something and then sent to live with Carol and Alan after they'd been on the Square for six months. It was much easier the way it was.

WG: Remember your first day on the set?

NC: Sure, it was with Wendy Richard (Pauline), and it was on the Square and it was freezing cold. Sonia was spraying graffiti on the launderette door and got caught out by Pauline.

WG: That's when she was a juvenile delinquent for all of two minutes.

NC (laughs): Yep!

WG: It's like when Ricky was a racist for two minutes, and they nipped that in the bud.

NC: They must have thought, "No, let's not do that. We like him." Anyway, I was a bit nervous that first day, but Wendy was lovely to me.

WG: Those of us who were lucky enough to meet Wendy and spend an evening at an Indian restaurant with her and John in New York think she's lovely, too.

NC: I'd love to come over to New York!

WG: Ever been?

NC: No. I have been to Los Angeles, though – I presented a holiday travel show for British television. We were there for four days this past June. Did the Universal Studios tour and some other things, but not Disneyland unfortunately. I would have loved to go to a taping of *Friends* but they were on their summer break. I didn't get to do half of what I wanted to do! Oh well, I had a great time anyway. It's a bit too industry-oriented in L.A. for my taste, though. I don't think I'd like to live there for that reason.

WG: I bet you'd love New York.

NC: I know I would. If I could just nip over there sometime between Christmas and New Year's on our two-week holiday break I'd be very happy. I really hope to. Words can't really explain how I feel about the September 11 attacks. We over here obviously have a very difficult time understanding an attack on such a massive scale. Why it happened, I mean, the mentality that went into planning it and carrying it out. We do know that it was a disgrace and an outrage and our hearts go out to everyone there. I've been told I have a huge heart and, well, it goes out to you right now, it really does.

WG: Back to Sonia. She may only have been a juvenile delinquent for two minutes but she swiftly became Albert Square's answer to Thelma Ritter for quite a long time.

NC (laughs): Oh, I know her from the old movies!

WG: That's right, she was a wonderful character actress in Hollywood movies during the 1940s and the 1950s. She always played wisecracking types. My favourite line of hers was in *All About Eve*. After Eve tells her sob story to everyone Thelma's character doesn't skip a beat, and she murmurs, "Everything but the bloodhounds nipping at her behind."

NC (laughs): Yes! Sonia was like that for the longest time – the lady with the one-liners! She was always the sensible, reasonable one in that crazy, messed-up family – maybe the most sensible, reasonable one in Walford!

WG: And the trumpet? Whose idea was it for Sonia to take up the trumpet?

NC: John Yorke, who was storylining then and is the executive producer here now. I took lessons and everything to learn to play that thing. At the beginning I was, of course, horrible. But as time went on I improved rapidly to the point where I was playing it too well. I was asked to pretend to play badly since Sonia was supposed to be playing badly, to the irritation of everyone else on the Square! (laughs) I still get it from people on the street, "Where's your trumpet, Sonia?" Well, I dunno where it's gone to. With the props that are no longer required on the show, I expect! (laughs) Sonia's grown up a bit since then. She must have left it behind wherever she and her family fled in 1997... thank God!

WG: I remember watching the episode when the Jacksons left the Square and thinking that it was you, Natalie, crying real tears because you thought you might be leaving *EastEnders* forever.

NC: Yes. Correct. Absolutely true. I was also crying because I knew I'd miss working with Lindsey Coulson, who played my mum, Carol. She had decided the time was right for her to leave, which is why most of the Jacksons got storylined out. It wasn't just that I thought I was out of a job here forever! I didn't come back to the show for about four months or so after that. And after Clare left the Square I was gone for another eight months. I just got on with school and all that – and eventually got the call to come back full-time. I was thrilled, needless to say.

WG: Did you and Gemma Bissix (Clare) get on well when you were both in the show? Even during the storyline when Clare was bullying Sonia?

NC: Sure. We were good mates then. I admit I don't see as much of her these days because she's at college, not acting at the moment and doing her own thing. She needed a break. Good for her. I'm sure she's enjoying herself.

WG: As you said, you've been on *EastEnders* for eight years. Now you're a veteran of it compared to other actors.

NC: I know, isn't that weird? I am very, very happy here. I am also very happy that in the years since I've joined Sonia has been given great storylines to play out and is no longer just Carol's daughter or Robbie's little sister or Bianca's little sister. She's now a character in her own right, and I couldn't be more pleased. I love my job and am always very aware that there are others who would kill to be in my shoes, believe me.

WG: Any other actresses you admire?

NC: Oh, yeah. Well, besides the actresses here at the show like Patsy and Lindsey and many others I love Julia Roberts and that Australian actress whose name escapes me – the one in *The Gift* and *Elizabeth*?

WG: Cate Blanchett.

NC: Yes – she's absolutely brilliant. Wow. I love the actresses in *Friends*, too. I love, love, love that show – like a lot of people, obviously.

WG: You love *Friends*, huh? That's interesting because I happen to have a videotape of the first six episodes of the new season in the U.S., which I can lend you in thanks for being such a great interview subject.

NC (eyes widening): You're kidding…. *I love you*! (laughs)

WG: But just one more personal interest question for our readers to wrap this up… any brother and/or sisters?

NC: I'm the youngest of three – I've got two brothers.

WG: Very impressive. You have earned your *Friends* tape.

NC: Oh, I can't believe it, thanks! I feel like I've won a quiz show or something!

We said goodbye by giving each other a big hug and promising to keep in touch. She is a terrific and talented girl – a joy to interview and a real sweetie. If I could snap my fingers and get her into a taping of *Friends* (or even a guest spot!), I would. I hope she gets to see New York first, though.

–Tim Wilson

Howard Antony (Alan Jackson), 2003

"If you told me that I was going to be in EastEnders as a regular character at any period of time in my life, I would have said you were crazy because it was never part of my plan."

When you first meet Howard Antony in person, you realise that his *EastEnders* alter ego Alan Jackson appeared much taller on the telly than he is in real life. But that's because his Walford better half Carol (played by Lindsey Coulson) was by her own admission "five-foot nothing." Howard was in town in early May visiting his mum, who recently celebrated her eightieth birthday and who has lived in Brooklyn for more than twenty years.

He's pretty familiar with the U.S., and in fact, if it hadn't been for his audition for *EastEnders* some eight years ago, he might very well emigrated to be with his family. *Walford Gazette* subscriber Bob Tulipan, whose business arranged for the actor's visa, set up this interview at a downtown, upscale Manhattan bar. Howard recently wrapped up working on his first American film, an independent production shot in California that is about to make the international film festival circuit in search of a distribution deal.

I show Howard a photo that the *Walford Gazette* ran of him years ago snapped by Brit teenager Darren Nelson at the rare mid-1990s *EastEnders* studio open house. "They asked me if I would sign autographs for an hour. When I got there, there was a queue down the High Street. There were about 13,000 people. I was there for four hours. It was my introduction to that whole kind of autograph thing. Wow. That's when I realised exactly how popular it was and what kind of attention we received."

Howard says he was "absolutely a fan" before he made it onto the show, but he never expected to land a role. "If you told me that I was going to be in *EastEnders* as a regular character at any period of time in my life, I would have said you were crazy because it was never part of my plan. It was never a goal in my life or an ambition, so when it happened it was a complete surprise."

Similarly, he chose acting as a profession almost by accident when a friend told him that in the mid-1980s a movie was being cast in east London and there might be a part for him. It turned out that master filmmaker Stanley Kubrick, who died a few years ago, was casting extras for his Vietnam film *Full Metal Jacket*. This film was shot on location, not in Southeast Asia like *Apocalypse Now* (filmed in the Philippines, for example), but rather in a neighbourhood not far from what's supposed to be Walford, oddly enough.

Howard grew up in London, primarily the west London section Notting Hill. When Antony was twenty-three, he followed up on a friend's suggestion that he go down and meet the casting director. "I just went yeah, yeah, yeah. I just forgot about it. About two weeks went by, and I got this phone call from the technical adviser of *Full Metal Jacket*. 'I've been given your name and number, and heard you might be interested in working on this movie.' I thought, 'okay,' I was really surprised. I went down to the East End. It was an old kind of gasworks, all these demolished buildings and stuff. And they had all these trailers there because they were in pre-production. They gave us pretend rifles that were supposed to be M16s, and we were supposed to pretend that we were in this hostile environment and could be under fire at any time. We had to go from point A to point B and run across this parking lot, and run straight at the camera and scream really aggressively like we were demented. I just said to myself, 'This is just like playing soldiers when you were a kid, right?' So I just did it. I didn't hear anything for four weeks, and then got this phone call, 'Stanley really liked you; he looked at the tapes and wants you to come down for a part in the movie. Are you interested?' I said, 'Well, yeah!' He said, come down to sign the forms. And that was it.

"Originally they said they'd need me only for six weeks, which transpired to six months. Because I wasn't featured that much, and I had this combat outfit, they said, 'The film is in two halves, there's a combat section and a boot camp section. Stanley thinks you'd be a really good drill sergeant. You look really smart in the uniform. Do you want to audition for that?' And they cast me in that, so I actually ended up doing another six months for that. So I ended up working on it for a year. That was it. I was totally smitten by the movie thing."

Howard was to get a few lines that he had prepared using a quasi-American accent. After all, his mum was already living in the States.

Unfortunately, those scenes ended up not being shot because Kubrick decided they weren't needed. Howard mentions that he was very upset four years ago when he found out that Kubrick had died. "I was coming back from Barbados. He kind of changed my life, you know."

Following the movie, Kubrick asked Howard whether he was going to stick with acting and suggested that he take acting classes. "He said, 'If I was you, I'd really stay in the business'." The fledgling actor then went to drama school, after which he embarked on an acting career in the theatre for the next five years. "I always wanted to say thank you to him in some way or work with him again."

Fast-forwarding to *EastEnders*: "The thought of becoming a TV actor on the biggest show in the country – 20 million two or three times a week. I think it took me the best part of a year to become more technically minded – know what camera to look at. There's never just one camera. Sometimes there's as many as four. You have to know which camera is doing what to give the best performance. You can give a really good reaction for camera two, but it's really camera three. It was little things like that. The executive producer once said to me, 'Howard, just think more technical.' And from that day everything just sort of made sense. That was great because you get the chance to practise your craft day in and day out. The only way you can do that is in a soap, it's ongoing."

When Howard started on *EastEnders* it was supposed to be only two years, to accommodate Lindsey Coulson's desire to stay on the show that long. "It ended up being four years. When she first joined the show she told me she'd only do it for two years. I always knew she was going to leave, and she was gracious and polite enough to tell me she was going to leave before she even told the executives. When she told them, they didn't believe her – 'Give her more strong storylines and more money.' But she wanted to do other things and not be typecast as this particular character."

Howard explains that the storyline regarding part of the Jackson family relocating somewhere north of Walford about four years ago for Billy's safety (after he witnessed a crime) was designed for Coulson's departure. "I was always meant to go back." In fact, during Coulson's hiatus, Howard says he was asked to come back a year after he left, but following his new agent's advice he decided not to become Alan again. "They said the character is incredibly popular, and we are going to bring you back. I said to myself at the time that I had only wanted to do three years, so having done four I thought it might be a good time to see what the big wide world had in store for me. I was worried about getting typecast as well. I'd saved enough money, so I didn't really need to go back."

In retrospect, Howard now realises that "it wouldn't have done me any harm to have gone back." And even though it's four years (U.K. time) since Alan left the Square, there's no reason why he and Billy can't return. "Yes, [Alan] is still alive living somewhere in London."

He points out that Lindsey ended up returning for three months to accommodate Bianca's exit. "That was really good stuff." When I interject that I hadn't yet seen the whole drama concerning Carol's new beau Dan, Antony courteously replies, "I don't want to ruin it for you."

He comments about Natalie Cassidy, who played his on-air daughter Sonia, "She's one of the best actors on the show. From Day One, she always had this maturity about her, and this appetite and desire to learn. When she was sixteen, I told her she was going to win an award for Best Actress in a soap, and she said she was just happy to be nominated. And she did win. I'm so glad she did because her mother died a few years later, but her mum saw her win that. Her mum used to bring her to the show because she was still a minor. I love [Natalie] dearly and she's a lovely person, and I think she has a wonderful future as an actress."

Howard had no problem playing a black man married to a white woman, and notes that in real life most of his relationships had been with other races. "What you saw was part of my life anyway," he says, adding that, like the fictional Jackson clan, he also grew up with siblings whose fathers were other than his own.

"Alan was so family oriented, but I liked that – a young black guy who was very responsible, mature. That was something that I was very comfortable with because it was something I grew up with to a point. To me, if you love someone you love everything about them. It's not 'I love you, but I don't love your kids.' It was something I was very glad to do. The whole black-and-white thing, I think we're at a stage now that people are more informed.

"I noticed things have changed in the U.S. over the past twenty years. When I first came here twenty years ago, it was a different racial climate than how it is now, when it's quite commonplace. We've had that England for forty-odd years. The whole point of a democracy is freedom of speech and freedom of action. Everyone should be able to choose who they want to be with. I don't think anyone should dictate whom someone should be with. It comes down to personal choice. I was raised in a way that I had that choice. There are good and bad in every race and that's how it'll always be. When I see racial intolerance and ignorance it just upsets me. One of the worst things that a human can do to a fellow human being is to reject that person or show animosity or be disrespectful to that person because he or she comes from a different racial background. And I don't mean that just from a black-and-white relationship. I think we should celebrate our differences."

Of his first experience working in California on an independently produced film called *Seizing Me*, his agent told him of the role: "A guy who kidnaps three people and brings them back to her house. And they all have something that she needs. I got this scene and realised it was really good. I read the rest of the script and said to myself, 'This is going to be a really good movie.'" His first audition went really well.

"I was in my car and within five minutes driving on Santa Monica Boulevard near Sunset the casting people called me on my cell phone and said they really liked me, and could I come back tomorrow for a callback. 'They want you to read with the actress playing the main character.' I said, 'Yeah.' I went back the next day and read for them."

Turning in a winning audition, Howard ended up landing the part, which he describes as "a transatlantic, he's more American than he is British. He's lived in the States for a while, but every once in a while you hear a little British out of him. The director said to me that I could play him any way I wanted. They asked if there was anything I needed to play this role, and I said, 'No. I'm an easy actor to work with, I don't make demands. I'm not Hollywood yet – unfortunately.'"

Elements of erotica make him a little nervous about his mum seeing it, but Howard says that "it's justified." Of the director, Howard says, "He's very art house, very cutting edge." The producers are aiming for the North American premiere to be at the Toronto Film Festival. The director of *Seizing Me*, Halfdan Hussey, had won an award for his first feature at the Venice Film Festival.

Four years after his *EastEnders* exit, Howard still thinks about how they could have taken Alan in another direction.

"Dramatically, what would have been interesting is if Alan got left with all the kids, to look after four kids. Of course, that would have meant something would have had to happen to Carol. There were various ways they could have dealt with that. They could have given me a new love interest. And there was the whole Frankie thing. Carol was no longer there, or it could have been someone else. There was so much mileage there. They tend to have these little family units, which is great because it's about these different families in this little community. They interact in the Square, and there's all this drama."

–Larry Jaffee

Martine McCutcheon (Tiffany Raymond Mitchell), 1996

"Tiffany hasn't been and isn't a prostitute. She just likes to date men who've got money!"

For once in my life I did not mind getting up at 5 a.m. because on this occasion I was doing a telephone interview with *EastEnders'* newest vixen, Martine McCutcheon, who plays that raven-haired temptress, Tiffany Raymond. I'd actually had the pleasure of meeting Ms. McCutcheon in person during my last visit to Elstree. She had generously invited me to hang out with her while I was waiting for Danniella Westbrook (who plays Ricky's estranged wife Sam) to come back in from the Albert Square lot for our pre-arranged interview.

For some reason it did not occur to me to interview Martine while I was waiting for Danniella. In my defence, I can only explain that Ms. McCutcheon is an enchanting person. I was so busy adoring her that I forgot I was carrying a tape recorder that could have been turned on to provide the basis of a terrific interview. (Honest, folks, it's not just that she's physically quite attractive and has a personality best described as "bubbly." There's also something very "winning" about her.) To be immune to Martine's charms, one would have to be both an Anglophobe and a woman-hater. I am neither.

Anyway, fast-forward six months ahead and you find me in New York at 5 a.m., dialling the McCutcheon residence in Britain. Martine's chirpy, East End accent takes over at the other end of the line, and I am entranced all over again. We're talking "charm…." If ever she decides on a career change to telemarketing, she could probably sell coals to Newcastle.

Walford Gazette: Thanks for taking the time to speak with us.

Martine McCutcheon: That's all right. Ooooh, you sound a bit rough!

WG: It's my morning voice, I swear. Last night I did not drink at all.

MM: Can't say the same for myself, I'm afraid. I'm a bit of a lightweight when it comes to drink… two glasses of Champagne and I'm done for. That's all I had. I went to an Oasis concert last night and I didn't have to work today and I thought, "Why not live a little?"… I just had two glasses.

WG: Well, you're entitled…. I've been told by some readers of the *Gazette* that they enjoy reading about how the actors got their roles – the audition process. Do you have a story?

MM: My agent heard through the grapevine that the *EastEnders* people were looking at a lot of girls for the role of Tiffany, and he rang them up about me. At first, I wasn't too keen on the idea of doing a soap because, at the time, I wanted to concentrate on working in film and the theatre. But my agent kept telling me that Tiffany was a character who was really different, that she was unlike anybody who had been on the show before, and that I was perfectly suited for it.

WG: That may have qualified as an insult, considering the way in which Tiffany was introduced to the audience. (Editor's note: One day she just suddenly showed up in the Square as Bianca's friend, and quickly landed a barmaid job at the Vic.)

MM: I know! Anyway, I went up to Elstree, pretty much dressed as I normally do, and read for the producers. They explained to me that Tiffany was a very feisty and quite bitchy character, quite worldly. They told me that they liked my reading but that, at the moment, I didn't look anything like the way they envisioned Tiffany. They said that Tiffany wears flashy clothes and junk jewellery and likes to show a bit of cleavage. They suggested that I come back and see them in a few days' time, dressed along those lines.

WG: Your transformation was obviously a success.

MM: I went out that night to a couple of, uhhhh… "gangster clubs," where you see these sorts of girls all the time and gave them a good looking over. A few days later I showed up at BBC reception wearing fishnet stockings, a tight black Lycra skirt, lots of junk jewellery, orange lipstick, and a fake tan.

WG: They must have thought you were the Evil Twin of the girl who had shown up earlier in the week!

MM: The producer said, "Great – you're perfect now. But we've got one more person to see." I thought, "Right! Terrific." It's happened before, where the powers that be had only "one more person to see" and they picked her. I waited bravely for three days after the last audition. On the third day I had to go to the doctor's because I needed tablets for my anaemia and I was feeling really down. I came home, and my mum was clutching the arm of the settee, and I asked her what was wrong. She said, "Nothing – just phone your agent." I said, "It's all right, Mum. I can take it. I didn't get the part, right?" She said, "Just phone your agent." So I did. And he started out by telling me I didn't get this and that and the other things I'd been seen for. Eventually, he said, "By the way, you got the part on *EastEnders*." I screamed. Mum screamed. She was really proud and happy for me. It was Christmastime when I got the part, and I remember we had the Christmas tree up, and everybody came round and we all watched *EastEnders* together. They were saying, "Oh my God, one day soon Martine's gonna be on that!" I'd watched *EastEnders* for ten years, from Day One, and I was really thrilled to get to be in it. Film and theatre work was just going to have to wait for the future, I figured. This was meant to be.

WG: You've had a very interesting background, professionally. You were in a pop group, weren't you?

MM: Yeah, it was called Milan. I'd been studying at the Italia Conti theatre school for six years and I saw an ad in a trade paper calling for a girl singer who should be about sixteen. I was about fourteen or fifteen at the time. I told two of my mates at the school about it, and we decided to go to the audition as a group. We rehearsed a routine in my mum's loft. It was Gloria Estefan's "One, Two, Three." (raucous, nostalgic laughter from Martine) Oh, and we did The Bangles' "Eternal Flame." I was the lead singer. We performed this routine for these people, and they said we weren't what they had in mind at the time, but they'd invest in us and see what would happen in a few years. We eventually got a deal at Polydor Records.

WG: Impressive. Did Milan release any records?

MM: Yes. Dance music stuff. Funky stuff. We got played in clubs a lot. I love singing. I actually began training as a ballet dancer but found that I really enjoyed singing and dancing better. I was in *Stop the World – I Want to Get Off* with Anthony Newley when I was thirteen, and a musical called *Bernadette* in the West End when I was fifteen. [Interviewer's note: Bernadette was a notorious flop. Unfortunately I lacked the courage to ask Martine if it was true that, during one performance, a theatergoer stood up and screamed out, "Can't something be done about this?"]

WG: How old were you when you began performing?

MM: Well, actually, I began my career when I was six weeks old. A lady from a PR firm over here chose me to appear on billboards all over Britain as a sort of representative of the Labour Party for the national elections that were then coming up.

WG: Little Martine McCutcheon, poster child for the Labour Party?

MM: That's right! I'd love a copy of that poster. I wonder if they have those posters in Labour Party files or something.

WG: I'm amazed that the tabloids haven't unearthed it.

MM: I wasn't naked, so they wouldn't be interested.

WG: Back to Tiffany Raymond. What's her family background?

MM: Well, it was all a bit sketchy when she was first brought on. But it's since been revealed that she has a mother, father, a brother named Simon, and that her dad made quite a bit of money, but when the recession hit England in the late 1980s, it all went wrong for him. Her mum walked out and her dad became a heavy drinker. Tiffany has had serious family problems. The show will go into a lot of why Tiffany is the way she is, why she's so determined to get what she can, without caring about the consequences. Audiences are going to see a lot more of Tiffany. She's much more than what you see right now.

WG: When I interviewed Pam St. Clement (Pat), she said that this process of gradually revealing a character is like the peeling of an onion, layer by layer...

MM: Yes, that's what this show is so good at.

WG: One early impression I had of Tiffany was that she is practically a prostitute. That scene in a sleazy club with Bianca and the two men. The guy Tiffany was with handed her some money.

MM: That episode got a lot of disapproving mail, and the BBC wasn't too pleased with it. But no. Tiffany hasn't been and isn't a prostitute. She just likes to date men who've got money!

WG: How has all the attention you've received from your work on the show been affecting you?

MM: Of course, it's affected me in many ways, but at the end of the day I like to be at home with my family. I like to think that they help keep my feet on the ground. I won't say that I don't enjoy the fringe benefits, like going to concerts and the theatre and film premieres, because I do. During my first year on the show I was also solidly involved with a man who helped me through the initial attention. I was very lucky in that way. We were engaged to be married, but we recently broke up. *EastEnders* did not contribute to the break-up, at least not in any major way. Anyway, we're still very good friends, and that's what counts. Gareth is a great guy.

WG: He's a music producer, right?

MM: Yes, and he'd travel all over as part of his job. We wouldn't see each other for long periods of time, and that's a difficult situation to get through.

WG: What's your fan mail like?

MM: I get fan mail from young girls who say they really like Tiffany. They think she's fun. I've also got some mail from men in jail who ain't got any honourable intentions when it comes to Tiffany!

WG: I can see where Tiffany might be a popular pin-up in jail cells…. Is it true to say that she has been slowly groomed to fill the void created when Sharon left?

MM: Perhaps, up to a point. But I don't think she's like Sharon at all. As you'll see, Tiffany will become involved with Grant on several levels. Sharon was quite a bit frightened of Grant at times, and she was considerate towards him in general. Tiffany, however, gives back as good as she gets. She doesn't put up with his rubbish.

WG: Do you see Tiffany becoming a permanent part of the Albert Square landscape?

MM: In truth, probably not. She will certainly become a major character for quite a bit of time on *EastEnders*. But she does have other fish to fry beyond Albert Square, I think. As it happens, so do I.

WG: What are the McCutcheon ambitions?

MM: I grew up loving Barbra Streisand and Audrey Hepburn in films like *Hello, Dolly!* and *Breakfast at Tiffany's*. *EastEnders* is allowing me to be part of a great show, and I am extremely grateful for that. But someday I hope to be up there on the big screen, singing my lungs out!

–Tim Wilson

Andrew Lynford (Simon Raymond), 2004

"As any actor on any soap will probably tell you, you even have to remind yourself that it is only pretend."

Editor's note: The following article was written by the actor in response to an article published in the Walford Gazette regarding how EastEnders portrays gays.

Before we really get into all this, let's get something clear. It was all a long time ago. Eight years to be exact, here in the U.K. Yes, people still approach me in the supermarket or on the train, recounting with either affection or horror how they remembered the character I played in *EastEnders* kissing another man, not only another man, but his sister's boyfriend to boot! Then usually they say how much they liked Simon and how it would be nice to have him back in Albert Square. I suppose this means they genuinely liked him and his storylines... or perhaps they're just being polite.

Would I like to go back? Well, never say never. After Den Watts's return from the daffodils, anything in soap land must surely be possible. Oops! Better not give too much away just in case you haven't seen it yet.

But going back would mean getting emotionally involved with the character all over again, like rekindling an old friendship, and defending him and his actions.

At times, as any actor on any soap will probably tell you, you even have to remind yourself that it is only pretend. However, I guess my "soft spot" for Simon still firmly exists, as here I am defending him (and, in a way, my portrayal of him) to you right now. It may be sad, it may be perfectly valid. Whatever your view, I shall endeavour to win your sympathy.

Phil Hansen's article, 'Queer As Walford', was interesting to read, and, assuming that he is a fan of *EastEnders* (*Editor's note: he is*), somewhat disheartening. To hear Tony and Simon written off as "ambitious failures" makes me wonder just what it was about them that was so fantastically abysmal in Mr. Hansen's eyes?

The two characters were long-standing and pivotal in many major storylines during their time in Walford. That in itself is unusual by any standards for a gay and bisexual character in an ongoing drama. Their continual inclusion in the everyday comings and goings of Albert Square saw them integrated in a way few gay characters have been in any soap.

Also, and I think refreshingly, their storylines were not just focused on their "orientation" and about "acceptance." There were issues that could have been directed at any couple struggling to survive life in a small community within a large city. It was about "life" and the best way to live it.

Perhaps then, this was the mistake. When a character such as Simon was representing a minority group, perhaps every opportunity should be used to promote a type of lifestyle and behaviour? In the U.K., the tabloid press has always used any "newsworthy" story centred around homosexuality as outrageous and scandalous, and Simon, sorry to say, was often featured in these quality journals.

Not Andrew Lynford, I hasten to add, but Simon Raymond. However, they invariably reported that Simon was dull and boring and not fun and upbeat like all gay men(?!). Perhaps the flip side of this was that the writers and myself had managed to show a young, gay man as perfectly "normal," and that in itself is surely interesting dramatically. If the *EastEnders* policy at the time was to "entertain and educate," then maybe Simon in all his mundaneness was saying something very important to the readers of *The Sun*, wasn't he?

But perhaps there were areas of the gay press at the time (and Mr. Hansen) who wanted some more stereotypical traits in the character? One character, and one actor playing him, could not single-handedly represent *every* gay man....

I am pleased that the article acknowledges the excitement surrounding the Tony/Tiffany/Simon love triangle. It was original and compelling I think, pure soap opera, but anchored to reality by strong writing and (I say this almost impartially) by well-judged performances. The added dimension of "Who was the father of Tiffany's baby?" only heightened the profile of these two already well-developed and sympathetic gay characters. Indeed, this storyline has since been "echoed" (I am hesitant in using the word copied) in *Coronation Street* and *Family Affairs,* big soaps in the U.K.

The Blackpool kiss, which sparked the start of the story, was never forty-five seconds. It was filmed at about three o'clock in the morning on Blackpool pier in the freezing cold. I think my lips would have frozen to Mark Homer's if we had taken that long over it. It was, however, edited by a second or two, and I personally think it did break the rhythm of the scene slightly.

The producers on the show at the time were disappointed the powers that were took the decision to cut the kiss down. At the time we felt it was shying away from the journey the two characters were taking. Looking back, of course, it made little difference, and the effect was still astounding!

Government ministers and even the Church of England took to commenting on that episode and its content. About two years later, *Queer as Folk* aired on Channel Four. The show was well crafted as a means to shock and cause outrage by showing elements of the life led by some men in the gay community. The Tony and Simon storyline in *EastEnders* never set out to do that. At the time, there were champions of *Queer as Folk* taking the line of "at last, real gay men on telly! Not like those two boring poofs on *EastEnders*." It was amusing to me at one level and saddened me at another.

We were broadcast at 7.30 p.m., aimed at prime-time "family" viewing, and *Queer as Folk* was at 10 p.m. on Channel Four, a channel in the U.K. renowned for its controversial programming. We were unable to compete, not that we ever felt we had to or wanted to. It was also around this time that the stories for Simon were becoming more dramatic and, as I have said previously, removed from anything purely tokenistic.

Mr. Hansen makes reference to the cliff top scenes with Courtney as almost homophobic. This is interesting and something I had never considered.

To my mind, the story was addressing mental health and the results of difficulty in coping with bereavement. To that end, it becomes a very strong image about family values from a gay point of view: Simon the homosexual was not destroying the family unit, but literally clinging onto the last fragment of stability within the family he had, having lost his sister, and maintaining no relationships with either his mother or father.

All Simon was looking for was a constant and nurturing home life. At that time, his young niece was the only chance he had of developing that, particularly as Tony was still dabbling with girls around that time. And rightly so.

This is, after all, telly drama, and Tony was a bisexual man. Eventually though, Tony and Simon ended up together. As they bade farewell to the Square (a decision reached mutually by myself, Mark Homer, and the producers at the time), Mr. Hansen shouted "Good riddance."

Apart from anything else, the two characters were integral to some major plotlines and affected the audience, whether they were liked or loathed. The main thing is, they caused a stir. And all this time on, as episodes are aired in the U.S. or repeated on cable channels here in the U.K., people still want to talk about it. We were noticed. People thought about it. Some may even have had a "rethink" about it all. So some good was done... I hope.

I know Mr. Hansen's comments have a degree of irony in them and are light-heartedly reported, and I don't want to sound too earnest about it all (after all, it is only pretend!). It is easy to accept a gay, camp character in comedy but so much harder in straight drama (excuse the choice of word!).

Will & Grace, Are You Being Served?, Gimme Gimme Gimme, every *Carry On* film... they all embrace a camp, overt, gay element of comedy, and it becomes acceptable as we are invited to laugh at it. But how then to ask your audience to feel for the character and sympathise when no laughs are intended?

Dr. Fonseca wasn't ever really about long enough to become integrated into East End life, he just happened to be gay. But no big deal was ever made of it. A lot of gay men I know don't want their sexuality to be emblazoned in sequins and feathers, after all, if it is no big deal to them, should it be a big deal to anyone else? I guess that it was what I always hoped for Simon: his sexuality was no big deal.... but *he* was.

–Andrew Lynford

Deepak Verma (Sanjay Kapoor), 1997

"Sanjay isn't one hundred per cent predictable – that counts for a lot."

Deepak Verma does not bring up the fact that I am twenty minutes late for lunch. I expected him to do so. But that would have been a typical "Sanjay" reaction, and Deepak, as it happens, is not much like Sanjay. I was late because of nervousness, which, combined with a temporary lack of common sense, caused me to get on the wrong train to Elstree. Fortunately, Deepak left word with the studio guards that I could locate him in the BBC cafeteria. That's where I find him, extending a friendly handshake over a plate of lasagna.

He is as good-looking in person as you might imagine. But it is his general demeanour that impresses me most, because Deepak is still a young man. As the saying used to go: He seems to have it all together. Which is to say that Deepak is confident without a trace of cockiness, with strong ideas about what he wants out of life and career. (Unlike Sanjay, who doesn't seem to have a clue about next week.)

Deepak, a graduate of the Central School of Speech and Drama, is a playwright as well as an actor. One of his works, *Kalyng*, has been produced at the prestigious Royal Court Theatre. Another, *The Bandit Queen*, was recently broadcast on BBC Radio, and, personally, I found it very moving. This led me to ask if he is tempted to quit acting for writing.

"God, no!" he replies. "Writing is something I know I can do and do well. But an acting career is what I've studied and worked hard for. Keeping options open is important though, and I think I'd like to juggle both." For the moment, he adds, "this role is keeping me very busy."

I asked him how he landed the role of Sanjay. "The way things work in this business is really funny," he replies. "Because you go into one audition for a very small thing and spend all day auditioning. Then you go in for something tremendous like *EastEnders*, and it takes ten minutes!" I ask him if that's really all it took, and he replies in the affirmative. "I read some lines, that was that. 'Thank you very much!' And five hours later, I got it."

"No screen test for an ongoing role on *EastEnders*?"

"No. I think in the early days there were screen tests. But, as far as I know, it doesn't really happen now. It didn't happen with me and Shobu (Gita). I was cast first. And Shobu came in to read a few days later, along with several other actresses. It was an interesting experience, reading with different Gitas."

Before I can ask the next question, Deepak answers it. "Yes, Shobu was the best of the lot. Sudha Buchar, who eventually played Meena (Gita's sister) read as well, and she was excellent – but not as right for the role as Shobu. So that's how the casting process has worked out."

I ask him what has been his favourite subplot so far, among the episodes involving Sanjay. "I suppose it's got to be the blow-up that happened after the affair between Sanjay and Meena was revealed. We had a very good director, Chris Fallon, on those episodes. He had an American outlook on directing. You know: 'Let's do this boom-boom-boom and not over-analyse it.' We've been fortunate with our directors on this show. I gather that, on other soaps, they haven't been too happy with theirs.

"Anyway, these episodes were well written and well directed. They were good. And we were happy with them. I also liked a recent storyline where Gita and Sanjay are constantly being threatened by racial thugs."

I had seen those episodes while in London (they have not yet been aired in America). I told Deepak that the "racial thugs" subplot seemed "tacked-on," without making any real or lasting impression on the characters.

"Yes, that's true to an extent," Deepak concedes. "But I'm really glad they gave it a go. I mean, the racism problem is an ongoing problem, and it's certainly a topical one. The story did grind to a halt just in time for Christmas, but I'm beginning to think that was the right thing to do. The show might have been straying into too dangerous a territory, and we [the actors] might find our security compromised. Anyway, if too much time was spent on it, it might have become boring to watch."

Which brings us to the whole subject of the portrayal of Asians on *EastEnders*. (In my opinion, this was one of the show's most glaring weaknesses before the arrival of Gita and Sanjay.) I ask Deepak if he feels that Sanjay and Gita have lived in a vacuum, segregated from their neighbours, except for the time Sanjay spent with Richard Cole and Gita with Cindy Beale.

"Yeah, sure. A lot of the time I do feel Sanjay and Gita have been in a bit of a vacuum. But that's all right as long as I enjoy playing Sanjay. He's human. He's an interesting character, and I wouldn't want to continue playing him if I didn't enjoy it. He's sometimes weak, but he's also sometimes strong. And he isn't one hundred per cent predictable – that counts for a lot."

I mention at this point that the chemistry between Deepak/Sanjay and Ian Reddington (Tricky Dicky) had always been terrific. Did the two actors get along in real life as well?

"Oh God, yes," smiles Deepak. "He was brilliant. We always got on well. And we loved our scenes together. He left the show because he felt it was the right time for him. I miss him. Sanjay misses him too because there's no one else around to get in trouble with."

I point out to Deepak that Richard's defection now leaves Sanjay to interact only with Gita and their infant daughter, Sharmilla. "Well, Sharmilla is Sanjay's Achilles heel," he observes. "Without her, I doubt the marriage would have kept on going. She's the one thing that holds the family together."

At this point in our conversation, Deepak adds that he gets along quite well with Shobu Kapoor and the child who portrays Sharmilla and that I "had better be sure to print that."

I ask him if he has ever objected to a plot development and demanded script changes. "No, actually," he replies. "It becomes a waste of time. I mean, look, it was sometimes hard to justify Sanjay's affair with Meena, of all people. But you can't walk around laying things on the writers. A lot of the time I get stuff from writers like, say, Tony Jordan, and I'll think, 'Hmmmm. I haven't heard Sanjay say something like this, but maybe it'll be interesting'. It's stupid to close doors, anyway. I do respect writers because I write as well. I'm not one for questioning things outright. I just say, 'Let's do it'. Of course I ask questions in my head but that's not the same, is it?"

Trying to veer the conversation back to the "vacuum" problem, I ask if Deepak hopes they'll bring in other members of Gita and Sanjay's family in order to generate more storylines for Gita and Sanjay.

"I've discussed that with the producers already and I really don't want that," he admits. "That would push Sanjay and Gita into more of a corner, more of a ghettoised environment. It's happened before – let's not give any examples, shall we? I just want Sanjay to cross over into as many storylines going on around the Square as possible, to interact with as many characters as he can. It's brilliant when that happens. I enjoy it as an actor, and that will show in the work."

Is there another character on the show he thinks could be a viable romantic interest for Sanjay? "No, to be very honest. Not at the moment, I can't think of anyone. But somewhere down the road it would be very interesting if someone else showed up in the Square who Sanjay seriously fancies. It just hasn't happened yet."

We get into his car, which is parked near the *EastEnders* lot, and drive through north London. I ask him if he plans on staying with *EastEnders*.

"For the time being, yes. I mean, look, I watched *EastEnders* from Day One and I really, really wanted to be on it, and I'm very happy doing it. I'll tell you one of my major ambitions, though. I'd love to work in America. That's a big surprise, huh? Everyone here has a secret dream to work in America. A few years back I took a Delta Pass and travelled all over America and absolutely loved it. I spent a few weeks staying at a friend's flat in Greenwich Village in New York, and especially wanted to stay there for a while. Got any ideas?"

I only half-jokingly suggest that we could swap apartments, and this definitely perks Deepak's interest. "Oh yeah?" he asks, raising his eyebrows. "Okay. Even if the kitchen and bathroom are the size of closets, I'll take it! Seriously though, someday I might well give America a shot." However, he adds, "As for right now, this job on *EastEnders* is my life. In a couple of years, maybe I'll take the risk."

–Tim Wilson

Paul Bradley (Nigel Bates), 1994

"I suppose he's a bit of a wallie. Nigel is very well-meaning. He was best mates at school with Phil and Grant. Where they would use their fists, he would use jokes to get out of trouble."

In addition to his talents as an actor, Paul Bradley can make beautiful music with such instruments as guitar, jigsaw, and Sellotape. That last item (which is U.K. terminology for what Americans call "Scotch tape") is not usually thought of as particularly melodic. Neither is the jigsaw, of course, but we'll get back to that in a minute.

"What exactly does Sellotape sound like?" I ask Bradley in the middle of our phone conversation. "Hang on a minute, you can hear for yourself...." He then proceeds to place his telephone on a table, grab a nearby supply of Sellotape, and to send out a rhythmic, semi-musical, thwacking sound in three-quarter time. It's not exactly Gershwin, but I can tell that in a larger combo, assisted by guitars and other, more conventional instruments.... Well, no. Even in that context, Sellotape would sound weird. When not emoting at Elstree, Bradley often performs with a band called hKippers (wherein, he assures me, the "h" is silent). Besides Sellotape, hKippers includes "a brass section, an accordion, a double bass, a violin, and somebody plays garden implements."

He further informs *Walford Gazette* readers: "There's usually nine in the band, but sometimes more." He defines their music as "all original numbers done in a style that might be best described as German Cabaret with French and East European influences. We call it 'Stupid World Music,'" says Bradley, "because the music is stupid, and so is the world, really." On the other hand, there are some very good professional musicians in hKippers, including Bradley's friend Stephen Warbeck, who has created themes for TV's *Prime Suspect* and the stage show *An Inspector Calls.*

As for the art of Sellotape-sonising, Bradley explains, "You wrap it round your hands and head. The more expensive, double-stick tape is dreadful, because it gets stuck in your hair." He recalls how this once led to a mini-disaster when he was appearing onstage in support of The Pogues. "I got my hand stuck to my head in "By the Side of the River," which is a dangerous song. One of the roadies had to come onstage with scissors.... Believe me, cheap Sellotape is better."

It is also safer than his previous hKippers instrument. "I used to have a jigsaw onstage and cut pieces of wood into shapes of fish. But one night I almost cut my leg off." Fish, however, remain the primary image of hKippers. The band members dress as they please for each show, "but we each wear a tie with a fish design on it." The costumes have got a bit bizarre of late, he adds. "In our last gig, one of the chaps wore a dress. I don't know why. There are two women in the band who don't wear dresses...."

Love of music has occasionally carried over into Bradley's portrayal of the Harpo-haired Nigel Bates on *EastEnders.* The most notable case was when Mark Fowler and Steve Owen held a "rave," and Nigel showed up wearing a cap with the "Dylan" logo.

"I'm a very big Dylan fan," admits Bradley. "In fact, that was my own cap. I've seen Dylan every time he came over here, and I bought that cap at one of his concerts."

This caused mild disappointment to numerous Brits who are fans of both Dylan and *EastEnders*, and who wrote in on the assumption that Bradley had access to some trove of Dylan hats. The mail also put him in touch with a fan who has since been sending him Dylan T-shirts and bootleg audio tapes. He adds that he made a special trip to an upscale London neighbourhood called Crouch Hill when the rumour got around that Dylan was buying a house there. "That rumour was presumably spread by the estate agents," Bradley reflects with a chuckle. "I dropped by in the hope of seeing him. He never showed, but house prices in Crouch Hill have gone up."

Before Albert Square, Bradley had done considerable stage work and also appeared in four episodes of a popular Britcom, *The Young Ones*. His character, "Warlock," was a friend of "Rick," who was played by Bradley's real-life friend, Rik Mayall.

The two graduated together from the University of Manchester in the same year as Ade Edmondson – who played Vyvyan on *The Young Ones* – and Tom Watt, better known to us as Lofty on *EastEnders*. "That was a good year for Manchester," remembers Bradley, referring to the comic breakthrough made by Mayall and Edmondson on *The Young Ones* and *The Comic Strip Presents*. "They broke the hold of the Oxford/Cambridge mafia on TV comedy. Bradley himself turned up in a couple of character parts on *Comic Strip*.

He goes on to explain that in the sixties and seventies, such comedy troupes as Beyond the Fringe and Monty Python had consisted almost exclusively of humorists educated at the elite Oxford and Cambridge colleges. With *The Young Ones*, "for the first time, alternative comedy from Manchester was given a chance." Bradley's tone leaves no doubt that he considers this a good thing for comedy.

Bradley, who spent a year with the National Theatre, found frequent work in stage productions of Shakespeare, cast for comic relief in such roles as Dogberry, Bottom, and Feste. He believes that his talent for bringing lightness to serious goings-on was a key factor to finding regular employment as an *EastEnder*.

"I was only supposed to do three episodes and I think they just liked the character. Nigel is kind of funny and light, and arrived just after Gill had died of AIDS and the show was accused of being a bit gloomy. I came back for one more episode, and then I've been back ever since."

At the time, that "one more episode" seemed like more of a chore than a major career opportunity. Nigel's scenes were taped early in the morning, after Bradley had opened the previous night in a play about Bulldog Drummond. He knew full well that, whether it succeeded or failed, there would be considerable post-curtain drinking with other members of the cast.

The play went quite well, with Bradley portraying an American detective and (in a series of surprise plot developments) that detective's four brothers as well. As a result, Bradley had to appear in the playbill in five different disguises "so as not to give away the plot."

An exhausted and drink-weakened Bradley showed up at the Queen Vic that following morning, grateful for the coincidence that Nigel was supposed to be hungover at the time. As for the character of Nigel, Bradley describes him as "harmless and amiable... I suppose he's a bit of a wallie. Nigel is very well-meaning. He was best mates at school with Phil and Grant. Where they would use their fists, he would use jokes to get out of trouble." Asked if Nigel is the favourite of all his roles, Bradley offers a very surprising comeback. "You mustn't laugh, but my favourite role was that of Albert Einstein in *The Life of Einstein*."

This raises two very interesting questions. First, what would Einstein have thought of Nigel? More important, how would Einstein have explained the phenomenon of music being made from Sellotape for a band called hKippers?

–Dan Abramson

Lucy Speed (Natalie Evans), 2003

"I showed up there with an attitude, not giving a stuff whether I got the damn part, and they responded to that. They liked it, liked my feistiness."

Getting Up to Speed. Okay, I know I've just used a rather too obvious pun to kick off this interview. However, since it's a much-used phrase from one of my two favourite TV shows (*24*), I hope I'm excused. And Lucy Speed is one of my favourite actresses from my other favourite TV show – *EastEnders,* of course.

In mid-January of this year Ms. Speed very kindly agreed to meet with me during her lunch break from the show at the BBC Elstree Television Centre's bar, which, incidentally, serves up a darned good lunch. I assured her that because of time constraints it wouldn't offend me if she spoke with her mouth full. She merely asked me to ask long questions!

Walford Gazette: Thank you so much for doing this, Lucy. I'm well aware that you have a busy day ahead of you, filming-wise.

Lucy Speed: Oh, it's fine. I'm happy to do it. Yeah, I actually have some pretty emotional scenes to do this afternoon and because of quick rewrites I haven't locked in all my lines yet so I'd better get going on that as soon as we're done!

WG: Let's get to it, then. Let me begin this by saying that I have always enjoyed your work on *EastEnders* so much. Natalie is a wonderful character, and you and she have proved to be a valuable asset to the show.

LS (smiling): Awwwww, thanks. That's very nice to hear. I think the viewers in general like Natalie a fair amount despite the mistakes she's made. That's the feeling I get when I speak to them in the bank or supermarkets or wherever.

WG: Well, that leads to my asking you about why you left the show in 1995 after being on it for just a year. I read in a newspaper interview a year or so ago that you "freaked out" at all the attention you had been receiving as the result of being part of a monster hit TV show like *EastEnders*.

LS: Yes, I've spoken pretty honestly about how I reacted to all that. I was very frightened by it quite frankly and certainly unprepared for it. I didn't like at all the attention that came with being on such a high-profile show. But I also have to make it clear that from the beginning when I joined I always intended to stay in it for just a year anyway. I honoured my initial one-year contract and then moved on. And that's what I did.

WG: I'm sure the show came running after you with another contract, right? At that point Natalie had just slept with her best friend Bianca's boyfriend Ricky. That storyline was certainly heating up.

LS: Yep, they did express their interest in signing me for another year but I politely but firmly declined. They were a bit shocked. I tried to explain in the best way I could my reasons for leaving at the end of my contract and they ultimately understood, and so I left on good terms with them. A good thing too, I could have ended up being run over and killed off out of spite by them!

WG: Ohhhhhh, you mean like poor Tiff the Stiff?

LS (eyes widening): You mean Tiffany? (laughs) Uh-huh, like her! That black-haired girl who was Natalie's replacement as Bianca's best friend! I heard she got out of B's shadow and ended up a pretty good character on her own.

WG: I risk the chance of seeming to harp on this but could you explain a bit further what you meant when you admitted to having been "freaked out" by appearing on the show?

LS: Oh, it wasn't like I suffered a nervous breakdown or anything like that. I was just frightened by what I found I'd got myself into. It simply wasn't what I signed up for in the first place – all that craziness. I was naive, I admit. Of course it does come with the job of being on the show and you have to learn to deal with it and cope with it. The advantages always outweigh the drawbacks, anyway, but it didn't seem like that to me at the time. I was very young and extremely shy, so it all became a huge difficulty for me.

WG: You and Patsy Palmer (Bianca) joined the show around the same time. Couldn't you have helped each other out coping with that difficulty?

LS: Patsy and I became great mates and got on really well together always during our time together on the show but her personal situation was so different to mine. She was a totally independent, young working girl with a little boy, Charlie, to bring up, and living in her own flat. She had grown-up responsibilities and had already been a crazy girl at clubs and all that. I had lived with my parents in a consistently "safe," quiet environment all my life. And then *EastEnders* happened and it shook everything up, is all I'll say. It was tough.

WG: And it must be stressed that when you left you did make it clear in the press that you wanted to take on other roles besides Natalie.

LS: Yeah, that's really how I felt, too. I was also afraid that being a young actress I would quickly be pigeonholed as a "soap actress" and also too strongly identified with my soap character and would find it difficult to get other work. I wouldn't have felt that way if I was a more mature performer who already had taken my turn at doing other roles. Being on a soap like this is a really good living and very satisfying for many reasons. Anyway it was the right thing for me to do at the time. I'd never advise others to do the same because each situation's different. I had some "growing up" to do and instinctively knew that "growing up" more or less in front of the British public for one year was enough! Not that anything too embarrassing was reported about me in the tabloid newspapers! (laughs)

WG: From what I remember your personal life was rarely scrutinized by the tabloid press, if at all.

LS (grinning): That's because the *really interesting* stuff didn't happen to me until after I left the show!

WG: Clever girl. So how did you join the show initially? I always love the stories behind the casting procedure, they're so varied.

LS: It was all pretty odd. I had suddenly been scheduled for an audition for *EastEnders* in the early evening and I had to rush up to it by leaving a dance class early. I really loved that dance class so I hated having to do that! I was in a strop, as a result, on the train up to Elstree. I was pissed! In the American sense. Pretty cranky. So I showed up there with an attitude, not giving a stuff whether I got the damn part, and they responded to that. They liked it, liked my feistiness, they thought it was the quality they were looking for.

WG: It sounds like you were more Bianca than Natalie at the audition.

LS: Yeah, that's true. But Natalie was a pretty gloomy kid if you remember, not a sunny showbiz kid, which is all they'd been seeing until I walked through the door. So I got the part. They called up a week later and told me to report to Elstree at a certain time, nothing more. I thought it was for a rehearsal or wardrobe tests with the cameras or something. No, it was my first day on the set shooting! Someone walked up to me and asked me if I knew my lines for my first day! I panicked, it was a nightmare, I didn't know where to go. I got hold of some scripts and learned Natalie's first lines *real quickly*. It's a good thing learning lines for me has never been that much of a problem or I would have been in big trouble.

WG: It sounds to me that the production people at that time were asleep at the wheel! They should have ended up in trouble, not you.

LS: Yeah, that was pretty unusual for them. I suppose the exciting prospect of my stunning first appearance on the show fell between the cracks somehow. They're absolutely brilliant about showing the newcomers around now and helping them to adjust to the production schedule when they first join. They even assign a more seasoned cast member to them as a "mentor," which is a really good idea. I wish I'd had one at the time.

WG: That sounds like a really smart thing to do. I liked Natalie from that very first day we saw her moping around the market, hanging around Bianca as her sidekick, egging B on to get her revenge on Tricky Dicky.

LS (smiling): Yes, that was her initial purpose, being B's sidekick. That's one of the reasons my return to the show was so interesting – I was no longer playing B's much put-upon sidekick.

WG: Bianca treated her like dirt, didn't she? She'd tell her to her face that she was plain and wouldn't attract boys. I remember when I'd get together with other *EastEnders* fans in New York and we'd talk about how mean B was being to Natalie and that she didn't know what she was talking about. Natalie was a cute girl with an adorable big eyes and a great husky voice!

LS (laughing): Awwwww, thanks! I love hearing that, obviously!

WG: And so when Natalie slept with Ricky we were actually rooting for her to take him away from Bianca because Bianca treated *him* like dirt, too!

LS (laughs): I *know*! But after it got out that she had slept with Ricky in that love shack also known as The Arches, she immediately got sent away to live with a relative by that horrible mother of hers. End of my one-year contract!

WG: What do you think happened to her during those four years away from Walford?

LS: Well, it was revealed bit by bit that she had taken a business course at college and had had at least one ill-fated romance. Guess the guy couldn't measure up to her memories of being with Ricky at The Arches!

WG: On her return to Walford in 1999, she opened up a dating service and ended up going out with one of her clients: Barry. I thought for a change I'd incorporate questions into this interview from some American viewers of *EastEnders*. This is from Sherry Lehman of New York: What were the circumstances leading up to your return to the show? Did you contact them or did they contact you?

LS: First of all, thanks for your question, Sherry Lehman! It happened in an interesting way. I'd actually kept in touch with Ross Kemp (Grant) over the years I'd been away, and one night over the phone I mentioned in passing that I wouldn't mind coming back to the show. He asked me if I really meant that and I said I did. He was having lunch at a very posh London restaurant the next day with Matthew Robinson, the show's then producer, and mentioned what I'd said. Matthew seemed pretty agreeable to it and asked Ross how they should get the ball rolling, should Ross call me up about it? Ross gestured over to my agent, who totally coincidentally was having lunch a few tables over! And they took it from there.

WG: Great story. We have a lot to thank Ross Kemp for now, don't we?

LS (laughs): You're telling me. I'm behind on my commission payments to him but he already makes a pretty good salary nowadays so I'm not too bothered!

WG: Matthew made a really good choice to bring you and Natalie back, that's for sure.

LS: It turned out that he'd been thinking of ways to introduce a love interest for Barry, and it crossed his mind that it could be Natalie. It was good timing. He thought I and the character fit the bill.

WG: I do think they look right together in a funny way. But a lot of people both here and in the U.K. have asked the question: Why Barry? In fact, Irene Feldman of New Jersey asked me to ask you what was it about Barry that attracted Nat in the first place?

LS: Thanks for your question, Irene Feldman! Uhhh, I think it has a lot to do with her childhood. Natalie really adored her dad but he couldn't put up with that horrible wife of his, Andrea, Nat's mum, and so he walked out on the family. Andrea is a total nightmare control freak, and it says a lot about who Natalie is, why she had no confidence in herself. Her mother probably emotionally abused her. So Barry represented safety and a secure family environment, believe it or not! He and Pat and Roy! (laughs) She feels safe with him and she felt she made the right choice at the time, although of course she was apprehensive about it.

WG: But after they got married and she became pregnant she became determined to abort their child.

LS: Oh, that's a complicated one. The safe environment she thought she'd married into became oppressive and stifling because she and Barry were living with Roy and Pat and never seemed to have any money. She couldn't see a light at the end of the tunnel and also didn't have confidence in being a mum. She felt trapped, and having a baby might have seemed to her like a nail in the coffin, sorry to use that term.

WG: The scenes between you and Shaun Williamson (Barry) during this storyline were very moving. I have a theory: Perhaps Natalie became pregnant with Ricky's baby back in 1995 and her mother forced her into an abortion, and so she never wanted to have another one for fear of always being reminded of the baby she wanted so badly – Ricky's.

LS (laughs): Interesting theory – that's all I'll say! Shaun is so brilliant to work with – a great, great guy, so nice and funny. I'm very lucky.

WG: Now it looks like Natalie and Ricky might be rekindling something this year.

LS: Well, Natalie's always had strong feelings for Ricky. And now she's grown tired of being a mother to baby Jack *and* Barry! *Really tired*! (laughs) Ricky perks her up. It didn't help when Pat said to her that you never can quite forget your first love. Ironic, considering she's her mother-in-law. We'll see. Quite frankly, I still don't know how it'll develop.

WG: I have to ask you about your time away from *EastEnders*. You were in the Oscar-winning film *Shakespeare in Love* – that must have been a good thing.

LS: It was. I had a very tiny role in it though, just a few lines of dialogue. I played a whore. A whore with very bad teeth! The hair people walked up to me shrieking, "We just found this faaaaaaabulously horrid wig for you to wear!" Somehow I think they expected me to be thrilled. (laughs) I ended up working on the film for a few weeks, though. I got to hang out a bit with Joseph Fiennes, who was lovely, and Geoffrey Rush, who was fantastic – so funny and nice. And Judi Dench is an idol of mine, so meeting her was amazing, of course. Everybody was in awe of her. The wardrobe people could never figure out how she seemed to float along the floor when she was wearing built-up platform shoes to make her appear taller! I made sure I scrubbed up and put on a nice frock to wear to the cast and crew party at the end of the shoot. I wanted to show everyone I could be cute in real life! (laughs) Joseph wasn't there – awwww!

WG: I read somewhere you worked as a nanny. True?

LS: True. Both here and in America. Although I only worked once as a nanny in America. It was in Boca in Florida and it was as a favour to a friend of mine. The kid was a right little terror – he chucked a milkshake on my lap and I dumped the rest on his head! (laughs) He was *so* much less well-behaved than the other lovely children I had looked after over here, like darling little Alexander of Clapham! (laughs) I love it.

WG: You've spent time in the U.S., then?

LS: At one time my aunt and uncle lived in Connecticut. My aunt married an American, and moved there. I went to visit them one summer when I was eleven, and it was my first time travelling alone on a plane. They were there to meet me at Newark Airport, of course. Another time when I was just hanging around bored in Connecticut my aunt's friend asked me if I wanted to join her on a trip out to Long Island in New York and I went way out there and lay on the beach for a few days! It was great! Incidentally, my brother also studied at university in Louisiana, and because of his scholastic achievements there his name is on a plaque they have up on a wall. My parents want to go over there to view it! (laughs)

WG: Awwww. What else did you do acting-wise from 1995 to 1999?

LS: I worked on two things for American TV. One was for a show called *The New Adventures of Robin Hood*. I played Maid Marian's cousin Iris, who was put under a magic spell by the wicked queen. I think it turned out all right in the end. That was shot in Lithuania, and those Lithuanians got me mighty drunk one night on orange vodka and cranberry vodka. I didn't realise at the time it was 100 per cent vodka! I didn't black out but... well, I'll leave the rest to your imagination.

WG: So *that's* what you meant about the interesting stuff that happened after your first year on *EastEnders*!

LS: Well, I wasn't a minor, I was of legal age. Needless to say, few experiences will be able to match up to that. (laughs) It was a lot of fun.

WG: And your other American TV job?

LS: Oh, that was for *Unsolved Mysteries*, hosted by Mr. William Shatner. I played this terminally ill girl taken to Lourdes by her friends and family hoping for a miracle. We actually shot that at Lourdes, and I almost didn't get to go because the night before I was to leave I realised to my horror that my passport had expired six months earlier! I managed to get them to change my flight for six hours later – it was on a Saturday – and so I spent the entire morning waiting on line at the passport office.

WG: That was the real miracle – getting your passport sorted.

LS (laughs): Yes! I simply had to appear on *Unsolved Mysteries*. I *had* to!

WG: I saw you on *The Weakest Link* in Britain. It was an *EastEnders* special, and your fellow contestants were your colleagues Wendy Richard (Pauline), Adam Woodyatt (Ian), Hannah Waterman (Laura), Lucy Benjamin (Lisa) and Shaun (Barry). You were funny on that. It didn't look at all like you wanted to be there.

LS (laughs): I didn't! I hated it. I'd been coerced into doing it by *EastEnders*! And I *loathed* Anne Robinson. I think she's the most horrid woman. I never wanted to vote out any of my cast mates intentionally. So what I would do during the time we had to vote is I'd just keep on typing everybody's first name until they told us to stop and the one which stuck on the electronic thingie was the one I had to use. We didn't write out the names like they do on the other shows for some reason. Anyway, the first time I voted the name which stuck turned out to be for the guy playing my on-screen husband, Shaun! Anne wouldn't let that fact go, not even during the breaks we took, when we weren't even on camera! She's hateful! True Evil. I'm glad she didn't last long in America!

WG (laughs): Too funny. I know you have to go now to lock in your lines for this afternoon so I'll end with a question from Esta Asteroff of Florida, but not Boca. Do you feel you'd like to remain in the role of Natalie for a long time?

LS: Thank you for your question, Esta Asteroff. Uhhhh, I don't really know. I've actually been on *EastEnders* for over four times this time around and I enjoy it here very much. I love acting. I've been a working actress since I was a little girl and begged my parents to let me get an agent! I hope to be acting for a very long time. Whether it's here will, I'm sure, depend on a combination of things. I do think Natalie has a lot left to do, character-wise. She's gone from being a young

141

girl with zero confidence in herself to a young woman with a certain measure of confidence back to someone with zero confidence. Life doesn't go easy on her but she's got strength. She's a feisty little thing and she gets on with things.

WG: We love her. Thanks again for doing this, Lucy.

LS: You're very welcome. When you met me last month here and showed me the *Gazette* I took a look at the Letters pages and I thought the passion and interest of its readers for our show was fantastic. We're very fortunate to get such interest by so many people in America, which I love. I personally think that kind of interest is a pleasure to receive!

–Tim Wilson

Shaun Williamson (Barry Evans), 1999

"When I first read the script I noticed that Barry was referred to as 'Blondie'. I then found out before my audition that Barry was initially conceived to be this big blond bloke."

The term "gregarious" must certainly have been coined for someone like Shaun Williamson, who plays Roy Evans' amusingly scrappy son Barry in *EastEnders*, a great guy to hang out with if my recent lunch with him at the BBC cafeteria is anything to go by.

During our interview at the BBC Elstree Centre several fellow cast members found themselves being politely shooshed away by Shaun only to happily return to our table when the grilling session was completed. This guy is obviously the life of any party much less a lunchtime communal gathering.

Shaun Williamson: So you're from America, no? I like America very very good.

Walford Gazette: Do you intend to use that quirky foreign accent throughout our entire interview, Shaun?

SW: Uh, well, no, I don't think it's a good idea to torture journalists... it makes 'em kinda cranky.

WG: Not if it's taken in the right spirit. What is it I'm eating again?

SW: Lancashire hotpot – a right old British traditional dish – really just a stew, innit?

WG: Just add noodles, and you've got goulash, I guess. Let's move the subject on to you.

SW: Ah, well, as for me I'm having bangers and mash – another right old traditional dish. You know for a canteen they feed us pretty well... (a mock scowl) Only problem is that they charge.

WG: Please don't be insulted but looking across to you and down to that plate of mashed potatoes I can't help but be reminded of that scene in *Animal House* where John Belushi stuffs some in his mouth and regurgitates it.

SW: One of the great canteen scenes of all time! And he says, "It's a zit... get it?" Classic comedy. I remind you of Belushi? I'm flattered. He was brilliant. Some of the antics that Barry gets up with his flatmates (not yet seen in the U.S.) are easily reminiscent of *Animal House*. There are lots of wacky goings-on in there, let me tell you.

WG: More about the show later. First, let's start with your America remark. Is it true or were you just being a tad smart alecky?

SW: You want visual proof I was sincere? (whips out a photo from his bag) There! There's your stinking proof!

WG: Well, from what I can see it's a photo of you and a very nice-looking young woman. Your sister?

SW: You know very well who it is, you pillock. I told you about this on the phone last week. I told you I'd bring it. This is my gorgeous wife Melanie I'm standing with. We had just gotten married amongst the boulders of Central Park, New York City, in October 1997.

WG: I guess I could think of something cutesy to respond but I'll mercifully restrain myself.

SW: You do that. Next to our daughter's birth, this was the happiest day of my life. We even went back there to renew our vows last October. You can print this picture in the *Gazette* if you like.

WG: Thank you very much. Why did you get married in New York?

SW: I love New York City and I managed to convince Mel that that's where we should tie the knot. It does have a reputation for being a particularly romantic wedding locale, you know.

WG: It sure beats Las Vegas in my opinion. Instead of an Elvis impersonator, who'd you get to officiate then?

SW: An interfaith minister who we found via the phone book. And she was terrific.

WG: What's in your wife's handbag?

SW: Mind your own business... I bet you'd ask the Queen what was in her handbag if you were ever lucky enough to meet her.

WG: I wouldn't, but Bette Midler has wondered aloud about what is the deal with that handbag.

SW: Bette Midler can do anything she wants because she's Bette Midler, and she's amazing.

WG: I gather that your wedding wasn't your first time in New York?

SW: Nah, I spent six weeks there back in '87. I was a summer camp counsellor down in Pennsylvania and took advantage of some time left when the gig was done. Actually a bunch of us hitchhiked to New Orleans first. It was one of those foreign exchange-type things... instead of a nubile Swedish girl, they got me. It was a camp in the Poconos that mostly catered to hyperactive kids. The whole lot of them was medicated to their gills on Ritalin. Ah yes. I remember it well. They were great kids, though. Our prime function was to keep 'em focused and engaged, and we succeeded in our mission. I enjoyed it a lot there. I'd already worked in quite a few similar holiday camps in England so I knew what I was doing. In England there were just us hyperactive folk minus the medication.

WG: I've heard of a few of those places. Butlins, Pontins...

SW: I worked at Pontins as an entertainer. I sing, too, you know, so I was useful. I also worked as a holiday rep for a place called Club 18-30 but I was sent home after five months for trying to live the punters' holiday with them as opposed to just being staff. I did a bit more than call the Bingo numbers, I'm afraid. At least I didn't screw up in Pennsylvania.

WG: And after Pennsylvania you hitched to New Orleans... a very good place to party hardy, I bet.

SW (nods): A great time was had by all. The rest of the gang had to head on back to England but I stayed behind to travel a bit more. I figured hitchhiking to New York from Louisiana might not be a particularly wise thing to do, so I flew instead. I stayed there for six fantastic weeks, and had the time of my life.

WG: Where are you originally from, Shawn?

SW: Oh, I see. This is the *This Is Your Life* portion of the interview. I grew up in a place called Maidstone in south-east England on a decent council estate. Very working-class and very happy. Mum's a cleaner, dad's a postman. I tried to follow in his footsteps after school but I thought I'd go mad so I joined the Royal Navy. Big mistake. I tried desperately to get out.

WG: How? Pretend to be gay or something?

SW: Nah, everybody was all too aware how girl crazy I was, so that wouldn't have worked at all. I found this book in the library that actually spelled out how to get released from the service. Wetting the bed worked a whole lot for starters! (laughs) Let me just say that after a while the powers that be realised I was a colossal waste of time and money and decided to cut their losses. They cut me loose and I couldn't have been happier or more relieved. So was the Navy laundry detail!

WG: Had you realised by then that you wanted to be an actor?

SW: I always knew I wanted to act but when you're young and in my environment you didn't have a clue as to how to actually make it happen. After the Navy fiasco and the holiday camp high jinks I learned about the Webber Douglas Academy for Dramatic Art in London. I enrolled there when I was 27, so I was a few years older than the others. Ross Kemp (Grant) went there as well, but he'd left and was already on *EastEnders*. I got a lot out of Webber Douglas. By the time I completed my training there I really believed that I might have a shot at actually getting work.

WG: Your belief was very soon justified, that's for sure. You were only six months out of graduating when you got the part of Barry Evans in *EastEnders*.

SW: I was a week out of there when I got my first part on *EastEnders*. Aha – didn't know I'd been on already, did you?

WG: My extensive research efforts failed me yet again, I'm afraid.

SW: I played a paramedic who tended to David Wicks in the Vic after Grant did him over for dancing with Sharon. My big line was, "How many fingers am I holding up, David?" Actually there's an amusing story tied to this auspicious debut. I was up for two parts, y'see. Paramedic #1 and Paramedic #2. Paramedic #2 had three lines of dialogue and Paramedic #1 had sixteen. No fool me – I wanted to play Paramedic #1. But I got Paramedic #2 instead. Well, at the time I couldn't drive, and for some reason Paramedic #2 had to be the one to drive the ambulance in and out of the Square. I 'fessed up about the driving bit, and so they switched our parts. I got sixteen lines!

WG: Why do I get the feeling that the other actor wasn't thrilled?

SW: He was gutted! I did feel bad for him. Honest. Not least because he wasn't a very good driver so the ambulance screeched in and out of the Square at about two miles per hour.

WG: Another classic *EastEnders* moment.

SW: Absolutely. Anyway I did a bunch of stuff in TV real soon after that and yes, I did learn how to drive. It quickly dawned on me that my blue collar-type of looks might just lead to roles in which the character drove a lorry or whatever. I was in *The Bill,* a cop show, which is sort of a running joke among actors here because everybody gets on it sooner or later. The same is true of *London's Burning,* the firemen show. I worked on that, too.

WG: And *EastEnders* came a-knocking five months after your auspicious debut as Paramedic #1?

SW: When I first read the script I noticed that Barry was referred to as "Blondie." I then found out before my audition that Barry was initially conceived to be this big blond bloke. I thought, "Well, that's it. That ain't me. Elevator shoes and a dye job won't cut it." The director said, "No, no, let's read this through – nothing is laid in cement." We read it through and it went okay. After that we spent a lot of time talking about. I got the job. It was just for four episodes at first. Barry came on just after Christmas to apologise to Pat for selling her a duff motor. He was really meant to be a vehicle, pardon the pun, to get Roy into the show. I found myself popping in and out over the next year and a half, as you may have noticed.

WG: Did you worry that you might not return to the show after they sent Barry off to prison for the car lot incident?

SW: Nobody ever went to great lengths to reassure me that I'd be returning. I'm not sure that I knew what would be happening. That was fine with me. I just went off and did a lot of other things. Singing in cabarets, theatre work, other television work. In a way, I was glad I wasn't on a long-term contract from the beginning. I got the opportunity to work in all sorts of venues, and if I was tied to the show that just wouldn't have been possible. I got the chance to sow my wild oats in a professional sense.

WG: You and Michael French (David) had great personal chemistry as actors.

SW: Thank you. Yes, we did. Michael's such a terrific actor and we always worked well. Barry and David's relationship was a brilliant thing to play. Each regarded the other not only as a best mate but as a brother. Barry was an only child and David hadn't been around Wicksy in many years so they treated each other as the brother they hadn't had.

WG: Was it me, or did you play Barry's friendship with Cindy as an unrequited crush as well?

SW: I see you've got a good eye for dramatic subtext. Yes, of course, I played it that way. Barry did have a thing for Cindy but he'd never dare make a move. There was David to think about, and besides, Cindy was too fast for him. She'd have eaten him alive!

WG: Without giving away plot information, what's next for Barry?

SW: There's something really horrendous coming up over there in the States over the next year which affects Roy and Pat in ways they (and the audience) could never have imagined. Barry becomes an unwitting pawn in a nightmarish situation. Barry loves his dad and is actually fond of and respects Pat. The troubles he gets in severely test everybody's love and respect. He remains unlucky in love for quite a while. Barry's love life does brighten up soon, I think.

WG: Last week I saw you on a television show over here called *Vanessa*, and you sang "I Feel Good." You were good!

SW: That was fun. I only hope James Brown wasn't in the country.

WG: You were obviously having a good time with it. Now that you've told me about your camp counsellor days I can imagine you entertaining the punters with a song or two.

SW: I certainly did. (sings) "You're just too good to be true... Thank you, ladies 'n gentlemen..." I sang stuff like that all the time. "Her name was Lola/She was a show girl..." Barry Manilow songs always went down well. "I Write the Songs" was a particular crowd-pleaser. It slayed 'em in the aisles every night, especially when there was a full moon.

WG: I also saw you over Christmas on a karaoke show called *Night Fever*.

SW: Yeah, I guess you can say I'm a hemi-demi-semi-regular on that. That show's really a silly, cheesy sort of thing but there's a place for it in the light entertainment sector on TV. I'm happy being on it occasionally but not much more that because the old credibility factor might get eaten away a bit.

WG: Have you sung on *EastEnders*?

SW: No, I haven't. Barry recently did a mean Boy George imitation in the Vic after a particularly teary funeral. It was meant as comic relief, no doubt. He wore beer mats for earrings. I began to think I was back at Pontins.

WG: How about doing an album some day?

SW: It's a childhood ambition of mine. Unfortunately, it hasn't quite worked out yet because the deal hasn't been quite right. I don't want to make some crap novelty record. If people are going to shell out their hard-earned money on a CD of mine it's got to be bit more... substantial. I'd be happy to creep in a rendition of "You're Just Too Good To Be True" somewhere in there, though!

WG: Why don't we end this with a few words about your lovely wife and child. Where did you two meet?

SW: I met Mel in an amateur theatrics group. We did a play called *Habeas Corpus* and in one scene our characters kissed. That scene needed a lot of rehearsal, in my opinion. The rest is history. We've got a beautiful one-year-old named Sophie May. I'm a good dad. I give the first feeding in the morning. Barry wouldn't have a clue, would he? Mel and I just like to relax and do what everybody else does, like conk out in front of the telly. We love to watch sports of any kind.... We used to cross over the road to a friend of ours who had satellite TV to watch stuff like *American Gladiators* and *World Professional Wrestling*. We've got a satellite now. We've certainly moved up in the world!

WG: Thanks for the interview, Shaun. Come back to America soon. Central Park beckons. You could throw an anniversary party on the Great Lawn. I'd come.

SW: There goes three months of my *EastEnders* salary!

—Tim Wilson

Tony Caunter (Roy Evans), 1999

"The show's made a distinct effort to make Roy more human and less perfect. He's gone from being Pat's knight in shining armour to a fellow who gets upset and angry and leaps about."

Yes, yes... I know many of you out there think Roy Evans (East End car dealer extraordinaire) is just too good to be true. *Walford Gazette* subscriber Lisa Williamson has even commented that he's "too nice for Pat – even though she has pulled herself together." I recently spoke on the phone with the gentleman who plays Roy, Tony Caunter, asking him to give his own viewpoint on this and several other matters. You shouldn't be too surprised to learn that he's extremely nice, too. He's one of the good guys.

Walford Gazette: So what do you make of this "too good to be true" business? It does appear that Roy Evans is the perfect man.

Tony Caunter: Uhh, did you happen to miss a certain crucial Pat/Roy episode, Tim?

WG: Okay, so he does have that little problem, that minor flaw.

TC: It's a pretty major flaw, don't you think? Impotency?

WG: I have great confidence that he'll snap out of it some day soon and then he'll be perfect. We have a popular sex therapist [in America] named Dr. Ruth Westheimer. Maybe he should fly her over.

TC: I've seen her on television over here! She's very funny. (sighs) Roy needs all the help he can get, poor sod.

WG: I watched the show over there a few months ago and there was a little scene where Pat slips and reveals Roy's impotency to Kathy. Kathy asks why he hasn't gone to get help for it. Pat says something like, "Oh, you know Roy, Kath. He's too proud to seek help." Come on! I think Roy is perfectly capable of getting off his behind and heading up West or wherever to get that problem sorted, don't you?

TC: Don't tell me, tell the writers! No really, even without the impotency problem, Roy wouldn't be perfect. It is true, though, that he really loves and respects Pat.

WG: And he's loaded.

TC: He also helped take good care of Janine when she was there. He's got on well with David and Ricky. And he's been a good dad to Barry.

WG: And he's loaded.

TC: (laughs): Right, right, that too! Although the writers have recently come up with a clever storyline in which Roy finds himself on... more of a level playing field with the other residents of

Albert Square. You're all quite a way behind in episodes over there so I guess you won't see that happen for many months.

WG: I admit I was a bit worried when Roy Evans was brought on to the show because it was established that he was an affluent fellow. I wondered how he and Pat could wind up together without her leaving Albert Square (and *EastEnders*) for a life of luxury.

TC: I think there was that concern in the beginning but the writers created a plausible reason for him to move into the Square. He's from that environment initially; he's an East End boy. He's not a posh gent although he does know about good wine and fine dining. He really loves Pat and she didn't want to leave because her family and friends were there and by then he'd have done anything for Pat. He'd reached a time in his life when he desperately wanted a good home life with a good woman. He was already semi-retired and could afford to sit back and smell the roses, so to speak – and he wanted to smell them with Pat! And to completely answer your original question, he's really not perfect at all. By now we've seen that he can lose his temper and he can sometimes not be terribly open to other people's views.

WG: A scene aired here not too long ago in which Pat said to Roy in the Vic, "You're the nicest man in the world" and Roy replied, "You didn't know me when I was younger." Was Roy a bit of a rotter before we (and Pat) got to know him?

TC: I don't really think he was ever a horrible person. I'm sure he had to be tough because he's a self-made man. In that area, in that business, he had to be tough. I don't think he was ruthless though. It would be nice if that remark of his is fleshed out in a storyline one day.

WG: A disgruntled ex-employee could show up at the Vic and accuse Roy of having been a total bastard.

TC (laughs): Yes, I'd like that. The ex-employee would have to be punished immediately for calling him a bastard in the Vic, of course. A lorry must run over him post-haste!

WG: For a nice guy you really have vivid ideas regarding punishment. Seriously, if I haven't already mentioned it, I really appreciate you taking the time to talk with me for the *Gazette*.

TC: Well, I'm very, very pleased to talk with you. I worked in America a couple of times in actual fact and I've always had a great soft spot for America and Americans.

WG: You've worked here, have you? Was it stage or film?

TC: Both. I came over first in 1963 to work on Broadway in a play called *Chips with Everything*. It was something of a traumatic period because we played in New York at the same time as President Kennedy's assassination. We did get very positive reviews by the local critics, but the play never quite gelled with the audiences, so we wound up running for five and a half months. We expected to run a bit longer. Oh well. It was great to be over there at that time, though, because there was quite a large British contingent working on Broadway during that season. It was a great deal of fun, despite the rather harsh winter and a transport strike! I absolutely adored doing *Chips with Everything*. It was about the Royal Air Force. I'll tell you one of the things I enjoyed most about being on Broadway. Every Thursday night, the casts from a lot of the shows would get together and go bowling! It was called the Broadway Show League. I'd be bowling alongside people like

George Peppard and a newcomer who was starring in *Barefoot in the Park* named Robert Redford. Kirk Douglas too – he was doing *One Flew Over the Cuckoo's Nest*.

WG: I've got to know for the benefit of my readers: Did Robert Redford or George Peppard or Kirk Douglas stink at bowling?

TC (laughs): No, everyone was rather good, from what I remember. Anyway, back to me and my career! The second time I came to America was for a two-part television film called *S.O.S. Titanic*... the title is self-explanatory, I guess! We filmed on board the Queen Mary in Long Beach, California. David Janssen was the star and Helen Mirren was in it as well. So was David Warner, who's now also in *Titanic*, I gather. I played Chief Officer Henry Wilde... he kept the working-class passengers from reaching the deck amongst the upper-class passengers. He's a baddie in retrospect, I imagine. *Titanic* just premiered here in England last week and I can't wait to see it. Both my American experiences, in a nutshell, were absolutely wonderful.

WG: You've appeared on *Doctor Who*, haven't you?

TC: Yes, three times as a matter of fact, opposite three different Doctors! I particularly enjoyed the last one I did. I played a drunken Victorian sailor.

WG: Is there any other kind?! Is *EastEnders* the first role you've played on a regular basis?

TC: Yes, it is. It's also the first time I've been subject to tabloid press interest and all that silly stuff, although so far I've been lucky in that they haven't been too rough on me or disrupted my family. I love to work, though, as all actors do. On *EastEnders,* I get to work on a highly regular basis, which is lovely.

WG: I'm sorry to dredge the impotency issue up yet again, but I wanted to ask you if you think it'll ever get seriously addressed?

TC: I hope so, yes. You know, the reason I think they decided to have Roy be impotent was that they were concerned about Pat falling into bed with someone, after Frank. The show since then has for some reason pulled away from dealing with it, one of the reasons most likely being that we air here at 7.30 in the evening and a large number of children watch. But by God, we deal with everything else, don't we? Homosexuality, homelessness, drug abuse. I was just talking to our story editor the other day and he claimed that the impotency issue will be addressed in the very near future. I hope by New Year's Eve, 1999!

WG: For Pat's sake, I hope so, too. Do you enjoy working with Pam St. Clement?

TC: Absolutely, she's a fabulous, fabulous lady. You've interviewed her, so you already know how very intelligent she is. She's a great person, just a joy to work with. Shaun Williamson (Barry) is a lovely lad, as well. I'm a lucky actor to get to work with extremely nice, extremely good people. I almost didn't get to play Roy. You know who almost got my part? Brian Croucher, who now plays Ted Hills, Kathy's brother. The show ultimately decided they didn't want to use him for Roy and because we shared the same agent, I was then suggested. Brian was cast later on as Ted so it all worked out all right.... except he hasn't got a lovely leading lady for a romantic interest, just two mixed-up kids!

WG: He's not impotent too, I hope.

TC: It wasn't infectious when last I checked the medical journals, Tim.

WG: That'd make for an interesting storyline. I can see the headline in the *Walford Gazette*: IMPOTENCY PLAGUE STRIKES ALBERT SQUARE!

TC (laughs): And it names Roy as Patient Zero and it's all too much for poor Pat.

WG: It should most likely happen at Christmastime because Pat rarely has a nice Christmas. One year she ran over a teenage girl and was arrested for drunk driving, and in 1995 Frank showed up.

TC: She has a nice Christmas in 1996, I'm happy to say. But oops, she had another bad one in 1997.

WG: I know, I watched. You're a very happy family man in real life, aren't you?

TC: Yes, I am, thanks for asking. I'm married to an absolutely wonderful lady named Frances and we have four children, three sons and a daughter. Our eldest, Nicholas, has been acting for the past five or six years. He just did a play last summer with Kathleen Turner. We also have twin sons, William and James. William is a first assistant director on a very popular series called *The Bill*. James is a political researcher for an independent channel, Parliament TV. Our daughter Sarah has three beautiful children – Mario Jr., Joshua, and Brinyan. In case you're wondering, Brinyan's a girl! Nicholas and I are the hambones of the family and the rest are the sensible ones.

WG: Where were you born and raised, Tony?

TC: Southampton, in Hampshire. I'm a real southerner. My mother died when I was eleven, so I was raised by my grandmother. To make a very long story short, I joined the Royal Air Force when I was seventeen and after that I went to drama school at LAMDA (London Academy of Music and Dramatic Art). Richard Harris, Donald Sutherland, Janet Suzman (Nicholas and Alexandra) and I were all in the same class together. Not bad company, eh?

WG: So do you intend on staying with *EastEnders* for a long time? I speak for many *Walford Gazette* readers when I say I hope so.

TC: Oh, thank you. Yes, I do. You know, this show came along at the right time for me. At times, I don't think I've ever been worked harder than on this show but I love it. Most men my age are considering retirement but I'm extremely happy at *EastEnders*. I don't even mind when my character's on the back burner from time to time. The show's made a distinct effort to make Roy more human and less perfect. He's gone from being Pat's knight in shining armour to a fellow who gets upset and angry and leaps about. He and Pat don't live "happily ever after," well at least not in that boring sense. There's a lot more turmoil to come.

WG: She hasn't admitted to him that she did sleep with Frank, for starters.

TC: Oh, yes, that's a biggie just waiting to blow up in her face.

WG: Thanks again for taking the time to speak with me, Tony. You're a really nice bloke, you know.

TC: You're welcome, Tim. Thanks for the very kind words. All the best to your readers.

–Tim Wilson

Paul Nicholls (Joe Wicks) 1999

"I work like a maniac to get the work done the best way I can. The residual effects can't be helped, really. I didn't go home and wrap tinfoil around the telly, though!"

"Bummed out" is the only way to describe my state of mind as I shuffled down Broadway in early January. I'd been back just four days from a six-week England-France trip, and the reclamation process was really getting me down. It certainly didn't help that it was a lot colder over here. I mutter "damned Canadian air" to myself as I passed the Coliseum bookstore. I mutter "damned *Cats*" as I passed the Winter Garden Theatre.

I was about to mutter something about Seattle-style coffee bars as I passed Java Coffee on Broadway and 49th Street, when for no apparent reason I peered in and saw a strikingly handsome, yet oddly familiar fellow, sitting at the counter, downing a huge cup of joe. It was actually Paul Nicholls, who plays Joe Wicks on *EastEnders*! Knowing a *Celestine Prophecy*-type thing when I saw it, I walked right in and introduced myself. The kid was floored.

Paul Nicholls: You interviewed Daniela (Denby-Ashe, who plays Joe's erstwhile girlfriend Sarah) five days ago? In London? That's really bizarre. You've just got back, then?

Walford Gazette: Friday night. Flight 138 from Heathrow to JFK.

PN: I flew in on Friday night as well but it was from Manchester. This is not only my first time here in New York, it's my first time visiting the States, period. This is wild meeting you like this. (staring down at his cup) Everything is so huge here, even the cups. And they don't stint on the food portions either, I've noticed.

WG: You'll never go hungry here. You're on vacation?

PN: I'm on holiday, yeah. I'd been down to Jamaica for a couple of weeks, and when I got back to England I thought, "F---, I'm back in England!" Coming here was a real spur-of-the-moment decision. It hadn't been planned at all. I had the time, so I figured, why the hell not?

WG: Indeed.

PN: This place is amazing. It's everything I thought it would be and more. It could be a little less cold, though.

WG: I know what you mean. I've noticed you already bought some tickets to the theatre. What are you seeing if I may ask?

PN: *Sideman*, with Christian Slater. I've heard it's really good, and I want to see Christian Slater on-stage after having already seen him in lots of films. I'll tell you a funny thing. The old lady at the box office scared me so much, I wound up buying three tickets when I only needed one! She didn't bully me or anything, she just asked me stuff like, "Do you want sit in the orchestra, young man?" I don't know what came over me. Do you want to come?

WG: That's a very nice offer, but sorry, I can't. I've got to go to a screening of a really bad film that I worked on as a stand-in last summer.

PN: Who's in it?

WG: Sarah Michelle Gellar, who plays *Buffy the Vampire Slayer* on television.

PN: Oh, I like her. She's really cute. Actually one of the reasons I'm over here is to meet the girl of my dreams. Think that'll happen?

WG: I don't see why not. You've obviously got several legs up on the competition, I would guess.

PN (blankly): What do you mean?

WG: You obviously haven't: a) looked in the mirror lately or b) read about yourself in the press. You are, as they say, a major catch. A babe magnet.

PN: I try not to read all that rubbish. It causes too much needless aggravation. So you're an actor, too, as well as a journalist for the *Gazette*?

WG: Right now, I've been working a lot in films as a stand-in. I'm on my way to the Screen Actors Guild to check out future work. Do you want to schlep along?

PN: Schlep away, then. I'm really curious to see what it's like. My union, British Equity, is pretty dull and boring to hang out in.

WG: I know, I've been there.

We headed down the five blocks to the SAG/MTV building and took an elevator to the 44th floor.) As we get out:

PN: I'm staying on the 39th floor at the Millennium Hotel downtown at Battery Park. The view is amazing, if a bit frightening.

WG: It certainly not for those with vertigo. Joe would freak out, wouldn't he?

PN: Uhh, yeah, absolutely.

I showed him the casting board, which listed various film and television projects currently in production. We then move down to a board that listed the nominations for the Third Annual SAG Awards.

WG: One of my friends was on the nominating committee for that so he'll let me borrow a bunch of tapes to watch so I don't go nuts in a movie theatre.

PN: My agent in London is a member of the British Film Academy, and I nicked a copy of the new *Psycho* from the office recently! I knew it wouldn't be missed by anybody. What a poor excuse for a film, especially when the first one was so brilliant.

An actress standing nearby overheard our conversation and without skipping a beat not only agreed with Paul but also launched into reviewing the actual nominees as well. After about three minutes of intense film critique, she took her leave, having realised she was late for her hair appointment. Paul looked at me in disbelief.

PN: That was great! That would *never* happen in London! Further proof that anything can happen in New York, right?

We head over to the Eighth Avenue Deli to get some lunch. Paul politely orders a "ham and salad sandwich to take away, please." The schmo behind the counter stared at him as if he was from Mars. I admit that this was one time when I had the spooky feeling that I was standing next to Joe Wicks, the character. By that, I mean the almost unbearable vulnerability and shyness on display. Paul smiled brightly and said, "Oh, sorry, I guess it's just another English thing." The schmo was obviously disarmed, and beamed back. The kid just has that effect on people. I made sure Paul didn't walk out with three sandwiches and we headed off to the Marriott Marquis Hotel and settled into a plush lobby section to eat our lunch.

PN: Do you think we're gonna get thrown out?

WG: Nah, I think that Italian designer coat of yours will help us out. They'll think we belong here. So what's it been like playing Joe? I have to thoroughly congratulate you on behalf of myself and the *Gazette* readers for your work on the show. It's a truly wonderful, heartbreaking performance.

PN: Thanks a lot, I appreciate that. It was an incredible opportunity to get to play Joe and work on the storylines regarding his schizophrenia. The writers undoubtedly do their homework as I do and it showed up on the screen and hasn't gone unnoticed. We all knew that this character was a first for a continuing drama series, and we'd better get it right.

WG: You have, from all reports. I correspond with a *Gazette* reader, who told me she knows someone precisely with Joe's mental disorder and swears that you really have nailed it in your performance. The scenes in which Joe is slipping into extreme emotional and mental distress are like watching a really bad car wreck. It's awful and you want to stop looking at it but you can't. Your work is absolutely a high point of the show.

PN: A lot of that credit has to also go to Michael French, who plays David, Joe's dad. What a brilliant, brilliant actor. I was beyond lucky to work closely with him and we also had a real laugh together, which helped keep the atmosphere light. It made the work we had to do so much more bearable.

WG: The old actor's cliche of taking your work home must certainly have been applicable in your situation, I would gather.

PN: Yes, a bit because I'm very serious about it and I work like a maniac to get the work done the best way I can. The residual effects can't be helped, really. I didn't go home and wrap tinfoil around the telly, though!

WG: May I change the subject a bit radically and mention that your accent is quite bit softer in real life?

PN: Is it? Yeah I guess that's because I've been living down in London for the last several years. I had to lay it on [his North of England accent] pretty thick last summer when I did a play, *Billy Liar*.

WG: You received some good reviews for that. I read a few.

PN: I was unhappy with that experience to be honest because the director was a young guy who was intimidated by my so-called celebrity from *EastEnders*, so he treated me with kid gloves. I desperately needed and wanted some direction, and I didn't get it from him. Oh, well, I guess I'll chalk it up to a learning experience.

WG: While we're still on the subject of your accent I have to mention that I saw you on a children's television serial before you joined *EastEnders*. Remember *The Biz*?

PN (flabbergasted): You saw *The Biz*? Incredible. So what does that have to do with my accent?

WG: In it you played a Leonardo DiCaprio-type rising star who had just come back from America after doing a film. I remember thinking, "not with that accent." We'd need subtitles over here to understand it. Your accent was three times as thick then.

PN: Uhh, no comment. God, is this city great or what? It reminds me of *Taxi Driver*, with all that steaming coming out of the subway grates. And that psycho character. What was his name?

WG: Travis Bickle. Okay, I get the message. All I really want to ask you now is... were you really as good playing Chandler of *Friends* as Daniela said you were?

PN: Oh, she's such a sweetie. Of course I was. I added new levels to the Chandler Bing thing. She made a great Janice. She made a great Joey too. That reminds me, Tim, it's time for me to head out once again in search of my dream girl. Got any suggestions?

I resisted my burgeoning yenta inclinations and spared Paul any further pain by just respectfully shaking hands and sending off the 19-year-old lad. The kid was on vacation after all and was obviously geared up to sow some serious wild oats. I suddenly realised I needed to follow up on something I'd seen earlier at the Screen Actors Guild and headed across the street. As I entered the building I realised I was walking directly behind Pamela Anderson and her entourage on their way to an MTV interview. I decided I'd had enough of celebrity *Celestine Prophecy*.

–Tim Wilson

Daniela Denby-Ashe (Sarah Hills), 1999

"I hardly watch EastEnders except certain times when I'm on and feel the need to pick apart my performance!"

Daniela Denby-Ashe, *EastEnders'* Sarah "I've Seen the Light" Hills, is as cheerfully well adjusted as her television alter ego is intense. I found this out during our lunch at the BBC Television Centre's cafeteria, and it was a great relief, indeed. Daniela's an extremely pretty, sweet, and likeable young woman with a truly disarming way about her, as you'll soon discover.

WG: Before we start discussing *EastEnders* and matters relating to it I just have to take the opportunity to tell you that I think you have a very beautiful name.

DDA: Thanks... I like it too!

WG: I once read about an Italian actress named Daniela Bianchi and remember thinking I wouldn't mind if my future wife wanted to name our daughter Daniela.

DDA: Hey, I've heard of her as well. There aren't many Danielas around, which can be quite handy. Of course, there's also Danniella Westbrook, who plays Sam, but she spells it differently, though.

WG: I also love your last name Denby-Ashe. It's so cool, very classy. I like to say it all aloud, Daniela Denby-Ashe.

DDA (looks around nervously and laughs): Okay, whatever makes you feel good, I guess! Believe it or not, there's a story behind my last name. My dad came here when he was twelve. My dad was born in Poland. His name was Miroslaw Pszkit (pronounced Shkeet). Needless to say, when he arrived some people wouldn't learn how to pronounce it properly. So just before he and my mum got married they had a look in the telephone directory. One found the name Denby and the other found Ashe. They couldn't decide between them which name to use so they just put them together with a hyphen in the middle. I'm not Pszkit like my dad; I was born with Denby-Ashe on my birth certificate. So that's where my birth certificate comes from.

WG: Great story. Was your mum an immigrant to Britain as well?

DDA: No, she was born here, but both of her parents were born in Poland. Her mum was raised in France, so my relatives are either French or Polish. Hardly any are English.

WG: Did your parents meet at an Anglo-Polish event or something?

DDA: I believe they met in a hotel lobby. Simple coincidence that they were both Polish.

WG: And you were born in London?

DDA: In north-west London. I've got a brother, who's two years younger than me. He's 18 and I'm 20.

WG: So it's now on to the acting questions. When did you start in show business?

DDA: Well, I began dancing at two and a half. Ballet. Then at about five came the tap lessons. You know, the sort of stuff a lot of little girls over here get into. By the time I was 10, I was dying to get into a theatre school for acting. My parents were dead set against the idea at first because they were concerned that I get a good education but I wore them out! I really wanted to act so badly and conveyed it well enough to my parents that they finally let me audition for a theatre school. It closed down after two months, unfortunately. Luckily I got into another one very soon afterwards called the Corona Academy in Hammersmith. I don't believe it had anything to do with the Mexican beer but you never know! After seven months that one closed down because the headmistress was retiring.

WG: Didn't you begin to think you might be some sort of a jinx?

DDA: No, no, no. It was all fate, nothing to do with me. Anyway, one of the secretaries at the Corona Academy opened up her own theatre school and simply brought all the pupils along with her. We didn't have to get a new uniform, which was a relief. That school was called Ravenscourt and I went there from the age of 10 to 16.

WG: So did you start working professionally at the age of 10?

DDA: Yes, at first I got silly jobs, like being used as a model to help determine clothes sizes for girls my age. I remember stretching out my arms so they could take down measurements and wondering if I'd ever get to act! Very boring. Eventually I began doing commercials and bits of TV work.

WG: I certainly wouldn't consider playing Saffy's daughter in the final episode of *Absolutely Fabulous* (in a flash-forward sequence) just a bit of TV work. You're a part of another classic series, along with *EastEnders,* aren't you?

DDA: (beaming proudly) I am, aren't I? That was only three days' work, but what a fantastic experience. I couldn't believe I got the opportunity to be on it. I knew I could do it when I got called in to read for it.

WG: It was a terrific bit of casting in that there's a real similarity between you and Julia Sawalha, who played Saffy.

DDA: Jennifer Saunders, who wrote the show and played Edina, really thought so too. She remarked it on several times on the set, which really boosted my confidence level. She would say, "like this" in a thoughtful sort of way.

WG: It's too bad that your sequence was in the final episode. They could have used the flash-forward sequence as a running gag.

DDA: I would have loved that. They did a one-off television film afterwards called *The Last Shout.* I was on *EastEnders* by that time, anyway, although I'd like to think the BBC could've worked out for a way for me to do both. They do own both shows.

WG: How about AbFab: The Next Generation?

DDA: I hope you read this, Jennifer.

WG: I'll send a copy to her agent.

DDA: Thanks, I'll take your word on that.

WG: How old were you when you started on *EastEnders*?

DDA: I got to *EastEnders* just before I turned 17. It was just a standard interview situation really, just something my agent sent me to. I went along on a Monday morning, read the script, was asked all the usual questions, blah, blah, blah. And the next day I found I got this part of this 14- or 15-year-old girl named Sarah and I started work the following week.

WG: Why is it that so many of the actors on the show appear to have very little time between auditioning, getting cast and starting work? In the States, it can take months.

DDA: I suspect that it may have something to do with the fact that the show wants to provide the press with as little lead time as possible so leaks are kept down to a minimum about who the new actors and characters are. That's just a guess on my part.

WG: It doesn't really give you time to be extra nervous, does it?

DDA: That's one way of looking at it! When Mark Homer, who plays Sarah's brother Tony, and I showed up on the set everybody told us how much we looked like Brian Croucher, who plays our dad Ted. That helped to put us at ease, much like what Jennifer Saunders did.

WG: The three of you are yet another example in a long line of traditionally wonderful casting work. In *EastEnders* the families always at least look right together.

DDA: Our mother Irene has been brought onto the show, and neither Mark nor I look like her, but somehow it works anyway. Roberta (Taylor) is a brilliant actress.

WG: I've always had a funny feeling that Sarah was in a sense conceived as a sort of younger version of Kathy (Ted's sister). Her initial storyline dealt with unwanted sexual attention, for instance. I realise that Kathy was raped as a young girl, and Sarah was actually sexually harassed. Another odd parallel I've noticed is that Kathy became involved with the Good Samaritans who do good works and Sarah joined a Christian group, which does good works. What do you think?

DDA: That's a very interesting analogy, which may or may not be accurate. But you've got a point. Perhaps the writers subconsciously intended for there to be echoes of Kathy's story in Sarah's.

WG: Kathy's schoolgirl rape certainly gave Ted a reason to be almost stifling in his protection of Sarah after the harassment incident.

DDA: Especially since there wasn't a mother around, yes. That harassment incident was really a very good way to pull the Hills family into the Square. They were on the run due to the harasser getting pushed off scaffolding at Ted's building site.

WG: Did you feel at all uncomfortable about the show deciding to transform Sarah into such as ardent Christian?

DDA: No, not at all. I thought it was a really interesting way to go with Sarah because she was such a confused and anguished young girl. Her shoplifting was genuinely related to her emotional problems at home. She wasn't just a thief. She desperately needed some help.

WG: I was worried that a cult storyline, which has been overdone in soaps and television movies for some time, might develop. I hope she doesn't eventually put on Nike sneakers

and kill herself along with a bunch of other sad folk who believe they'll get beamed up to some comet.

DDA: No chance of that ever happening on our show. The entire storyline is being handled so responsibly. The leader of the group, Alistair, is not meant to be perceived as a devilish character out to destroy souls. He's a really human person whose weaknesses are eventually revealed as a sort of hypocrisy. The audience doesn't feel the need to see him explode in flames!

WG: I loved the Blackpool episodes where Sarah was unwittingly slipped some Ecstasy tablets and goes tripping. You were wonderful in conveying Sarah's initial confusion, which then led to false exhilaration during the E trip.

DDA: Thanks. I'd never taken the drug myself so I spent a month doing research on it by talking to friends who had taken it, as well as reading about it in periodicals and police leaflets. When I got onto the disco set where Sarah is slipped the E, I was fitted with black contact lenses to make my pupils look dilated. It felt like I was wearing ten pairs of sunglasses so I already felt disoriented! I'm glad you think they turned out well. The disco scenes were taped out at BBC White City because the studio space here at Elstree was full up.

WG: And now on to a purely frivolous question. What was it like to be the envy of millions of females all over Britain? You know what I mean?

DDA: Oh, you must mean Paul Nicholls. *Great, lovely!* (a wicked laugh) Paul is a truly lovely guy. We actually became so close that it began to feel like we were brother and sister, which is quite common on this show. One thing we loved to do together was to act out scenes from *Friends* for anyone who'd listen. Paul played Chandler and I played his whiny girlfriend Janice. We knew all the dialogue by heart! He's an absolute sweetheart. We bicker sometimes too, but it never comes to much because we get along so well. It's part of that brother-sister thing.

WG: You make *EastEnders* sound like a happy experience.

DDA: It is. I know it sounds boring but it really is. I'd gone to Ravenscourt with Dean Gaffney (Robbie), and so when I started here he took me by the hand and showed me around. There are many lovely people here. Who am I to complain?

WG: Do you have ambitions beyond *EastEnders*? Sorry, I had to ask that.

DDA: That's okay. It sounds so corny to say "I wanna be in films," but of course that's a dream of mine. It wouldn't necessarily have to be a big-deal Hollywood film. A nice low-budget British film with a good cast and a good working atmosphere would do very nicely, thanks. I'm also gagging to do some theatre. I've only done one play, a prize-winner at a playwright's competition at the Royal National Theatre. I certainly hope to do more in the future.

WG: One more trivial question. Do you watch anything else on TV besides *Friends*?

DDA: To be honest, I really don't watch that much television. I'm sorry, that sounds boring. When I get home from work I like to take my shoes off and start kicking with a bit of music on. I love to read. I hardly watch *EastEnders* except certain times when I'm on and feel the need to pick apart my performance! I can't bear to watch it with other people, that's for sure. I already mentioned *Friends*. Hey, you bribed me to do this interview with some brand new episodes. Cough 'em up, will ya?

WG: I will. I promise. Thanks for the interview, Daniela.

DDA: It was my pleasure. All the best to your readers, okay?

Postscript: In addition to *Friends*, I decided to send her a few episodes of the new series *Felicity*. Felicity's a fresh-faced, earnest, and appealing young woman, and I think Daniela would like her. She'd also be an obvious choice to star in a British adaptation. Stranger things have happened.... Hey, the Brit version of that 70s show has just aired.

–Tim Wilson

Nadia Sawalha (Annie Palmer), 2000

"[Annie] always believed that she was better than those people.... It's nice to play such a devilsome lady."

Nadia Sawalha, the actress whom *EastEnders* fans know as Annie Palmer, was nearly cast as Polly, the *Walford Gazette* reporter, and vice versa. She tells me this as we settle for an interview in the green room, following a taping of the Granada-produced TV series *Soap Fever*, for which Nadia is the presenter.

Reared in an acting family, her father and sister (Julia Sawalha, best known for playing daughter Saffron in *Absolutely Fabulous*) are also both thespians. But back to the story of how she ended up as Annie. She points out that she got the audition only two weeks after she told her agent that she wanted a soap opera part.

"I always had seen myself as jobbing actress. I never had any dreams of being a big star. I always wanted to earn good money and have a regular kind of job. A soap kind of fits the bill for that. Unbelievably, two weeks later I got a call for an audition." Nadia auditioned with a slew of other actresses. She thought it was going well when she realised that during the interview process, she was in with the casting director for 45 minutes.

"They asked me to talk about myself. I'm chatting away. I do that when I'm nervous. I noticed that everyone else was out the door after a minute. The next day they asked me to come back for a screen test. 'Blimey, I thought I'd never get this far.' The only two they screen-tested were Victoria Gould and me. We were always going to get the job. They hadn't decided which way they were going to go (who was going to be Annie and who Polly). They always have a vague idea of what they want, and then they build the character around the person they choose. I was pleased when they turned it around."

I tell her that I'm glad she ended up with the role that she did – it suited her. She agrees. I also score a few points when I tell her that Annie always seems a bit more posh than the others in the Square – she dressed better, spoke better, etc. "Thank you. She always believed that she was better than those people."

Annie Palmer is described in the BBC-published *Who's Who Guide to EastEnders* as "a rather terrifying creation, a kind of dominatrix without the dungeon. A verbal Miss Whiplash, she tore strips off anyone who crosses her." Nadia says of the character, "It's nice to play such a devilsome lady."

She thought she didn't look right for *EastEnders*. "My father is Arabic and my mother English. I just thought that I was too exotic – that there wasn't enough call for a foreigner."

Besides *EastEnders*, Nadia has acted in a couple of films, including one with Ewan McGregor. She says that she prefers television to the sitting around and waiting process of a movie set. "That's like, 'Just learn your lines and don't bump into the furniture'. They then take four hours to talk about it." Nadia recalls working on a film with Sherilyn Fenn, who kept on having to stop in the middle of a scene to nurse her baby "every time I had a close-up. That was very annoying."

Reverting to *EastEnders*, I tell her I recall a scene when she first arrived in the Square and the character Lenny immediately hit on her. Nadia says that such treatment is almost a ritual on the set when a new female character joins the cast. "Isn't she lovely?" – no matter what you look like, the back end of the bus."

I also mention that I had lunch with her [then] real-life boyfriend two days earlier at the *EastEnders* studio, Marc Bannerman, who plays Gianni di Marco. "I know, he told me," she replies.

"It was lovely for me to meet Pam (St. Clement) today," Nadia says, of her special guest on *Soap Fever*. Even before she made it to *EastEnders*, Nadia apparently had a talent to mimic Pat mixing and taking a swig of gin and tonic. My sisters would tell me, "You're doing Pat." Speaking of her sisters (there are three), she's looking forward to starring with Julia later this year in a West End play. They've worked together before. She adds that Julia is also about to start work on a reunion with her *Absolutely Fabulous* co-stars Jennifer Saunders, Joanna Lumley, and Jane Horrocks in a new series, all playing different parts.

Nadia sees the irony of her speaking with the *Walford Gazette* – remember Annie Palmer wasn't too fond of the rag. I tell her that I was pleased to find out a character on *EastEnders* was named Annie because that's my two-year-old daughter's name. Nadia says she's planning to take a holiday to New York – her first time – in a few months. "And thanks for being in our [*Soap Fever*] audience," she adds.

–Larry Jaffee

Michael Greco (Beppe di Marco), 2002

"I'd watched EastEnders from Day One. I always knew one day I'd be on it."

Michael Greco caught the acting bug at eight years old. Not surprisingly, given the ladykiller image of his *EastEnders'* alter ego, he initially was interested in theatre mainly to impress a girl. "She was my childhood crush, my sweetheart," reminisces Greco, in the lobby of the Jurys Inn hotel in Islington. "My school was doing a production of *Alice in Wonderland*. She was cast as Alice. So I went out for the part of the White Rabbit, the male lead, and also the Mad Hatter, thinking that after-school rehearsals would be a great way to get to know her better."

The young Michael didn't get either part that he coveted; rather he was the Mock Turtle, stuck with a huge shell on his back and a stocking on his head, "looking like a complete fool." But he didn't give up his thespian itch, and soon was in the school production of *Peter Pan*, although it was a few years before he was getting the male lead parts that he wanted.

He took a year off after graduating from high school at 18 and then enrolled in drama school, the Guildford School of Acting in the county of Surrey, outside London, where he studied for three years and where his classmates included future *EastEnders* alumni Des Coleman (Lenny) and Howard Antony (Alan Jackson).

Before coming to *EastEnders*, Greco spent six years throughout Britain acting in classic plays by Shakespeare, Chaucer, Ibsen, and Chekhov, as well as those of contemporary writers. "I was always doing different types of roles. Money was pretty scarce because doing theatre isn't lucrative." Four and a half years ago, he was acting in Shakespeare's *All's Well That Ends Well* when his agent called about *EastEnders* casting a new Italian family. They wanted to see him for one of the parts.

"I thought okay, that would be interesting. I wanted to break into film. TV wasn't my idea, but I'd give it a go. If I got it, I could always turn it down. If I didn't get it, they've made up my mind for me. I'd watched *EastEnders* from Day One. I always knew one day I'd be on it. When I was struggling as an actor people said to me that I should be on *EastEnders*, that I'd be perfect."

The next morning, he drove several hours to Borehamwood (where the *EastEnders* studio is located) for the audition and then back to southern England for that night's performance. His agent called to tell him that they wanted to see him again. He did a screen test for the role of Beppe, and *EastEnders* offered him a year's contract.

For the Shakespeare play, he was wearing the now familiar goatee. Although facial hair wasn't what the creative team originally had in mind for Beppe, they liked the look, and told Greco to keep the beard because the character was supposed to be a cop in the vice squad. It would help him fit in on the street. Since then, it's become his trademark. Greco tells of women who have asked their boyfriends to grow it the same way, and guys whose girlfriends also want them to look like Beppe. Greco's flattered by all the attention.

The celebrity he's gained from playing Beppe led to Greco twice working with Jennifer Saunders, first in a sketch for the U.K. charity Comic Relief and then in a cameo on *Absolutely*

Fabulous, in which Michael played himself. A very drunk and bad-smelling Edwina and Patsy grope a very uncomfortable-looking Greco, who calls for security to get rid of them. "It was great to be asked to do that, really good fun."

Greco laments that *EastEnders* never worked the vice side of his work into storylines, but that would require additional characters, and *EastEnders* is typically family based. "When a new family hits the Square, *EastEnders* tends to introduce them with a bang," he explains. "People wonder who they are. The only way the audience gets to know them is by seeing more of their life, what they do as a job, where they eat, where they go, how they talk, how they are perceived by people."

Speaking of family, Greco's own family is very important to him, and he thanks his parents for a wonderful upbringing. They grew up poverty-stricken in Italy and moved to England to make better lives for themselves without knowing how to speak English. "Dad was a chef and mom was a nurse who looked after sick children. They wanted me to have a really good English education. I had a brilliant upbringing. I'll never forget where I came from. I can't thank my parents enough. I earned more in the last four years than they did in thirty years. That's not me bragging. That's me thinking 'Crikey, there's no justice out there. My mum and dad worked so hard to bring up a family. They couldn't speak English. They had no friends here. I've always been told to keep my feet on the ground.'"

Having an Italian heritage also didn't hurt Greco's chances with the *EastEnders* producers. He still has many relatives living in Italy, which he visited every year with his family up to the age of 18. Although Greco doesn't speak Italian fluently, he does understand quite a bit of what his relatives say in conversation.

It's also probably no accident that when asked which actors influenced him, he quickly cites Robert De Niro, John Travolta, and Al Pacino – all three Italian-Americans. He praised De Niro's versatility, and in particular, *Mean Streets,* as the film that prompted him to want to become an actor. Travolta in *Saturday Night Fever* and *Grease* also made a huge impression.

Among film actors closer to his own age, he cites Sean Penn, Ed Norton, and John Cusack, all of whom he thinks regularly turn out stellar work. After a recent visit to Los Angeles, Greco hooked up with an agent there, and he's hoping to make it big in the States. "New York is the only place other than London where I'd actually live. The city is very similar to London. The people are very friendly. Brits are really accepted there. I know a lot of Brits go to America to try to crack it."

–Larry Jaffee

Leila Birch (Teresa di Marco), 2003

"If you look at [Teresa's] relationships, she's a psychotherapist's dream really, isn't she? She just shacks up with all these different blokes."

The following interview with Leila Birch took nearly a year to happen. When I was in London the previous January we spoke on the phone, but her schedule in the pantomime production of *Dick Whittington* didn't allow for a meeting. She's reprising her role in that panto again this holiday season, but this time I caught her while it was in pre-production. We did the interview in the lobby of central London's swanky hotel, One Aldwych.

Walford Gazette: So tell me a little bit about your background. How did you become an actor?

Leila Birch: I grew up in south-east London. I knew I wanted to act when I was five. That's when I saw the Fred Astaire and Judy Garland films, and all of that. I started training when I was five or five and a half and started to go to stage school on Saturdays. And then when I was nine, I did that full-time. So I didn't go to a regular school. I went to a school where in the mornings we'd have ballet, tap, singing, dancing, acting, things like that. And then in the afternoon you'd do a limited amount of subjects, just enough to get you by – English, biology, things like that, but you didn't take chemistry. It was really fun because we had dance studios that we'd go into at lunchtime and play music and dance around.

WG: Is anyone else in your family an actor?

LB: My great-aunt, who was one of the "Gaiety Girls," 1919 to 1924, around that era. We have loads and loads of her theatre programmes [*Playbills*].

WG: While we're on family, I was curious whether you have any Italian in your blood.

LB: My grandmother's Italian and was born in Italy.

WG: Did that help when you went for the part of Teresa?

LB: I think maybe. I get taken for Jewish, Italian, Arab, Spanish, all kinds of different things. And I think it's funny because I'm as much Irish actually as I am Italian, but no one ever says I look Irish! I still see my grandmother. She was one of the evacuees during the war. She's fantastic. And then on my other side, my grandfather and grandmother met in the Second World War. My grandfather's a major and he's very "jolly good," all that kind of thing, very, very British. And she's very, very Italian. And it's great because I see those grandparents every week. On Sunday we go round and have a four-course meal. The whole family gets together and it's kind of very Italian that way. I'm very family-orientated. I think it gives you a really good base, especially in the world of show business.

WG: When did you start to do serious theatre?

LB: I had my first job when I was nine. And then basically I did a whole myriad of different things – bits here and there really. I did the Children's World Variety, and that was dancing. I did things for children's television programmes and little bit parts in British films, adverts, voice-overs. When I was 15 I went to Yale University in New Haven, Connecticut for a five-week drama course. I don't think they were supposed to let me in because you know how the Americans and the English write the date and the month the other way round? They thought I was older than I actually was. They thought I was already 16, but actually I had my sixteenth birthday during the course. I don't think anyone ever found out, so I didn't get shipped home. This course opened me up to a more adult way of working with drama. There were people from New York, Alabama, Los Angeles, Connecticut. There was a girl from France. She and I were the only Europeans. The course was really intensive, nine in the morning till ten at night. It was really, really hard work.

WG: How did you get selected for that?

LB: Well, my mum knew someone who said, "Your daughter should find out about these courses that go on at Yale, because they produced a lot of good actors."

WG: What was your first big break?

LB: It was a small part, but it was the first thing that was prime time. I did an episode of a series called *Thief Takers* for Carlton. I played a sexually abused teenage girl. I then did two years of college, a whole lot of physical theatre and experimental theatre. In my third year of this performing arts thing, it was more about putting on plays. When I finished, I wrote to 190 agents and found one. I did a television production about a reject football team, and I played this Italian girl called Gina, who just came on and basically told some guy who was pretending to be an Italian, "Oh, you can't be an Italian." He scores a great goal and then we walked into the sunset.

I then got an audition for *EastEnders* to be a baggage handler at an airport. The episode had to do with Cindy running away with David to Italy. As I walked to the lift the casting director said to me, "I'm going to persuade the director not to use you for this." And I was devastated. Then he said, "Because there's an Italian family coming into the show. Would a six-month contract scare you?" And I said, "No!" There was this massive gap – five or six weeks – in between going for that audition and then coming back again. Of course, every day's slipping by and you're going, "Oh, no. They just didn't want me at all and they lied."

They asked me to come back again, and I knew I was among the last five, including one of my friends from college. We had a chat and said, "Whichever one gets it takes the other one out, meal, as much champagne as they want." So we're down to the last five to read. And then I got re-called back again, and I wasn't sure whether it was just me. The lady who played Stella – the lady who played my grandmother – walked through, and I met Marc (Bannerman, a/k/a Gianni) and Michael (Greco, a/k/a Beppe).

WG: They were in the same boat, basically?

LB: We were all going for the screen test. We all met and it was very nice. And then I had to do a scene where I was pretending to be Nigel's girlfriend. And I'm thinking, "Well, maybe they want me for the girlfriend, that maybe they don't want me as Teresa."

WG: Your mind plays tricks.

LB: I got worried and waited for hours until maybe seven at night, just waiting. So I was, "Why would they leave me hanging around so long?" And they were quite appreciative that I stayed. But, of course I'd stay. I wanted the job! And then I found out two days later that I'd got the job. Obviously I was ecstatic. I screamed on the phone to my agent!

WG: So once the family was set, did you bond with Marc and Michael?

LB: Very much so. You know, we bonded as a family, yeah. Well, not so much as siblings. Maybe at first, but recently I saw Marc and Carly [Hillman, the youngest di Marco, Nicky]. Carly did a gig somewhere – she sings – and me and Marc and one of my other friends went to see her. They all just ended up staying at my flat. It was fantastic, like a family reunion! When we were working with each other, we bonded in a completely different way then because there was almost like a kind of family edge to our relationship with each other. I felt quite responsible for Carly.

WG: How old was she then?

LB: I think she was about 13 or 14, but she was playing a year or so younger than she actually was. I think my character was two years younger than my real age. I was 19 when I got the job.

WG: Do you have any older brothers?

LB: I have an older brother in real life, yes.

WG: Was he as protective as Gianni and Beppe?

LB: Yeah, but in a different way, not quite as hands-on, a bit more kind of like taking a step back but having knowing looks. (laughs)

WG: Well, how much difference in age between you and your brother?

LB: Four years.

WG: Wasn't Gianni supposed to be about four years older than Teresa?

LB: Yeah, but Gianni was like hot-headed and like a bull in a china shop, but with a good heart.

WG: What did you like about Teresa?

LB: When she came into the show, she was very much a party girl who didn't realise the consequences of her actions. You know, she'd go out and buy drugs, but she didn't ever think, "Oh, I might get caught," or "Oh, mum might find out." She was rebellious. Her dad had just died, and like I don't think she'd gone to any counselling! So of course, she was going to all of a sudden turn into this rebel because I think she was daddy's little girl. And then her brothers obviously step in to attempt to take the role of the father figure, but she's like, "You're my brother. Go away." If you look at her relationships, she's a psychotherapist's dream really, isn't she? She just shacks up with all these different blokes, and then she finds Matthew. He trusted her in a way that really she hadn't ever got in a relationship. It was like, "Oh, I've got a problem, and you've got a problem," but it was all quite superficial. Matthew is actually the first time you've seen her show any loyalty to anyone really, outside of her family.

WG: *EastEnders* gave you recognition and put you in the public eye. How did you deal with fame?

LB: I'm starting to grow my hair out, and it's like it was when I was on the show. On the way here I had three or four people just go, "Yeah. I know you," or, "Yeah, hey." But people are very nice about it. I think my character appeals to certain cultures, because I don't get as many white people recognising me now as I do with Caribbean or Asian people. Maybe it's because I played an Italian, an apparent ethnic minority, and also because my character went out with black people, white people, criminals, old people!

WG: Before Matthew, Teresa had to deal with Tony turning out to be gay.

LB: I know a lot of people who that happened to. From Tony's point of view, you can't help whom you love and you can't help what you are. People get into a kind of verbal contract really when you're in a relationship with somebody and one of the stipulations in that contract is you don't sleep with anyone else, you don't kiss anyone else. Male or female, not the point. The fact is he two-timed her with an ex. The fact that it was a man just made it more obvious she couldn't compete. But she felt, "What have I done?" She had a chat with Tony and at first she was like, "I don't want anything to do with you." After a while, she just moved onto the next guy! (laughs) I think she thought, "I can find someone a bit more exciting."

WG: I think personality-wise, Matthew made the most sense.

LB: Yeah, he was a club deejay. He was a bit more exciting. And he was really a bit more her age. Tony was a bit older, and he'd kind of done his really, really cool things. Now he was nice, but I think he was a bit too settled really for her at that stage of her life. And then, she found Matthew, and obviously Matthew was cool and he kind of ran a CD stall, and he was quite nice. And he had this secret. As soon as he told her, he let her in really to a level where she was not only a girlfriend. It kind of awakened something inside of her in that protective way that was very much like her mother or her brothers had been to her. This is the first step where you actually saw her grow up a bit.

WG: Matthew's prison plight really captured the imagination of the British public.

LB: I had this one woman come up to me in a department store. I didn't have the heart to tell her it wasn't real. She just said, "Oh, you're a good girl, you are. My bloke's in prison and I'm waitin' for him, and you just carry on. You wait for him. You're a good girl." And I was just like, "Yeah, I will, but." I didn't have the heart, you know.

WG: But that woman's living it, so it is real.

LB: Yeah, she's living it. And I was thinking, "God, I hope, for her sake the scriptwriters don't just suddenly make me have an affair with someone!" I was happy that they allowed Teresa to stand by her boyfriend and do the whole "Free Matthew Rose" campaign, because really everybody else just turned their back on him.

WG: Well, there was also this interesting rivalry with Sarah, though. They were both competing for his affection. You were talking about how Teresa was a psychotherapist's dream. Remember Sarah's kleptomaniac phase, and how she was saved by Jesus? I didn't think Teresa would turn to religion to solve her problems.

LB: Teresa was a Catholic girl, but, she's like, "Well, we go to church for Christmas and that's enough for me."

WG: I remember an episode that had Sarah going to the prison and saying to Teresa, "Do you want to come, too? He really wants to see you." And she couldn't handle that.

LB: Yeah. I think that kind of freaked her. She did go a couple of times. I remember being in the prison set, but it was all a bit too real, I think. Teresa was constantly escaping from who she was. And to be dealing with, "My boyfriend's in prison. No one's asking me what I feel about this." You know, she had no real friend to turn to. She had Robbie to a certain extent. She had a competitive thing with Sarah. Everyone else really who was close to her had left the Square. And there wasn't really anybody who she thought she could really open up to.

WG: You just mentioned Robbie. He really fancied Teresa, but she was only interested in him as a friend.

LB: Robbie had own problems really. I mean look at that family for a start, you know. You think ours is in big trouble. What about theirs? (laughs)

WG: There was not really a lot of closeness between Louise and Teresa.

LB: There were scenes off-camera that we discussed, but at the end of the day it's a soap, it's fast-moving, and you have to realise that. I liked it when I was in the restaurant, where I was able to give a lot of comic looks.

WG: Is there any of Teresa in you?

LB: I don't think I could be further away from Teresa. She wasn't a baddie as such, but she was a bit of a minx, and sometimes that's quite fun because it's something that I would never do. So it's almost like getting to live out this strange lifestyle, like be a fly on the wall and look at how you could have been in an alternate reality. So I think that's really fun about her and I quite miss her in certain ways actually. People have said, "Oh, would you go back to *EastEnders*?" And I said, "You know, I think it would be quite fun," you know, because I would have to like refine my character. They didn't kill us [the di Marcos] off, which is a nice thing.

WG: Has playing Teresa made it difficult getting other parts?

LB: When you're in a soap, you get this high amount of recognition, but then when you leave sometimes they don't want to touch you with a bargepole because the general public won't necessarily believe you as another character yet. So you have to have this cooling-off period as such, which can take people ten years, three years, five years, it depends. I've managed to get quite a lot of theatre things.

WG: What are you working on next?

LB: I'm going to play the character Fairy Bow Bells for a Manchester theatre panto production of *Dick Whittington*. He was the Lord Mayor of London. It starts on December 10th and it finishes the 4th of January. Pantomime I think is one of those things that you have a responsibility as a performer, whether you're a magician or an actor or a dancer or a comedian, because you get the children to realise the magic of the theatre. I did it last year, the same part. I jump onstage and go, "Hello, boys and girls," very, very cockney and a lot of the comedy. I didn't even realise I was being funny. The audience laughed. So for me as an actor, with the audience so much on my side because my character's amusing and funny and a goodie, it was really, really fun last year. It's so high-energy, panto, and it's Christmassy and it's lovely. So I'm very much looking forward to doing it.

–*Larry Jaffee*

Russell Floyd (Michael Rose), 1999
"The first time I was seen I asked, 'How cockney would you like me to be?'"

There's more to Michael Rose, *EastEnders'* Bridge Street market inspector character, than his clipboard, assures his alter ego, the extremely affable Russell Floyd, who came over to New York for a few days in early March to lend a hand with WLIW/Channel 21's pledge drive.

"I've tried to ditch that clipboard. That's become the bane of my existence," Floyd joshes. In a wide-ranging interview with Paul Field and myself, the classically trained actor shed light on what life is like inside the closed set known as Albert Square and shared some thoughts about American and British history and politics.

It's been several years since Michael replaced "Tricky Dicky," a fairly unsavoury character. He's had his share of minor storylines, such as intervening in a market squabble between Mark Fowler and a new stall owner who tried dirty tricks (ultimately unsuccessfully) to drive Mark out of his fruit-and-veg business. He's also been seen moping around the Square looking for love in all of the wrong places, such as with Carol Jackson's sister who was on the rebound after being jilted at the altar, and with Carol herself.

"Michael's in love with Carol," confides Floyd, who had no problem with that storyline since the actor was already friendly with Lindsey Coulson, who plays Carol. When he began on *EastEnders*, Floyd and Coulson had the same agent, and she helped him get familiar with his new surroundings. "She showed me the ropes the first few months. We became mates, and it was great to work with her." In contrast to Tricky Dicky, "Michael's a nice guy," notes Floyd, explaining that there was a conscious effort by the creative team to make his character different from the previous inspector.

Although most of his acting work since graduating from the U.K.'s Royal Academy of Dramatic Art has been in the theatre – performing in everything from big West End productions of *Romeo and Juliet* to regional shows – Floyd was ready for prime-time telly. "*EastEnders* had been on for ten years. Like any actor and being a Londoner, you wonder, "Why haven't I been seen for this show?"

Floyd received some encouragement from Susan Tully (Michelle Fowler), with whom he appeared in a play in a North of England theatre group. "She was great and gave a lot of advice."

He arrived for the first time at the BBC's Elstree studio with a beard, which he grew for a play that he was in at the time. "The hard thing is to get your face in the door. It doesn't make a difference how good you are, like any job I suppose. The first time I was seen I was offered the job. I asked them, "How cockney would you like me to be?'" What was especially refreshing for Floyd was that he was getting a chance to use his native south London accent, compared with the upscale standard English accent used in most costume drama.

Having grown up in London, Floyd was familiar with street markets. He then did some research on how markets operate in contemporary London. "The producers and directors didn't require me to do that. They hand you the part," he says, noting that may be he had "too much information" for the part. But generally the market scenes are pretty realistic.

Floyd dismisses the notion that Michael appears a bit more upscale than the rest of the people working in the market, bellowing, "Have you seen those clothes?! They're sad old corduroys, multicoloured shirts, and those ties that will give you hay fever!" and sounding as though he was describing Nigel's wardrobe more than Michael's. Larry asks, "Well, what about Bianca's silver jacket? That's not exactly high fashion, now, is it?" Russell responds, "That's style compared to what I'm wearing." Getting serious, he adds: "I'm sure the costume is absolutely right for the type of character and kind of income he has. He's banged around. He's divorced and he has a child." As Michael's character develops, people come into his life from his past. Without giving away any plots, Floyd admits that Michael "gets more unlucky in love."

Walford Gazette webmaster Paul asks whether Russell encounters the public confusing him with the character. "It's not been a problem. It's part of the job. The only time it's a problem is when people are rude. They just butt in. But I'd rather have that problem than not. It's not like I'm famous for being Russell Floyd the actor, the same way that Mel Gibson is. People see me in their living rooms three, four times a week. People believe you are that person. Most people don't know the names of the actors. If somebody says, 'Hello, Michael!' You turn around and say, 'Hi! Fine!' There's no point in getting worked up about it and saying, 'I'm Russell Floyd!'" He notes that some of the younger members of the *EastEnders* cast have a bit of a problem coping with being recognised in public.

As far as working with the production team, Floyd says that sometimes the actors can object to a storyline or particular line, but there's "usually no time to discuss anything. We're handed a script." He remembers once doing a scene with Sid Owen (Ricky) in the Queen Vic where Michael is telling him a story that "some bully comes along. I thought, this is a guy in his thirties. He's an East End market inspector. He wouldn't say that. So I changed it to 'Some bloke....'"

Despite the hectic shooting schedule, the cast members and crew engage in fun from time to time. He tells of a heavy scene involving Grant sitting in a church when somebody set off a fart machine that has occasionally interrupted the proceedings followed by much laughter.

The one thing about Floyd that's immediately apparent is that he enjoys his work, and puts his everything into it. He also has a quite separate personal life, being happily married and recently a father. As a result, he turned down a touring stage show to be with his wife and newborn son.

An actor who stays with a soap long can be unfairly stigmatised, leaving the impression that he or she can't do much else. "It's a kind of artistic snobbery. I don't think it's the actors' fault; it's the people who cast films and television shows." Besides *EastEnders*, Floyd has appeared in popular British series *The Bill* and *London's Burning*.

Well read in history and political science, Russell moves the conversation to his affinity for things American. In fact, he and his brother grew up fans of American football, particularly the New York Giants, when NFL games were broadcast in Britain.

This is the second time Floyd has made it to the colonies. A few years ago, he and his wife spent a few days in New York and a week up in New England, where he spent time visiting Revolutionary War sites. "What amazes me about American history is that it's not an objective view; it's propaganda. We replaced one set of middle-class rich people with another set of middle-class rich people." On the other hand, he says that he doesn't fault the colonists for breaking away from the Crown considering the circumstances, and he recently read a biography about the American patriot Thomas Paine.

While in New York that first time, Floyd had a Bill Clinton encounter. "There was this motorcade. And then all the sudden all of the cars pulled away, and there was one left behind. The window was rolled down. I could see him as clearly as I see you. There was no security around. I yelled 'BILL!' He waved back with a big grin. This woman came up to me and asked (Russell turns on his female American voice) 'Is that Bill Clinton? Isn't he a dish?'"

He notes that the British Parliament has its share of sex scandals, providing the tabloid press plenty to write about. Floyd takes a libertarian view of such transgressions and thinks politicians should be prosecuted or driven from office only for corruption. Like Ross Kemp (Grant), Floyd is a supporter of the Labour Party and occasionally his extracurricular political activities make it to Albert Square. "I once found myself explaining taxation to Dean Gaffney (Robbie Jackson)."

Floyd is very content with the work he's done on *EastEnders* and expects it to continue. "They (the creative team) look at you on the screen. They can see what you can do and they start writing for you. So in a way, the character becomes the actor."

–Larry Jaffee and Paul Field

Perry Fenwick (Billy Mitchell), 2004

"June Brown asked, 'Who are you playing?' I told her, 'Billy Mitchell'. She said, 'Oh, there's another one'."

When you enter the dressing room of Perry Fenwick, you can't help noticing a giant poster of the British rocker Ian Dury, who died a few years ago. There's also on a chair a stuffed replica of Terence the dog that Billy gave to Janine as a gift.

Walford Gazette: I ran an obituary of Ian Dury in the *Walford Gazette* when I learned he died. I wrote although Ian was not a cockney, he certainly lived the cockney spirit.

Perry Fenwick: He's great. He's more of an Essex boy really, but I mean he's a brilliant bloke, absolutely brilliant bloke. I was in a film with him that Bob Hoskins directed called *The Raggedy Rawney,* and we filmed it in three months in Czechoslovakia in 1987. He played a bit of a rock star in it. It was before the Berlin Wall came down. So it was still very communist and kind of, you know, very secret and lots of KGB people around. That was the only time in my life that I've actually seen a television set get thrown out of a hotel room window. (laughs) And it's quite a weird thing to see.

WG: Who threw it out?

PF: Dury. He was just so fed up with this place and just one night we'd had a few schnapps too many and he said he was gonna do it. So everyone went out onto their balconies and just looked and you just saw this television come out of a thing and it just went slow motion. And just smashed into a million different bits, but it was very funny. Pointing to the poster, Perry says, "I got that from the [*EastEnders*] set, a smaller one of it, and they blew it up for me."

WG: Let's talk about the Billy Mitchell character.

PF: Yeah, sure. Ask away.

WG: You have this interesting relationship with Phil. I mean you're related by blood, but at times Phil can turn on you at any second and disown you, like in *The Godfather*.

PF: It's a funny one really because I mean it's like you say. When I first came into the show, it was only for four episodes. It was to introduce the character of Jamie Mitchell. It's kind of like they put the show on hold for a week just to concentrate on a certain family or just to kind of make everything easier and swifter for the public. So I got a call and I'd never had an audition for anything in my life. I'd been acting for about twenty years before I got an audition. *EastEnders* had been up and running for about thirteen years. People everywhere would just constantly say to me, "You should be in that *EastEnders*. You'd be perfect for that because you are from the East End of London." And I always used to say, "Yeah, but, you know, they haven't asked me and I've never had an audition." Anyway, eventually they asked if I was interested in a contract for up to four episodes. I was immediately deflated and just went, "Well, you know, that's not that much." They offered me the job and I asked, "Well, what's the likelihood that this character, you know, returns?" And in the words of the casting director, she said, "Well, he's a Mitchell." So, you know, they were the big mainstay family of the show. "So you can really make it your own – it happens quite a lot – then he'll return."

WG: Were they looking for positive feedback on the character from the critics or the public?

PF: Both. I mean it's a good job, but it can be really so fast. I mean you walk onto the set and that's it basically. You get one camera rehearsal and then you film it, because there's so much to film, especially now it's four times a week. And so it's a bit daunting. You've got to be able to keep up with the pace of it. So, anyway, I got cast and looked at the character and luckily for me, I mean it was – he was a nasty piece of work. The whole story about how he was beating up Jamie. I'm in the last one where people suddenly go, "Oh, Billy Mitchell. He's really nasty." So it kind of gave me two sides to do. Rather than just being, "Oh, he's an out and out villain," it was more to play with. Steve (McFadden) is an old mate, so he kind of showed me the ropes a little bit and said, "Look, you know, you find stuff in it. You don't have to do exactly what's written now. It's a guideline, but you know, make it your own and stuff." And I decided, well, I could do it and at the end of that, they said, "Oh, we're pleased and would you be interested in coming back?" And I said, "Yeah."

WG: How long did it take for you to find out if Billy was going to be a regular character?

PF: Six weeks, a long time, because even if they think that you're fantastic, they can't alter the storylines they've got put down.

WG: So the year is pretty much plotted out?

PF: They'll know upstairs what's happening to me up until like, say, next May already, but I only know what's happening to me up until just before Christmas. So it's that far ahead. So when they say "Well, we might, you know, be interested in getting you back," it's then going to be a case of you're available to do it and, two, how serious are they. But then the next thing that happened was that Ross Kemp (Grant) announced he was leaving. And so that was gonna leave a gap in the Mitchell family to be filled. Billy was still a baddie, the character, and at that point I'm not sure whether they were thinking, "Oh, he could be possibly a replacement in the same mould as Grant and Phil or he could be like a Nick Cotton-type character." I wasn't really interested in doing that.

Fenwick explains that he was more interested in working the "quite likeable" side of Billy's personality, exemplified by his taking an interest in Janine when she was down and out, and no one else cared to lend a helping hand.

Once it was decided that Billy would be a regular character, the creative team also came up with a storyline for him that explained his dark side, dealing with physical abuse by a former teacher. "A guy turns up in the Square, and you see Billy being nasty to an old man. It gave him a reason for always being the black sheep." Fenwick has fond memories of the two-hander episode in which Billy confronts his former abuser because it further developed his character, as has his romance with Little Mo.

The fact that Fenwick is a real East Ender gives the show a touch of authenticity. He tells of a story when he first joined the cast and ran into June Brown (Dot Cotton), who asked "Who are you playing?" When Fenwick announced, Billy Mitchell, Brown replied, "Oh, there's another one." June then enquired about where he was from, and Fenwick said, "The East End, Canning Town," and Brown responded, "Oh, really?"

He explains how on this day he's been at the studio since 7 a.m. – it's about 1.30 in the afternoon when we chat – and he won't be leaving until 7 p.m. He's expected back on the set for some scenes in the late afternoon. Hoping to run some errands on the Borehamwood High Street before then, he apologises about having to end our chat prematurely.

Before I go, Fenwick shows me a photo of the *EastEnders* soccer team, of which he is a member. He played seriously up to the time he was seventeen and still plays.

Fenwick enjoys being recognised while shopping or at the post office, and appreciates how much people enjoy his portrayal of the character, as he points to a stack of fan mail that he plans on soon answering. "People believe Walford does exist."

–Larry Jaffee

Martin Kemp (Steve Owen), 2006

"They wanted [Steve] to buy his clothes in Walford Market like everybody else. But in the end, I think the character was taking 90 per cent of the wardrobe budget."

Want to know what a good bloke Martin Kemp is? The actor known to *EastEnders* fans as dashing Steve Owen stays on the telephone with me at an early stage of the 2006 World Cup match between England and Trinidad and Tobago. The dumb Yank (me) forgot that the Brits take their football so seriously. Martin, who remembers me from the last time we spoke via a transatlantic phone call eighteen months ago, gently explains after a minute of small talk that he needs to get back to the game on the telly (the score was nil-nil at the time), and I should call him back at the same time the next day.

"It doesn't matter how we win, at least we win," Martin tells me the next day, as we trade notes on how lucky the England team had been so far in the competition. "That's the best it can be," he adds. The north London native, forty-four, is an avid Arsenal supporter.

I explain to him that the impetus for my call: *The Krays*, the 1990 gangster film in which he co-starred with his brother Gary as the title characters, is kicking off "Pulp Month" (June 2006) on the U.S. cable network, the Independent Film Channel (IFC). (The second was *Pulp Fiction*.)

"That's fantastic," comments Kemp, who was glad to hear that the film is still appreciated, and that for the time being Steve Owen is alive and well on U.S. screens. "They remastered [*The Krays*] for a new DVD. Myself, my brother, and Peter Medak did a commentary. It was the first time I saw it in a good ten years. I think it's one of those movies that's better with age, in a way. Lots of the actors in that movie have passed away. It's one of those films that's holding its own the older it gets. I think the styling of *The Krays* has been copied several times in recent gangster films. The styling of Tarantino's *Reservoir Dogs* I think was based on *The Krays*."

Kemp's first brush with entertainment stardom came earlier as bassist in the 1980s band Spandau Ballet, which were huge in their native U.K. and Europe, and even scored a Top Ten U.S. hit with "True." Gary Kemp was the lead singer and principal songwriter. "The band was Gary's deal," Martin explains. He looks back fondly on his Spandau Ballet days.

"Gary was the leading force in it, but I was in there playing at the top of the game for twelve years. In England we had a fantastically long run. Most pop groups, which describes Spandau Ballet, I suppose, only get four or five years at the most. Spandau was kind of my brother's thing. Me going into acting, and *The Krays*, *EastEnders* and all the stuff I've done since, is nice because it's my own thing. Gary and I spent seven or eight years in drama school when were kids. Acting wasn't new to us. When I started drama school at nine years old, I had already totalled twenty TV shows when I was a kid. So going back into acting in *The Krays* when the band finished I was going back to something I felt at home with anyway."

Following his *Krays* success, Martin in the mid-1990s tried to make it in Hollywood, where he learned he had two life-threatening, but ultimately benign, brain tumours. He counts his lucky stars, and recently visited the Hospital of St. Cross in Rugby, England, to open their MRI scanner. At the appearance, he was quoted as saying: "One of these machines saved my life so I was delighted to be asked here today. I know the help these machines can give people."

Kemp doesn't regret the time he spent in Hollywood trying to make it as an actor there. "I didn't find it frustrating. It was a really big learning curve. Going over and living in L.A. wasn't a hardship. I have to say I loved living there. It's beautiful. I did quite well in a way. I was constantly working, maybe not in the films that I wanted to do at the top level. But it was always in those kind of 'B' independent movies. But I was always working, which was really nice. When I look back it now, it was a fantastic experience, and an experience that I still use today."

While *The Krays* is a film cult classic and Spandau Ballet has made its mark in the annals of pop music, it's Kemp's portrayal of *EastEnders*' Steve Owen that gave him a continuing television career, and landed him such honours as Best Actor at the British Soap Awards in both 2001 and 2002 and Most Popular Actor at the 2000 National Television Awards.

I mention to him that Mal Young, the BBC's former head of drama, once told me that he decided to bring in Kemp based on his stellar work in *The Krays*. "I don't know whose idea it was to cast me in *EastEnders*. Several people have said it over the years. Matthew Robinson, who was also an executive producer, always said it was his idea. I don't mind. I had great fun working on *EastEnders*."

Kemp sheds some light on the wardrobe decisions made for the cast. "When I first took on the role of Steve Owen, they put him straight away in the regular jeans and black leather jackets that they always put their characters in. It took me about six months to talk them into getting Steve into suits, ties, shirts. I wanted to smarten him up a little bit. They wanted him to buy his clothes in Walford Market like everybody else. But in the end, I think the Steve Owen character was taking 90 per cent of the wardrobe budget. Everybody else was left with hand-me-downs!"

I ask him if he caught the *Extras* episode last year in which Ricky Gervais's female sidekick has trouble distinguishing between Ross Kemp (Grant Mitchell) and Martin Kemp and the Mitchell Brothers. He did see it, and agrees it's funny. Despite sharing a surname, he and Ross are not related.

"I think we (Martin and Ross) had about a year that we worked together. By the time I joined he was going to leave." Was it ever confusing to have two Kemps around the set, such as having their inter-office mail mixed up? He responded jokingly, "Noooooo."

Besides *EastEnders*, Kemp in recent years has worked regularly on British television for rival channel ITV, for which he starred in several series, including *Serious and Organised* and *Family*, as well as six or seven one-off dramas. "ITV is really good at that. It's kind of the equivalent of the 'NBC Movie of the Week.' I did lots of those. I did one (*Can't Buy Me Love*) with Michelle Collins (Cindy Beale), which was a lot of fun. It was really nice working with Michelle because I've known her for years. But I never worked with her on *EastEnders* because our paths never crossed. There was none of that kind of first-day nerves. Usually you meet each other [for the first time] and get on with it straight away. We had a kind of hidden rapport without knowing it. She's a good girl."

I suggest to Martin that he and Michelle are among the exceptions of *EastEnders* acting alumni who have been successfully able to go onto other roles, and not get stereotyped forever as their Walford characters. "Soaps are funny that way. The danger there is if you're straight out of drama school and *EastEnders* is the first thing you ever do then I think you're in trouble because its very hard to do something after *EastEnders*. But I think if you already have a CV and a back catalogue of work, and then go into *EastEnders*, people will know you for something else, I think it's quite an easy step to get out of it."

Kemp is about to start production on an independent British movie, a remake of a horror thriller called *The House on Straw Hill*, with Jane March, who was in a movie with Bruce Willis. "I start work on that in three weeks' time." Asked whether he might give Hollywood another try, he says, "If I'm invited then I would. I'm a bit too old now to say, 'Let's go over there and give it a shot like a lot of young actors do. I don't think I'm up for banging on a few doors. If I was invited to go over there to work I think I'd jump at it."

I mention that the actress behind Steve Owen's better half (Melanie), Tamzin Outhwaite, last year had a brush with Hollywood, co-starring with Wesley Snipes, albeit in a movie that went straight to DVD. "I think if you've got a movie that opens the door for you then that's fantastic."

Kemp is at a loss to come up with a funny anecdote about life on the *EastEnders* set. "*EastEnders* is one of those shows that's constantly fast and full on – there isn't time. As soon as you laugh in *EastEnders* and start enjoying yourselves, you can't, which I found kind of frustrating, because you have to shoot another scene. They shoot so many pages. I remember we once shot thirty pages of script in one day, which is unheard of. You just don't have time to enjoy yourself really. When I wrote that book (*True*, his 2000 autobiography), the hardest thing I could think of was coming up with any anecdotes out of *EastEnders* because there just isn't time to have anecdotes."

While *EastEnders* might have spent more money on his wardrobe than other cast members, they also broke the bank on his exit. For fear of revealing a spoiler, I won't describe the particulars, but let's just say that Steve Owen didn't leave Albert Square in a taxi driven by Charlie Slater.

"It was quite brave of them really because you build up a show like that for somebody's exit then obviously the show has to come down the other side. That's how things work. I was quite pleased that they wanted to get rid of me in a big way."

Kemp also reveals that it was his idea to leave *EastEnders*. "I said, 'It's up to you whether or not you kill me off or keep me on'. It didn't really make any difference to me. It wasn't in my agenda that I'd go back to the show. They often shoot themselves in the foot [by killing off popular characters]. I have to say if it was my show I don't think I'd kill off the big characters."

–Larry Jaffee

Sylvester Williams (Mick McFarlane), 2008

"I always suggested that my character, Mick, should own the cafe. They'd say, 'Great idea', and then it would never go anywhere."

Upon reaching Sylvester Williams on the telephone to congratulate him on his debut feature film, *Jingle Blues Jingle Bells*, the first Christmas movie to feature a black British cast, I tell him that besides publishing the *Walford Gazette* I am also currently managing a New York jazz musician, and that Sylvester's character Mick McFarlane played a mean saxophone on *EastEnders* for about six years (from 1996 to 2002 in the U.K. episodes).

"Those were the days," he quips, adding that he's embarrassed that after all these years he wasn't aware of the *Walford Gazette*. I also mention that Mick is still fairly fresh in American fans' memories since we're at least five years behind the current BBC One storylines.

When asked what he missed most about *EastEnders*, Williams half-seriously jokes, "the money." Williams admits that when he left *EastEnders*, which was a mutual decision, things didn't work out for him regarding new acting opportunities as easily as he had hoped. That's why two years ago he launched Ebonywood Productions to concentrate on making his own feature films, the first being *Jingle Blues Jingle Bells*, which he wrote, produced, and directed.

It was preceded by *Simple,* a short film he made and starred in in 2002 that landed him a best actor award from *bfm* (*Black Filmmaker*) magazine. *Simple* was co-produced with Troy Titus-Adams (*EastEnders'* Nina, who also played Mick's one-time girlfriend). The 10-minute short film is about a writer who gets writer's block. Stuck at his computer with a deadline to meet, Wesley is accused by Pamela (Titus-Adams) of being a two-timing cheat. He says he is not; she says he is. But the answer is really... Simple!

Titus-Adams told the *Walford Gazette* four years ago in an interview that she was also disappointed how *EastEnders* didn't better develop storylines for minority characters, and lamented that her relationship with Mick could have had a better storyline.

Although Williams is a first-time feature film director with *Jingle Blues*, he has much experience directing fringe theatre productions. "I've been in the game for 32 years," says Williams, who caught the acting bug as a child in Anna Scher's troupe. In fact, he used Scher's theatre/agency as a model for his own drama school/talent agency called Characters, which he launched in 2001 to train young actors in east London.

Jingle Blues Jingle Bells was shot in the East End over twenty-four days in September 2007. He raised £40,000 from family and friends for the production. The film is currently available on DVD in the U.K. Williams chuckles over the irony that he had to trek to America to the Hollywood Black Film Festival this past June to find a British DVD distributor, Jetstar, for the U.K. market. Distribution through cinemas remains a harder nut to crack. But he expects a future Ebonywood production to go that route.

He has finished a first draft of the script of the company's next film, which he hopes to put into production in 2009. This will be a love story/comedy about a music producer, featuring "sweet soul music" and aimed at young adults between nineteen and thirty-two. He bristles over the images of how blacks have been depicted in British films, especially males virtually always carrying knives and guns.

"I like a big action picture as much as the next guy, but..." says Williams, who can't fathom how there can be such a dearth of family-oriented films for blacks in Britain. So in that sense, *Jingle Blues Jingle Bells* represents "a milestone," of which he is proud.

He agrees with many of the black actors the *Walford Gazette* has interviewed over the years that *EastEnders* often falls into tokenism, and that the plots didn't fully explore the possibilities. "I always suggested that my character, Mick should own the cafe. They'd say, 'Great idea,' and then it would never go anywhere. Why couldn't they tell a variety of stories from different perspectives? Why do they always have to look for 'a black story'? Why couldn't the same story apply to Grant, Barry, or Mick? My colour could do the rest."

In the U.S., Williams says he's impressed how blacks now regularly play judges and doctors, which is not the case in Britain. "Sammy Davis, Jr. once said on [the U.K. talk show] *Parkinson* that in America black actors had 'opportunity without equality, while in England it's equality without opportunity'. That's still a good description."

–Larry Jaffee

Hannah Waterman (Laura Beale), 2004

"It's fairly well documented my father's not a massive fan of EastEnders, but they're both immensely proud that, you know, I'm working."

Hannah Waterman's Laura Beale represents the archetypical female character on *EastEnders*: long-suffering yet resilient. One minute she's practically homeless, the next she's running a business in the Square. Classically trained and hailing from a drama family, Waterman is not afraid to find deeper meaning within *EastEnders*. Several years into Laura, Waterman has ridden an emotional roller coaster surrounding her domestic circumstances. The following interview took place in October 2003 in an office at the *EastEnders* studio at Elstree.

Walford Gazette: Since the U.S. broadcasts of *EastEnders* run at least four years behind the U.K. episodes, I became aware of Laura probably six months after she was introduced, when I was on a trip to London. To me, all of a sudden, Ian had a new nanny. And there seemed to be some sort of romantic thing going on between them.

Hannah Waterman: Boy, hasn't that changed! (laughs)

WG: That's true. So I made another trip – probably like six months later – and then I realised the two characters were engaged and it was when Laura was about to inherit some money.

HW: From her grandmother, yeah!

WG: So then I was like, "Oh, now I've figured out Laura." But Hannah, I want to talk about you. Your dad's an actor, right?

HW: Yes.

WG: So as a little girl, did you want to be an actress?

HW: I did. Both my parents, my mother and my father, are actors, and I supposed "inbred madness" is one expression for it. And my sister is just completing her training as well. So all the Watermans – perhaps I prefer that we be a bit like the Redgraves, but not as posh, yeah. So, yeah, we're all actors as much by design. Me and my sister wanted to do it, and I kept it a secret, in fact, from both my parents for quite a long time really. I was still doing school plays, and I was in a big British theatre company that takes kids, and it's quite prestigious. So they had an inkling that something was going on because I was working for that and I was sixteen or seventeen then. And then eventually I came clean, and we negotiated that I'd go to university first and then have a go after that, you know, get a bit of training to fall back on, a bit of education just in case.

WG: What did you study in school?

HW: English and theatre, yeah, joint honours. I think I needed to go to university personally, to do my three years' growing up there. I did a lot of fringe theatre and things like that while I was at university, got my agent and was lucky to start working pretty quickly.

WG: So in the household were they watching *EastEnders* all along?

HW: Ahm, it's fairly well documented my father's not a massive fan of *EastEnders*, but they're both immensely proud that, you know, I'm working. And that, for any actor, is an achievement in this day and age. So, yeah, I mean really, you know, they watch my work and they enjoy it from that angle.

WG: While you were keeping your acting aspirations a secret, did you also watch *EastEnders* in secret with your sisters?

HW: We watched *EastEnders* at school. I went to rather a posh boarding school, and certainly there were some girls there who used to kind of be under the impression that you should watch *EastEnders* to "see how the other half lived," you know. (laughs) How sadly deluded were they. But there you go! So, yeah, I was watching it at boarding school – it was always on there. So it was definitely part of my life growing up, *EastEnders*. I just wanted to work as an actor, didn't particularly aspire to just be in *EastEnders* or anything like that, but, my gosh, it was a wonderful job when it came along, three and a half years later.

WG: Was that your first big break?

HW: Yeah, really. I pretty well jobbed for four years before I started here, but certainly I had a dreadful ten months before I got this part. So it was a real saving grace, and I got it just before Millennium Eve really. So it was a great Year 2000 present, you know, apart from tummy ache with nerves (laughs) worrying about my first scene. I was terrified. For six weeks I was shaking in my boots.

WG: Playing against Adam Woodyatt (Ian) and all his experience on the show [he's the last member of the original cast].

HW: Adam was fantastic, fortunately, not at all like his evil counterpart, yeah. Otherwise, it would be hard work! (laughs)

WG: The thing I like about Laura is the drive. Obviously, she's had lots of problems, but she's been able to overcome them. One day she's next to homeless and the next day she's running a business.

HW: Yeah, she bounces back. She's definitely a survivor, Laura is. And, in fact, I think that's where she and Pat have quite a close relationship now, and in some ways I think that's quite a common bond between them. They have faced adversity and have actually managed to retain most of their dignity and kind of come out intact. I think Pat's a good role model for Laura in that respect. I remember when she said to Pat, you know, "You taught me about what it means to be a survivor and to, you know, stand up for yourself." Laura can take that too far. I think she's at her best when she has a reason for that drive. You know, when her back's against the wall and she has to protect her child or go out and do something in order to survive, that's when she's most impressive really. She gets a bit sidetracked along the way and she does make decisions that I thoroughly disagree with. But that's not my job, you know.

WG: Looking at Ian's history with women, Laura in no way is as vindictive as Cindy, for example.

HW: No. Laura genuinely loved Ian, but he just let her down. And in some ways I think she still – it's a bit of a love/hate thing, but I think there was a genuine love there for him which had gone for Cindy a long, long time before. So the difference between Cindy and Laura, yeah, Cindy was definitely more vindictive and more malicious in her intent. Laura's more about protecting herself or, as will be, her child from hurt, you know. That's when she gets more aggressive, but, like you said, it's not vindictive particularly.

WG: I can't imagine Laura ever trying to get Ian killed. I mean even at her worst moment.

HW: I don't think she'd bother. The thing about her is she does get emotional. She does react with anger and can be quite physical with that and everything else, but essentially I don't think she'd make that sort of life-changing decision to something that extreme because I think she sees a future as she will move on, you know? I think she's got more hope for the future than having to kind of get him out of her life.

WG: I think the infidelities that engulf Ian and Laura can resemble real life, to some extent?

HW: I think it probably does. In Janine's case it was pretty much quite a lot more than a mistake, really. It wasn't a drunken one-night stand. It was a pretty thought-out affair until he got caught. That particular evening that Laura was drunk and it was a mistake – it was more of a mistake than what Ian did. Ian's was kind of a bit more considered. Laura's was a genuine drunken error.

WG: I saw that episode, and it was interesting because you didn't know which one Laura would go off with.

HW: Yeah. It could have been any of them. Garry was almost the outsider, I think, really. (laughs) Yeah, yeah. It could have been any of them. It wasn't particularly Garry that she was going for. She was very vulnerable. She was angry with Ian that night because they'd had a fight and she felt rejected, and I think she'd been fighting against that for so long. He'd worn her down really. So it was inevitable that something would go wrong.

WG: I also liked the scene where, and I thought this, again, resembled real life, when a woman in that position, Laura had to choose the name of...

HW: Of the baby, yeah.

WG: And she wanted to do the honest thing.

HW: For the child. Weirdly enough, I think that Garry was the person that actually made her aware of how important it was for him as a child to know who his father was. Although he didn't get on with his father, but he kind of brought it all into perspective, which made her think that she couldn't actually lie to her child about who his father was. So, ultimately, she's going to have some explaining to do. She might continue to lie and say it was just because it was her married name at the time. She could get round it, but I think you're right. I think she did have honourable reasons actually, and I think it was a terrible wrench for her. So I don't think she really wants to let Garry down. She does want Garry to – it's kind of self-motivated, but it's more about she's more selfish for her child than she is for herself really.

WG: Any catfights with Lynne (Garry's wife)?

HW: Oh, I should think maybe one or two! I can imagine. I can feel something bubbling definitely. (laughs)

WG: Again, this goes back to the relationship with Laura and Pat. I mean Pat had that type of adversarial relationship with...

HW: Mo.

WG: Well, I was thinking...

HW: Peggy?

WG: Peggy, yeah. I was thinking when she threw the plate and that whole thing?

HW: I think that when certain things come to light, there could be a heated discussion at least. (laughs) My stories have been very female orientated. Women relate to Laura's stories a lot better than men do, because for men it's more black-and-white than it is in some ways. Like the decision she makes with the father in not telling the real father and not telling Garry and everything about the child, a lot of men understandably found that totally deplorable, but a lot of women went, "Aha, yes. Okay. Yes, that happens. People do forget to tell the truth sometimes." Like you said, it's the reality of the situation. I like to think that if I'd have been in that situation, I would have made a different decision, I'd have stuck to my guns and brought the child up on my own. I do sympathise with why she did what she did, and, like I say, it's a revelation how many women have come forward and either told me, you know, related to her making that decision. And I've heard stories of people who've done similar things

WG: Do you think *EastEnders* might not get enough credit that it can be intellectual?

HW: I think so. In university, we have mediaeval literature, epic literature, and all different kind of facets of literature. The best literature is about real life, and that's what we're trying to do. And it's all about human emotions. Any kind of writing or drama goes around in circles. You can't really do anything new because it's existed for hundreds of years, people living together and being written about and so on, but what you can do is meet with the genre and develop it, continue to move it along. And I think soap particularly is a very organic thing, and the characters change and shift and different situations occur because of that, and situations change characters and circumstances change characters. My character's changed beyond all recognition. She doesn't bear any relation to what she was, but then if you look back and take into account what she's been through, then it's sort of understandable that she's grown up and developed into what she's become, you know?

WG: I agree with you that *EastEnders* resonates with women.

HW: I think it appeals across the board to all sorts of different people. I mean I think each character has a job in some ways to reflect someone that exists in society. So that we're all playing – obviously they are fictional characters, but they're as true to life as we can make them within the constraints of making television, you know. And obviously therein, the necessity of having dramatic moments and peaks and troughs and all of that. So obviously it isn't what happens in real life, but it's as near as we can reflect like society. And I think *EastEnders* is, further, very successful. I mean the female characters in *EastEnders* are sort of famously the most successful characters there. I mean you've got Kat, you've got Pat, you've got – those are sort of unfortunate names to put together – Sharon. Pauline, in her own way, is, you know, a successful matriarch.

They're all very powerful women, and the men in some ways are kind of a bit sidelined by that. It's centred around, you know, Peggy, Pat, and Pauline.

WG: You just reminded me of an article I reprinted some years ago written by Jacquetta May, who played *EastEnders'* Rachel Kominski, about the show's matriarch aspect.

HW: I'll be interested to see that, definitely. I think it's pretty relevant. I suppose traditionally soap has been watched more by women than by men, I guess, but I don't think that's the reason behind it. I mean I think, you know, strong female characters are good dramatic parts really. It's better than saying, "Yes, sir" and "No, sir" all the time. That's for sure!

–Larry Jaffee

Nick Bailey (Dr. Anthony Trueman), 2003

"You'd think he'd be sensible to leave well enough alone with those two [Kat and Zoe]. Tangling with the Slaters is a big mistake."

My interview with the extremely affable and charming Nick Bailey (official British Equity name: Nicholas R. Bailey) somehow found itself developing into a two-part deal. The first time I met with the actor (who portrays *EastEnders'* uptight if well-meaning Dr. Anthony Trueman) was on a cold and dry January afternoon in a West End London club called Teatro.

Many months later, on a hot and sticky summer afternoon following an impromptu fan luncheon, we sat down in a midtown Manhattan Starbucks. Nick is an absolutely great guy to hang with.

Walford Gazette: It's really good to meet with you, Nick. I worried that over the Christmas/ New Year's break you'd change your mind about doing an interview for us!

Nick Bailey: Why would I, mate? We've all seen copies of the *Gazette* lying around the studio and we've been totally impressed by it. You guys obviously love the show and you seem to know more about it than we do at times!

WG (smiling proudly): We do. Where should we start? I did my homework on you; the Internet is invaluable these days.

NB: Oh dear God, you probably know more about me than I do, then.(laughs)

WG: No, no, no. I read an interview you gave on the BBC website about *EastEnders* which was excellent. The one you did alongside *EE* writer supremo Tony Jordan?

NB: Oh, that was a great day. Yeah, I actually got to sit right next to Tony for the webchat and a phone was placed between us to use for it. We had a game going to compete who would get the most questions because that ultimately meant the fans were more interested in what I had to say than what *he* had to say, and vice versa.

WG: That's a funny picture. Knowing Tony I bet he used his low-key, every-man humour to mask his competitive streak.

NB: So did I! He'd say to me stuff like, "Well, I'm the principal writer, get back in the queue, you," and I'd shoot back something like, "Well *I'm* an actor and I'm actually *in* the show, so *you* get back in the queue, you lowly writer," and so forth. (laughs) We had such a laugh doing that thing. I love Tony – great guy. Great writer, too.

WG: I agree. Did Tony create the character of Dr. Anthony Trueman?

NB: No, actually it was John Yorke's idea. John was *EE*'s executive producer at the time and he also wrote for the show many years ago. He wanted to bring on a classic bad boy character, who turned out to be Paul Trueman, and he felt he needed a good guy in the same family to spar with him and that's how Anthony came about. Anthony was established on the show first though, about six months earlier than Paul. John thought it would be more dramatically effective for the viewers to start warming up to Anthony and then to have Paul come in and wreak havoc in his life, to have him storm in and shake up his world. Along with the rest of Albert Square, hopefully.

WG: Not to mention their mum, Audrey.

NB: Exactly. Paul was meant to be a cat set amongst the Walford pigeons. I think John's idea was fully realised.

WG: I think the actor who plays Paul actually *looks* like a cat at times – he's got a cat-like face. And he makes as much mischief as a cat does, albeit in a somewhat human manner. Gee, it felt like a year in between the time when Dr. Fonseca left the surgery and Dr. Trueman stepped in. I started to wonder where Dot went to for all her supposed aches and pains.

NB: I dunno... Catford?

WG (laughs): Yes, very funny, she probably did go off to Catford. On the bus. I don't know why but an image of you appearing in a television film shown on BBC America often has just flashed before my eyes.

NB: You must mean *Sex and Death*.

WG: Yep. I could only watch the first few scenes because its freneticism gave me a headache but I noticed you in it. You played this hunky performer on a reality TV show.

NB: Yeah, I did although I don't know about the "hunky" bit. I played an actor who regularly appeared on one of those extreme TV-type shows that air here in the U.K. on Friday nights—only *Sex and Death* took it to another level. I had on a very strange multilayered magician's costume, and attached to the top of my head were devil's horns applied with spirit gum!

WG: I forget. Did you have hair on your head then?

NB: A bit of stubble! (laughs) My character in that was quite similar to Anthony's actually in that both were rather shy and retiring when it came to women but had a bit of the devil underneath which was let loose on occasion.

WG: You can say that again. Anthony had relationships with Kat Slater and then her daughter Zoe – scandalous! That little devil.

NB: Ahhhhh, but Anthony never actually had sex with Zoe; they only kissed. She even threw herself at him half-naked once and he wouldn't take her upstairs. Now *that's* willpower, mate.

WG: I stand corrected about Zoe. But he was still involved with them both.

NB: But that's what I have loved about playing Anthony. He hasn't been utterly predictable all the time, has he? You'd think he'd be sensible to leave well enough alone with those two, for starters! Tangling with the Slaters is a big mistake.

WG: I must ask this: What was actually supposed to happen to Zoe and Anthony the summer of 2002? I know the actress who plays Zoe (Michelle Ryan) had to temporarily leave the show for personal reasons, and a lot of plotlines had to be changed as a result. I assume the Zoe/Anthony wedding was the first casualty.

NB: The writers had to rework fifty-four scripts if I'm not mistaken. Zoe and Anthony were to get married after all, but she would soon find it very rough going. She'd get bored in the marriage, I'm sorry to say! Here's a clue about what was supposed to follow: Madame Bovary.

WG: Ohhhhh, I'm sure all our French literature-loving readers will know *exactly* what you meant by *that*. Thanks, Nick!

NB (laughs): You're so welcome! I had mixed feelings about their storyline anyway so in a way I'm glad it never got to play out.

WG: Who do you feel Anthony loved more: Kat or Zoe?

NB: I hate to sound like a bit of a wuss with my answer to this but I feel he loved them both equally but in a totally different way. Kat was exciting, unpredictable, down and dirty. He also loved her tender, vulnerable side. Zoe was this fresh, lovely, kittenish (pardon my pun as it relates to Kat) creature whom Anthony felt compelled into moulding into an elegant and "respectable" doctor's wife. Americans call them "trophy wives," don't they? Zoe would certainly qualify. He did genuinely love them both, though. He might have told Kat something different but I'm not sure he believed his own words! He was caught up in the heat of the moment between them. Maybe he didn't want to hurt Kat by actually articulating how he felt about Zoe all that time. I doubt she wanted to know the details, anyway. No wonder she went off to Spain to get over the abortion and Anthony.

WG: And now he's moved on to a new job in the A&E at Walford General to mend his broken heart.

NB: He's moving on with his life – which is brilliant. I hope he stays away from those naughty nurses of Walford General and the broom closets: He's got that little devil I mentioned! I've always thought of Anthony as a pressure cooker with the lid screwed on tightly but the steam seeps to the surface and he's constantly trying to press it down. (laughs) Anyway, now he's finally reached something of a turning point in his life. He was clearly a mama's boy and she's dead. The personal issues between Patrick and Paul have been resolved, more or less. The same is certainly true of Zoe and Kat in that he knows he can never be with either of them. We'll see what happens. (looks at his watch) Oh my God, I'm sorry, mate, I've got to run off right now to an appointment with, uh-oh, my accountant. Please let's continue this another time, yeah? I'm so sorry.

Since it was my own fault the interview had to get cut short because I was late meeting him at the Teatro in the first place I readily forgave him. We decided to postpone the second part of the interview until he actually visited New York City, which he did in mid-August. After the hugely enjoyable *EastEnders* fan luncheon at an upscale Indian restaurant called Utsav, we attended a performance of the Broadway revival of *Gypsy*, starring the magnificent Bernadette Peters. Afterwards we chose a Starbucks just blocks away from the theatre to unwind.

NB: Was that show absolutely brilliant or what? Awesome. I didn't know *Gypsy* all that well. I'd only seen the first hour of the movie version years ago, actually.

WG: That was one of the best things I've ever seen on Broadway. But what was that strange tiny sound you made next to me when Louise (who eventually grows up to be stripper Gypsy Rose Lee) was singing "Little Lamb?" It sounded like you were crying and although it was

a poignant moment I didn't think it was a tear-jerking one. I couldn't bring myself to look over to you to see what was up.

NB: (laughs): Oh God no, mate, I was trying to stifle a laugh! That lamb onstage was looking all around during her big song and I could swear it focused on me for a bit. The look on its face was priceless. I started cracking up!

WG (laughs): Oh, you're so vain, Nick. Even lambs can spot you in the audience and make eyes at you now, huh?

NB: Maybe he recognised me from *EastEnders*. No one else in the theatre did! (laughs)

WG: True. But those folks at the fan luncheon sure did – they obviously adored you and you were just great with them. Thanks.

NB: Thank you for setting that up. Yeah, I really enjoyed that although I wish there had been more time for me to chat with everybody. They were such lovely people and I was gagging for a curry besides.

WG: Oh, you Brits with your quaint expressions.

NB: Don't start, Tim. (laughs)

WG: I still can't believe that earlier you defended the Brits mocking Americans for pronouncing "Anthony" with the "h" by saying that pronouncing it like "Antony" just *is* the way it's done and that's it. Some answer.

NB: I'm afraid that's all you'll get on that matter, sorry, mate.

WG: An awful lot has changed in your life since we last met in London back in January, hasn't it?

NB: Uhhh, yeah, you could say that. Would you consider my leaving *EastEnders*, forming a TV/film/theatre production company, moving house from London to Gloucestershire and getting engaged to constitute change in my life?

WG: In a word, yes.

NB: In fact, if you'll remember I had to cut our interview short to head off to see my accountant that day. I had to get some financial matters sorted to see my way through to making these changes in the first place.

WG: You had to find out if you could afford to leave *EE* for starters, right?

NB: Right. Amongst other things. The house didn't come cheap either, but Lisa and I both love it so it's well worth it.

WG: Congratulations on behalf of all *Walford Gazette* readers on your engagement. So when's the big day?

NB: Next summer, God willing. I can't wait.

WG: Lisa's a Scottish lass, isn't she? I spoke to her briefly on the phone a few days ago.

NB: Indeed she is.

WG: So will you be wearing a kilt to the wedding?

NB (laughs): It's under consideration. But we're actually getting married in England so perhaps a black tux is in order!

WG: You're actually from Birmingham, aren't you, Nick?

NB: Yes, I'm a Brummie Boy! From Birmingham in the Midlands. I also attended a public (boarding) school in Staffordshire in the Midlands.

WG: What happened to your Brummie accent, then?

NB: Attending public school initiated the process, I think. They tend to frown on local accents. They also beat it out of me, figuratively, when I attended LAMDA later on.

WG: Ah yes, the London Academy of Music and Dramatic Art. You studied there to ultimately play Shakespeare and such.

NB: Yes, but I'm not in the position to be that selective in my career! I'd certainly love to get my chance to play Edmund in *King Lear* some day. I was in a production of *Lear* at the Royal National Theatre starring Sir Ian Holm and it got filmed for television. I played a much smaller role in that, however. That's one of the reasons I wanted to develop my own production company. It's called Divided Child and I hope to generate projects which I can perform in. There will be some projects I won't appear in at all, though. Right now I want very much to do a London production of a show that was a huge hit on Broadway quite a few years ago. I don't want to jinx it by naming it though. But that's one of the reasons I'm in town – I'm going to try and get the rights to do it. And I won't be appearing in that should it come to fruition.

WG: Well, good luck on that, Nick. You once played a guest role on the popular ITV cop show *The Bill* before you joined *EE*, would you join that on a regular basis like Todd Carty (Mark) recently did?

NB: I'm not saying never to anything because that would be closing the door on options. Who knows what will happen? I am firmly committed to my production company, though, and I'll work extremely hard to get my projects off the ground. That's all I can do right now.

WG: Did you feel comfortable about leaving *EE*? It was your decision to do it, after all.

NB: Yes, absolutely. Of course when I first spoke to you I was putting the final elements together to do it. I definitely feel it was the right time. It was the right time for Anthony to leave Walford and for me to leave the show to try and do other things. As I said to you in January Anthony was at a turning point in his life and he was at the perfect time to make a major change. He chose to head out of Walford and end up in Estonia of all places!

WG: Yeah, Estonia... what was up with that?

NB (laughs): Okay, that was the result of an in-joke on the show about me. I had a Finnish girlfriend once and we spent a holiday together in Estonia. All the cast of *EE* take their holidays in places like Spain and Florida and the Canary Islands but never in places like Estonia. Anyway, I was in a supermarket in England a few weeks before I got here and someone walked up to me, and said: "I thought you was in Estonia." I didn't know what the hell he was talking about. I later found out that Patrick had got a phone call from Anthony – and he was in Estonia!

WG: Perhaps Anthony is romancing a mother-daughter Estonian accordion duo or something these days.

NB: Ha ha, very funny, Tim.

WG: But getting back to your leaving *EastEnders* – you weren't tempted into staying in it for as long as you could for the money and the fame it brought into your life?

NB: Of course, I was tempted by that stuff but at the end of the day I knew it was the right thing to do for me. There's that expression about fame and money and how all that is the icing on the cake but you've absolutely got to focus on the cake or you're in trouble. And by the cake I mean the work.

WG: Darn, that's profound. Did you just make up that about the cake symbolising work? I'd heard the one about the icing before. Although usually performers who get nominated for things like the Emmys or Oscars say it's the "icing on the cake" to get nominated and I never believe them. That expression is right up there with "the nomination is the award."

NB: Yes, I did just make that bit up about focusing on the cake. Thank you. Perhaps I can take up writing someday, huh?

WG: Never say never. Do you miss the folks on *EastEnders*?

NB: Absolutely, I made a lot of friends on that show but I'll still see many of them socially. I've invited many of them for my and Lisa's engagement party next weekend, as a matter of fact. The [actors playing the] Trueman family is invited, of course, as well as folks like June Brown and Wendy Richard. Wendy's an angel – we got along very, very well during my time on the show. It was just one of those things – we clicked immediately as people. She is a very kind lady indeed. I hope Jessie (Kat) can make it, too. I wish her well. I hear she's engaged, too. She deserves happiness with a good guy. And I hope she stays on *EE* for a long time – she is such an asset to that show and she's so happy to be working in it.

WG: Which actors' careers do you admire? I know you want longevity and variety as an actor – which is why you left *EE*.

NB: That's a good one. I've always loved Jimmy Stewart and Paul Newman. Newman even more so than, say, Marlon Brando because Brando, in my opinion, only gave four great performances in great films over a very long career but Newman has been astonishingly consistent all these years and has rarely picked a stinker to act in! Daniel Day-Lewis, Gary Oldman, and Gérard Depardieu, too, they've had great careers and been totally brilliant in everything they've done.

WG: What will you miss about *EE* besides the people?

NB: The really good writing material I often got to work with. Anthony sometimes got criticised in the press for being something of a stick-in-the-mud but I do think he was a complicated character. I hope he was interesting to watch as a result, and I know he was someone who people understood. He always tried to do the right thing, for instance. He was, however, always playing up to someone else's idealised image of him, like his mother's or his dad's or Kat's. He needed to get the hell out of Walford and be his own man, so to speak.

WG: Perhaps he'll show up in an extreme TV show in Estonia wearing a magician's outfit with horns on his head.

NB (laughs): If that's what he wants to do. Hey, Den Watts is coming back from the dead so I wouldn't be surprised at anything. That's one thing I'm sorry about with the timing of my leaving *EE*. I would have loved to have been in a scene with Dirty Den (Leslie Grantham). Anthony could have treated his long-festering bullet wound! Oh, well. Things happen for a reason.

WG: Well, I think you've got a great future ahead, Nick, so if you asked me I'd say you did the right thing, too. We'll all miss seeing you on *EE*, though.

NB: Thanks. I appreciate that, Tim.

–Tim Wilson

James Alexandrou (Martin Fowler), 2007

"I sort of have memories of dancing to the theme song while I was still in nappies."

For the past decade, Martin Fowler has provided teenage *EastEnders* fans with a laundry list of how not to grow up. Let's briefly recount young Martin's various transgressions: childhood truancy and stealing; more of the same in adolescence; general misbehaviour at home, including consistently letting down Mark when called on to help at the fruit-and-veg stall; abandoning his girlfriend after getting her pregnant; and driving with an expired licence that results in the accidental death of a mate, to name a few.

Therefore, a revelatory opportunity presented itself when it was learned that James Alexandrou and his [then] girlfriend Kara Tointon, who plays the stunning Queen Vic barmaid Dawn, were planning a pre-Christmas holiday in New York.

The duo were the special guests at an impromptu meet-and-greet fund-raiser for WLIW 21 at Swing 46, a Manhattan restaurant owned by an *EastEnders* fan who originally hails from Manchester. Several dozen local-area fans came out to meet the actor who gave Pauline repeated heartache.

James is having a great time meeting us Yanks, and he handily fends off a heckler's questions addressed repeatedly to "Martin." I hand James a vintage copy of *WG* issue #26, which contained *Gazette* co-founder Dan Abramson's analysis (written circa 1997 or 1998) of the Martin character ("Me 'n Arthur Watching Young Martin Grow"). He accepts this tribute with thanks and immediately shows it to Kara. James and I arrange for a time for a telephone interview from his midtown hotel before he flies home to Blighty.

Walford Gazette: Glad I caught you before you took off.

James Alexandrou: Yeah, I'm checking out in a few minutes.

WG: I was curious about what it was like to grow up with a character who, like you, was going through adolescence. My question is: Did you find Martin a model of what not to do?

JA (laughs): Exactly, yeah. Be the opposite. It was strange growing up, going to school and working. I started working on *EastEnders* my first day of high school. But it was okay. It was sort of like the fat kid or the spotty kid who stands out at school.

WG: How old were you when you started on the show?

JA: Eleven.

WG: Were you already going to a drama school like Anna Scher, which trained many *EastEnders* alumni?

JA: Yeah, I went to Anna Scher. It's basically a youth theatre group after school and an acting agency for young actors. It's for kids off the street, as compared to kids whose parents have loads of money and can send them to fancy drama schools.

WG: How old were you when you started at Anna Scher?

JA: Eight.

WG: Back then, did you realise you were going to be an actor?

JA: I just enjoyed it really. I remember being in the Nativity play. I didn't think too much about it [that he was going to eventually make his living as an actor].

WG: Were you surprised when you got the job?

JA: Yeah. I was still in what was called "elementary" school. I got called to the headmaster's office, and I thought I was in trouble. My mum cried, she was so happy.

WG: Was watching *EastEnders* a ritual in your household?

JA: Sure. I sort of have memories of dancing to the theme song while I was still in nappies.

WG: Did you have favourite characters?

JA: I vaguely remember Grant, Phil, and Sharon, and also Arthur Fowler.

WG: Did you ever get to act with Bill Treacher? [Treacher played Arthur, JA's on-screen dad].

JA: No, his character had died already. *(Editor's note: Martin was first played by a different child actor.)*

WG: It must have been strange being a character that was started by someone else?

JA: Not really. Before me, Martin didn't really have many words. It was really like creating an entire new character.

WG: Yeah, I guess he was like Cindy and Ian's kids in their early days, they were always there in the background but you hardly ever heard them open their mouths. As a viewer, you always wondered if the kids were incapable of doing more. But did Martin go from 6 years old to 12 overnight? That's what it seemed like.

JA (laughs): Yeah, pretty much, yeah.

WG: So you lived in New York while you took a course at the New York Film Academy. How did you like that experience? And do you have plans to become a director like your on-air sister, Susan Tully (erstwhile Michelle Fowler)?

JA: Maybe. I made a documentary in 2005 about an island off Spain, Ibiza, where it's like a 24-hour party. It's a series of interviews.

WG: After doing *EastEnders* for ten years, are you afraid you'll always be labelled Martin Fowler of *EastEnders*?

JA: In the last four or five years, it's become more acceptable for a soap actor to do high-class TV. Michelle Collins, Tamzin Outhwaite, and Ross Kemp have all gone on to do other shows. Michael Caine reportedly wants to be on *EastEnders*.

WG: Have a good trip back home, and I'll be sure to look you up when I get to London.

JA: Cheers, Larry. Yeah, that'll be good.

–Larry Jaffee

Ian Lavender (Derek Harkinson), 2008

"A person's, let alone a character's, sexuality shouldn't have any bearing on how you feel about them for real, or whether you should play a character who is gay."

Ian Lavender's portrayal of Derek Harkinson provided Albert Square with an older male role model, who has carried himself with dignity. The character was introduced as an old schoolfriend of Pauline Fowler. He supported Pauline through various crises and acted as a father figure to Martin, even taught him how to drive. Brought on as a potential love interest for Pauline, Derek, in true soap fashion, turned out to be gay; alas such a coupling was not meant to be.

While *EastEnders* in recent years brought Lavender back into U.K. telly consciousness, he's perhaps better known in Britain for his portrayal of a young soldier in the classic comedy *Dad's Army*. He reminisces with the *Walford Gazette* here about both shows.

Walford Gazette: You've had a long acting career. What are the highlights in your mind?

Ian Lavender: Being part of what was arguably the biggest comedy programme that the BBC has ever had. Only this last week there have been complete evenings devoted to *Dad's Army* and programmes to celebrate the fortieth anniversary of the first broadcast. I'm obviously very proud of that. It continues to be shown and repeated here [in the U.K.], collecting an audience across the whole family from grandparents to grandchildren whose parents weren't even born when we made it. It became the programme that everyone wanted to do an episode of, and was where I first met Wendy Richard. She played the girlfriend of one of the leading characters in four or five episodes. Some years ago I was in the West End production of *The Merchant of Venice*, starring Dustin Hoffman as Shylock. It was the event of that West End year, the hottest ticket in town. Great to be part of that event and it wasn't a bad production either! And just recently another highlight was being in the National Theatre's production of the American musical, Tony Kushner's *Caroline or Change*, starring Tonya Pinkins and directed by George C. Wolfe, Tony award winners. Great experience all round.

WG: Did you feel typecast at all after *Dad's Army*?

IL: Literally typecast yes, I am in that the public tend to expect me to appear in comedies or light comedy, but they don't expect me to play the same character. I have found that friends and other actors who have become well known for playing in straight series or soap operas find it much more difficult afterwards in that the audience seem to want to see them only playing that character.

WG: Was it nice once you arrived on *EastEnders* to act with Wendy Richard? Wasn't it sort of art imitating life in that Derek and Pauline were old friends?

IL: The experience started off very easily because I had known not only Wendy for thirty years or more but also June Brown, Derek Martin, Johnny Bardon, and Barbara Windsor to name only a few. It was like old friends' week in possibly what could have been called an old actors' home! So life imitated art with Wendy, but I never got to play golf with Jim Branning or Charlie Slater!

WG: My favourite Derek moment is him not taking any nonsense from the Mitchells during the mini World Cup competition. (That played in the U.S. only about six months ago, by the way). How about yours?

IL: You are obviously quite early on in my period in *Enders*. There are several moments that are more favourite for me than the World Cup but I would be giving things away. Suffice to say that there is a lovely story to come yet when Derek's former partner reappears for a while. It's a nice storyline that interweaves with a holiday trip for Dot and Jim, and Pauline and Derek. Great fun to do but shot on location in the middle of the winter. It can get very cold here at times!

WG: Did you have any trepidation in taking on a gay character?

IL: None whatsoever. I have played several gay characters in my career and I have too many friends who just happen to be gay for me to worry about that sort of thing. A person's, let alone a character's, sexuality shouldn't have any bearing on how you feel about them for real, or whether you should play a character who is gay.

WG: How are you feeling? I read about your recent heart attack. Any advice for readers regarding taking care of one's health?

IL: I had my heart attacks three years ago now. I feel fine. Apart from the pills that I shovel down my throat daily I find it hard to remember that they happened. I am still working and still doing everything else that gives me pleasure. One of the greatest pleasures is coming over to visit with my son, daughter-in-law and granddaughter in Los Angeles. I think I would have another heart attack if I couldn't do that. Advice? Surely there is enough out there about lifestyle and diet without me adding more. What I would like to shout at everybody is that you don't necessarily have the pains in the arm or in the chest when an attack happens. If you think there is something wrong get in there and find out. Not only for yourself but it also makes the doctors' job easier if they get their hands on you right at the start. My team told me that they once had a man walk in with his food shopping with him. He had started to feel unwell in the supermarket, but thought he would just finish the shopping and then go to hospital. Idiot!!!!

–Larry Jaffee

John Bardon (Jim Branning), 2005

"[June Brown] takes it to extremes. I love her to bits really. But she's got to know what's in her handbag. She's got to know where she's come from, why she's there, where she's going, what she's had for breakfast."

The first time I met John Bardon (Jim Branning) was in the BBC canteen at the *EastEnders* studio. I was about to grab a sandwich when Michael Greco (Beppe di Marco) and Marc Bannerman (Gianni di Marco), who both remembered meeting me the year before in their dressing rooms when they had just started on *EastEnders*, asked me to join them. John, whom I hadn't met before, was with them. John was impressed by my being from New York, and immediately asked about "the lines round the block" for *East Is East*, a well-received film about the assimilation of a Pakistani family in northern England, in which he had a featured role.

I told him I wasn't sure about the queue, but it was a pretty full house the night I saw the film in Greenwich Village. "Did they tell you I made only 150 quid on that?" I responded, "Wasn't it a small independent film by a first-time director?" "It wasn't my first film!" John replied, with the three of us laughing. The exchange perfectly captured the wit and wisdom of his alter ego, the inimitable Jim Branning.

We met again a year or so later in the foyer of the interior sets, and we vowed that one day we'd make the time to do a "proper" interview. Thanks to Wendy Richard, that took place in November 2005. Wendy had emailed me that John and his wife Enda were taking a pre-Christmas holiday in New York.

Eileen Fulton, a long-time actress on the American soap *As the World Turns* and a massive *EastEnders* fan, asked me to invite John and Enda to a small dinner party at the famous Friars Club in Manhattan while he was in town. He's also going to make time to meet his New York-area fans. The following conversation took place over the telephone. John did not disappoint.

Walford Gazette: Did you watch *EastEnders* before you landed the part?

John Bardon: Not really. I knew about it. But I wasn't an avid watcher.

WG: I think discerning *EastEnders* fans know your character Jim was introduced as Carol's dad.

JB: Right, it was first at the wedding. I suppose they thought he was a smashing character, and they brought me back three years later. They had me to the office, and asked, "Would you like to be a regular character?" They said, "It will change your life forever," which it has done. And they put me in a nursing home. I was recovering from a hip operation to bring me back. That was my first appearance. They took three months to write the character in.

WG: At what point did they decide to make you a couple with Dot?

199

JB: There was a bit of courting that went on first. She was just a mate really, just a friend. No way did the pair of us want to get married because we thought if we got married, we'd sit indoors and watch the telly every night. As it happened, we've had some nice things to do. And we are married, and it's worked out all right.

WG: I remember watching a scene of yours with Jim chatting up Dot, sitting and flirting on the stairs. And that point, she wasn't interested.

JB: She didn't want to know, at all.

WG: Eventually she fell under the spell of Jim?

JB: Yes, she softened to my charms, yes. That's it, mate.

WG: To what extent is your wife is similar to Dot?

JB: Is she what? Nothing at all, thank God! Larry, please! Nothing at all. No.

WG: Do June and Enda compare notes at all?

JB: They get on very well together. We took June on holiday with us this year for a week to our place in Turkey. She had a wonderful time. People don't recognise June when she doesn't have the wig on. They know me. I get spotted wherever I go. But with June, it was sort of an after thing. They'd say, "Oh, you're here as well!" It blew their mind to see me and her walking down the street in Turkey.

WG: So *EastEnders* is on in Turkey?

JB: Yes, BBC Prime. We've had Turkish people come to us and say, "It's Jim. My wife is English. She watch you, and I watch too. I learn English." We get that as well, yep.

WG: Getting back to when Jim was first introduced, it seemed like the character was somewhat bigoted, not unlike your character in *East Is East*. But then, his best friend becomes Patrick Trueman. Can that really happen?

JB: I see what you mean. You can't get away with it (prejudice) anymore. Everything needs to be PC. Politically correct stuff, that's what it is. He was bigoted, yeah, yeah. But he's softened.

WG: Right, at first he objected to Carol getting married to Alan.

JB: "You've not married *that*," was what he said. But you can't get away with it now, not over here any way.

WG: I was looking at your CV and I noticed that you're one of the few actors on *EastEnders* who has also appeared in *Coronation Street*. Jill Halfpenny (Kate) is another.

JB: Yeah, she was a regular character.

WG: I was just curious with the big rivalry between the two shows, whether it ever became an issue.

JB: Not much. In prize-giving, one side gets the hump of the other side. But that's it really. They're all actors earning a living, that's all.

WG: I noticed on the official BBC *EastEnders* website when you recently gave an interview, you said, "June works in a different way from me." Could you please be a little more specific, different in what way?

JB: We're all Method actors because that's the way you do it. Otherwise, you wouldn't get it right. But you do it at home. She takes it to extremes. I love her to bits really. But she's got to know what's in her handbag. She's got to know where she's come from, why she's there, where she's going, what she's had for breakfast. She takes it to extremes.

WG: I guess that helps establish the relationship between the characters on-screen (i.e., opposites attract)?

JB: I suppose that's what comes across on the screen, but I do love her to bits, as it happens.

WG: And a couple of months ago the two of you won "Best On-Screen Partnership."

JB: We've won that four times actually, me and her.

WG: It must be a great honour for both of you.

JB: Of course it is.

WG: I noticed that you personally won the Laurence Olivier Award for your performance in *Kiss Me Kate*.

JB: I'm very proud of that.

WG: I wonder if at some point we will see you sing on *EastEnders*?

JB (big laugh): I'll tell you what I can do. I'll give them a verse at the fan brunch. I'll also brush up the Shakespeare because that's what I did.

WG: Is your wife in the entertainment business at all?

JB: No, no. She's a lovely lady. We're only married three years. I was 62 when I met her, and she's the jewel of my life. I'm so lucky. I've got a lovely job, a lovely wife. Everything's wonderful.

WG: One thing *EastEnders* also brings out is your versatility, in terms of being able to do both comedy and drama. Obviously Sonia has gone through some really rough periods over the years, and you were there to help her through it. And obviously the comical side of you comes out fairly often. I think one of my favourite moments in *EastEnders* history was Jim inadvertently vacuuming up the budgie.

JB: That's everyone's favourite. (laughs) It's clever how they did that; they reversed the tape.

WG: Also I wanted to let you know that the *Walford Gazette* is running an advert for the "Viva Jim" t-shirt from Tonic Shirts, to benefit your favourite charity, Help the Aged.

JB: Yes, that's them. They sell hundreds of the bloody things.

WG: It's a great shirt. It really captures the essence of Jim.

JB (big laugh): It is great, innit?

WG: Also, I looked you up on imdb.com, and it says your given name is John Michael Jones.

JB: Yeah, that's it.

WG: How did you settle on Bardon?

JB: That's my grandmother's maiden name. I couldn't use my own mother's maiden name because it was Alcock. That wouldn't look too good on the billings. (more laughter)

WG: I also wanted to ask you about your stand-up comedy act. How would you describe it?

JB: I did a one-man show about a comedian called Max Miller. I did it for five years, eight weeks in the West End, and showed it all over the place. I did see Max Miller work. In 1933, he was in a film called *The Good Companions* made from a novel by J. B. Priestley. Then later I was in a musical of *The Good Companions*, for which Andre Previn and Johnny Mercer wrote the music and words. J. B. Priestley said, "That film made a star of Max Miller, and this is going to make a star of you." He wasn't too right about that. But it gave me the idea of getting stuff together to do this show. I'll bring a copy of the tape and you can have a look at it. It's an hour long. Very simple gags he does. I do it every now and then. I don't get the time any more.

WG: I'm sure the New York fans would love to see a little glimpse of that, and see another side of your talent. Eileen Fulton from *As the World Turns* told me the reason she likes *EastEnders* is that they give such meaty parts to the older characters, unlike the American soaps, where she said after 40 they just put you into the background.

JB: Well, we're the mainstay of the bloody thing. June Brown and Wendy Richard are sticklers for the whole history. They know when somebody died, and they'll say she wouldn't have done that because so and so. And they stand up for it. And if it wasn't for them, the thing would fall apart really. I've got a little bit of history now.

WG: I have to thank Wendy for telling me about your holiday here.

JB: She's a funny old thing, Wendy, but she's got a heart of gold. She's a good soul really.

WG: You mentioned that the last time you were in New York was 1958. What were the circumstances of that visit?

JB: I worked in a shop on Regent Street called Austin Reed, and they had shops on the boats, the Queen Mary and Elizabeth. It was just my turn to go. It wasn't very nice. I didn't enjoy it because we were staying on the boat. We had to go back through the docks every night. It was a bit like *On the Waterfront*.

WG: Well, New York has changed a lot since then.

JB: It's the wife's birthday and Christmas present combined.

WG: Has she been here before?

JB: No, her brothers and sisters have. I think she has relations out there. She's Irish from Belfast. So they've all got relations out there somewhere.

WG: You mentioned that you belonged to a club similar to the Friars Club here in New York.

JB: It's called The Grand Order of Water Rats.

WG: I was in London last year and went to a concert at a pub called the Water Rats near Euston Station.

JB: That's where we have our meetings – over the pub. It's nothing like the Friary, of course. That's what they're hoping to make it like some day. I wish I knew you were there because upstairs in the museum it's amazing. Bob Hope was a Water Rat. Laurel and Hardy were Water Rats. Maurice Chevalier. George Raft. Peter Lorre. Sidney Greenstreet. There are quite a few of them.

WG: Any other *EastEnders* actors?

JB: No, not really. They don't really have actors these days. They're variety acts. I'm very honoured to be amongst them.

WG: Have you done panto at all?

JB: Yeah, I normally play Dame, female, the Ugly Sister. I've played Cinderella's dad in a couple.

WG: All right, Jim. I mean…. John.

JB: Only once, Larry! Only one time allowed. That's all. You better warn the others as well.

WG: I will. I'm glad we did this after having met briefly twice before. We'd put it off.

JB: Yeah, we did. God bless, Larry mate.

WG: Give my best to your wife. See you both soon.

–Larry Jaffee

Laila Morse (Big Mo Harris), 2006

"I live just over the water from the East End and know a lot of people who have to make a living out of that [dodgy] way of life. Good luck to 'em."

The Slater family stormed into Albert Square over six years ago (just a year or two ago for stateside public television fans), and life in Walford never has been the same. Keeping the often unruly clan in order is none other than "Big Mo" Harris (never to be confused with "Little Mo"). You don't want to fool with Big Mo, whose comical side emerged when she ran a phone sex chat line, among the numerous schemes she's come up with to make ends meet for the family.

Advises the official *EastEnders* website of Big Mo: "Woe betide anyone who messes with matriarch Mo or the family she rules over. She's hard as nails and doesn't suffer fools gladly," and what she is likely to say is: "Look what I got down the market," while her profession is listed as "Dodgy dealer."

Laila Morse, the fine actress behind Big Mo, recently gave the *Walford Gazette* an exclusive interview, demonstrating her quick wit and the indelible mark that her character has left on *EastEnders*. Laila and I met briefly a few years ago, when I also made the acquaintance of two of the four infamous Slater girls, Elaine Lordan (Lynne) and Jessie Wallace (Kat), in the foyer leading to the *EastEnders* internal sets.

Acting is in Morse's blood, as she is the real-life sister of the great English actor Gary Oldman, but she's a late bloomer in the vocation. Laila made her acting debut in Oldman's 1997 film (which he wrote and directed), *Nil by Mouth*, loosely based on his own life growing up in London with their abusive father. (Through Gary, Morse is also the ex-sister-in-law of Uma Thurman.) After *Nil by Mouth*, she made episodic appearances in several U.K. television series, including *The Bill*, and got her big *EastEnders* break in September 2000.

Morse's *EastEnders'* co-star Wendy Richard (Pauline Fowler) implored her to get a lump checked, and as a result her doctors caught her breast cancer in time. The *Walford Gazette* thanks Wendy's husband, John Burns, for facilitating this interview.

Walford Gazette: When the Slaters were first brought on six years ago, did you realise what a phenomenon the family would become?

Laila Morse: Actually I suppose that would have been from before we first turned up at the Square. We had meetings and press releases, which had not been seen on *EastEnders* since the first episode, because of the number of new characters introduced all in one big hit.

WG: How much background did they give you for the character of Mo?

LM: I suppose just being the grandmother of an all-girl family living with my son-in-law. I was glad Mo was a ducker and diver.

WG: Obviously Mo has a bit of history with the likes of Pat. Did she relish going back to Albert Square and settling old scores?

LM: Mo loved it... the history between Pat Wicks and Mo and the scores to settle – it was just great because Mo knew the history, held the trump card, and played it very well.

WG: Mo is the matriarch of a house of women (except for Charlie, of course). The sisters' various love trials and tribulations have dominated the proceedings for several years, but do you feel that Mo should also get a romantic storyline now and then? Maybe she has, but in the States we're five years behind the U.K. episodes.

LM: Maybe I do, maybe I don't. Speak to me in five years' time. (hopefully)

WG: Did you ever object to the dodgy deals that the scriptwriters are always giving to Mo? For example, last week here we just saw her supplying Paul Trueman with perfume bottles filled with water to sell to unsuspecting suckers in the market.

LM: Never, because I live just over the water from the East End and know a lot of people who have to make a living out of that way of life. Good luck to 'em.

WG: Any favourite moments behind the scenes on the set, such as practical jokes?

LM: I have had so much fun on set. But the green room is the main source of fun – mostly instigated by Wendy Richard and Leslie Grantham, particularly picnic lunches in Walford Park.

WG: When did you decide to become an actress and what did you do before that?

LM: Before being an actress, I had done a variety of jobs including driving a medical van. Then when my brother offered me the part in *Nil by Mouth*, I thought, I'll give it a go, and I went from there.

WG: I'm a big fan of *Nil by Mouth*, and in fact reviewed it in the *Walford Gazette*. I wrote that the menace of Ray Winstone's character would scare even Grant Mitchell. Do you agree?

LM: Absolutely, but never mind that. I think he'd even scare Pauline Fowler.

WG: What was it like to work with your brother Gary on it, and is he still thinking about directing more films?

LM: It was fantastic to work with my brother. You'd have to ask him about other projects.

WG: Does Gary watch *EastEnders*? Did he even before you were on it?

LM: Yes, he's watched it when he has time.

WG: Any chance of an emailed photo of you and Gary together?

LM: Sorry Larry, that is family business....

–Larry Jaffee

Derek Martin (Charlie Slater), 2008
"Originally I was up for Leslie Grantham's part (Den Watts)…. Julia Smith called my agent, and said, 'I like Derek very much, but he's not the ladies' man type.'"

The first thing Derek Martin wants to know as we meet each other in the lobby of the posh Royal Garden Hotel on Kensington High Street is whether I'm related to the semi-legendary actor of yesteryear, Sam Jaffe. I explain, well not as far as I know, but I wouldn't mind if it was the case. As it turns out, Derek is a first-rate Hollywood buff. He reels off his favourites of the silver screen: Bogie, Cagney, Raft. He knows all the classic gangster flicks by heart. "I could have easily been a gangster because I'd seen Cagney. I was born in 1938 in Bow. The East End was full of cinemas. I'd go three or four times a week."

This July Derek celebrates his eighth year playing Charlie Slater, Albert Square's affable cab driver and dad to a brood of grown, sometimes out-of-control daughters. "I can't wait to go to work. That's how much I love it. I feel actors and actresses are very lucky to be able to do a job that you love doing and get paid for it. We've all got to work, bills, commitments, mortgages, whatever. I go to work with a big smile on my face. Even if I'm there for 12 hours, I come back with a big smile on my face." Of *EastEnders*, Martin comments: "Let's face it. Four nights a week; it's like a mini-movie."

Martin was something of a late bloomer as far as the acting game, and first worked as a stuntman. "I didn't come into the business until I was twenty-nine. Before that I was a professional gambler, motor racer, worked at the meat market, debt collector, national service in the RAF [as in Royal Air Force]."

While he's never been a cabbie, Derek is quick to point out: "I know my way around London. I just got a brand new cab in the storyline. It's got twenty-five miles on the clock."

He talks like a proud dad of his on-screen offspring, the latest dramatic, non-*EastEnders* endeavours by Kacey Ainsworth (Little Mo), Jessie Wallace (Kat), and Michelle Ryan (Zoe). Of the last-named, he says, "She's a beautiful girl. In England, she has what we used to call a 'box of chocolates face.' She has one of those faces. Lovely, lovely girl, really down to earth."

Martin points out that he had TV success before *EastEnders*, as the star of an early 1970s series called *Law & Order*, which has just come out on DVD in the U.K. When *EastEnders* was still on the drawing board, Derek was asked to audition for the part of Den Watts. But at the time he had another work commitment, and series co-founder Julia Smith decided to go younger for the role. The ironic twist is that Leslie Grantham had once worked with Martin in a play about gangsters. The two actors also crossed paths on the set of *Ragtime* at England's Shepperton Studios, and were both in awe of Cagney.

"Meeting and talking to Cagney is one of the highlights of my life," Martin says, vividly remembering the day. "When he arrived at the set, the place erupted. The entire cast and crew clapped and cheered for ten minutes until he gestured [enough]. The stuntmen were crying their eyes out because we all loved him. He told me that *White Heat* took sixteen days to make. When you worked for Jack Warner you could be on the set until midnight, you had to be back the next morning at 5 a.m. That was a great honour to work with Jimmy in the pictures. I have a signed photograph of him in my dressing room."

At this point in the interview, Derek notes that he serves as editor of a weekly newsletter, dubbed the *Walford Gazette*, distributed to cast members and crew at the BBC studio. "It's not a proper newspaper like yours," he says, making my day. We talk about me watching the previous night's BBC One episode.

WG: Since the *EastEnders* episodes we see in the States are five years behind the U.K., more than half the cast seems to have changed. It was nice to finally see a recognisable face – yours. You must have one of the longer tenures on the show these days.

DM: Eight years this July. Besides Adam, Barbara, Pam, Steve, and June, there's me.

WG: You come from the East End.

DM: Yes, born and raised in Bow.

WG: How similar was Bow to Walford in the way it's depicted?

DM: It's very similar the way it's built – the terraced houses, the local pub. But the East End now has changed; it's completely different from what it was. What it was like in the 1950s and 1960s – that's Walford. Now fifty per cent of the East End is made up of Asian residents. In the East End, the shmata (clothing) trade was predominantly Jewish. When we'd have fish on Fridays, my mum would cook with matzoh meal, not bread crumbs. We used to have a Jewish cake at Christmas. By the 1970s, that was gone. It's now the Asian shmata trade... know what I mean?

WG: You worked as a stuntman before becoming an actor. What was the most dangerous stunt that you were involved in?

DM: I did a lot of *Doctor Who*. I crashed a few cars, fencing, fighting, running through a brick wall. In war films I played a German and got blown up. When I became a stuntman you didn't have to become qualified. Whereas now they have to be sub-aqua (underwater), they have to do skydiving, horse riding, karate. It's a completely different game now, so technical. Stuntmen of my era did the job; we got it done.

WG: You must have been pretty fit.

DM: Yes, I was fit, still very fit.

WG: But you never landed in hospital?

DM: There was a series called *Elizabeth R.* with Glenda Jackson in 1971. In the episode, Elizabeth I sends the troops to Ireland to quell the rebellion. It was down in a forest in Surrey (a county close to London). I'm at the head on horseback in full armour. A shot rings out. All the hooligans and Irish rebels come running out and they're stabbing and killing. The director says, "Derek, I want to do another take. Is that all right?" So I say, "Fine." He says, "Same thing again." This time my foot gets caught in the stirrup. I can feel my neck or collarbone break. They carted me off on a stretcher to the local hospital. The director says, "Don't forget, you're at the studio in three weeks. You're playing a horseman named Cecil when Elizabeth is dying." In three weeks' time I've got my arm in a sling and I'm in pain, and my line was, "Ain't she dead yet?" I realised I was too old to do this any more.

WG: How old were you then?

DM: About 38 or 39. I always wanted to be an actor like Cagney in the films. I packed it in as a stuntman and got myself an agent. I got some acting bits until this thing called *Law & Order*, which put me on the map. From then on, everything's been great. I'm still playing the same character. Because I never went to drama or stage school, my repertory is from the street. A lot of my characters are based on people I knew: villains, coppers. But it's all Derek.

WG: *Law & Order* got a lot of attention in the U.K. because it was about corruption, right?

DM: I had to testify before the House of Commons. I said, "Wait, I'm just an actor."

WG: How much are you like Charlie Slater?

DM: Charlie Slater has got a bit of me in it. I put me into the character. That's how I've gotten away with it for forty-odd years. I came into the business in 1962.

WG: *EastEnders* certainly has given Charlie some dramatic moments, such as when he finds out that his brother Harry was responsible for getting Kat pregnant.

DM: We were always under the impression that it was some schoolboy behind the bicycle sheds. I went apeshit when I found out it was Harry.

WG: The actor who played him died a few years ago.

DM: Yes, Michael Elphick. He started off as an electrician. Remember when I spit in his face in the kitchen? I could have killed him. I tell him, "I never want to see you again." We went to the studio canteen for lunch, and he had a pint of Guinness and a triple whiskey. He couldn't do the scene when we got back. They cleared the set. He came out crying. I said, "Michael, go home and sleep it off." Nine o'clock next morning. Two takes, done. Good actor. He was in the film *Gorky Park* with Lee Marvin.

WG: When they gave you the character sketch for Charlie, did you think to yourself, "Can't I have at least one son?"

DM: Yes, I did. It's funny. when I went to the audition for *EastEnders,* there were five dads, five Charlies. They already cast the girls. You had to do a little speech, "I'm Charlie Slater. I'm a cab driver, I've been a lorry driver. I love my girls [daughters]. At the end of the day, this was a Saturday, one of the producers says, "Thank you, everybody. Even if you don't get the part, I'll still use you in future things. We'll let you know in two or three weeks. On Tuesday, my agent phoned, and said, "You've got it. Charlie Slater." John Yorke, who was then the executive producer and is now head of drama at BBC, lovely man, said to me, "Derek, we don't want anyone to act. We want everyone to be normal." I said, "John, I've done that for the last forty-odd years." There's always been a bit of Derek in my characters. They don't want me to put an accent on; they just want me to be natural.

WG: That comes off on the show. Weren't you also considered to play the role of Frank Butcher at one time?

DM: Yes, I was. Originally, I was up for Leslie Grantham's part (Den Watts). It went down to the last five and [*EastEnders* creator] Julia Smith called my agent. I worked with her on a series called *Angels* about nurses. Julia said, "I like Derek very much but he's not the ladies-man type. He's more the hard man, so thank you very much." So Leslie got it, and of course, it did wonders for him. A few years later, Julia called my agent and said: "We got this part, Frank Butcher, that Derek would be perfect for." I'd just started the second series of my own show, *King and Castle*. It would have been four months before I would be available, and they needed me to start in three weeks. So I didn't get that either.

WG: Otherwise you would have taken it.

DM: Yeah, yeah. Of course, Mike [Reid] did it wonderfully. Mike and I started as extras in war films together, back in 1962. You can't do everything.

WG: So it's three times the charm with Charlie Slater.

DM: They've told me they want me to stay forever.

WG: You mentioned Leslie Grantham. Didn't you work with him early in your career?

DM: We did a play many, many years ago. He played a small hoodlum. I was playing the lead.

WG: You have great chemistry with Laila Morse (Big Mo), Charlie's mum-in-law.

DM: She's the same way: She is what you get.

WG: People in show business are tight-knit. Aren't they?

DM: I'm a member of The Grand Order of the Water Rats.

WG: John Bardon told me about that group. When he was in New York, an American soap actress had a small dinner party in his honour at the Friars Club.

DM: He absolutely went ape. He said, "Derek, that is Mecca." He told me all about it, and said it was "absolutely stunning." He loved it.

WG: Have you ever been to New York?

DM: Since the 1940s I have been more American than I have been English. I'm not saying this because you're American. Whether it's Brooklyn, the Bronx or Queens (*Editor's note: three of New York City's boroughs*) I understand every single word. In New York, I know certain alleys where Cagney's character got killed in the movies. I know all those places, so I'd never get lost in New York. Interesting. I know the American civil war backwards. I've always wanted to go to America, to Hollywood. The nearest I've got to the U.S. recently is Heathrow. I've got twin boys, David and Jonathan. They'll be thirty this July. When then they were eight, I took them to Florida. We had two wonderful weeks. I will go back [to the U.S.]. Remember Dick Martin, of Rowan & Martin who died this past May?

WG: Sure. Any relation to you?

DM: No, but the lady he was married to, Dolly Read, we were all extras together. They lived in Malibu next to Frank and Barbara Sinatra. She said, "Derek, you should come over and play golf. Thursday nights we have a poker game, Barbara, Angie Dickinson, Gregory Peck's widow, and Jack Lemmon's widow."

WG: Your CV lists appearing on the American TV series *Hart to Hart*.

DM: They did an episode here. The casting director needed a police inspector. I was recommended. Before I came into *EastEnders* I always played villains and coppers. So I got to arrest Stephanie Powers at the Tower of London. Everybody said, "You lucky bastard." She's a lovely lady. When you got close to her, her face was full of freckles. I still get money for that, also *Doctor Who, Upstairs Downstairs*, many others.

WG: Didn't you go to the same school as the Krays?

DM: I'm older than them, but I knew their older brother Charlie better than Ron and Reg. In the East End, you'd see each other in the pub.

WG: Can you please share any behind-the-scenes information about being on *EastEnders*?

DM: About three or four months ago I was on set, and got back from lunch. I'm in the Vic waiting to do the scene. A young designer about twenty-two is fiddling around with bits and pieces. I asked, "What time are we supposed to be back?" She said 2 p.m. "It's two now." I said, "If I was Robert Mitchum, I'd be pissed off." She asked, "Who's Robert Mitchum?" I said, "Are you winding me up? I'm the winder-up, not you." She said, "No, I never heard of him." I said, "He's up there with Heston, Wayne, Peck, and Stewart." All these young people don't know these actors. It's sad in a way.

WG: Americans who are obsessed with British culture are called Anglophiles. What are Brits who are obsessed with American culture called?

DM: I don't know. But I've always wanted to be in a Western.

–Larry Jaffee

Epilogue

The following brings readers up to date with career highlights of what the actors in *Albert Square & Me* have done since their *Walford Gazette* interviews.

June Brown (Dot Cotton) still is a regular member of the *EastEnders* cast. In 2005 she won a Lifetime Achievement Award at the British Soap Awards. In 2008 she was appointed as a Member of the Order of the British Empire (MBE) for services to Drama and Charity.

John Altman (Nick Cotton) returned to *EastEnders* in 2009, repeating what he has done several times since appearing in the very first episode. Outside of *EastEnders*, he's been in demand on the British stage, such as playing Billy Flynn in *Chicago*.

Leslie Grantham (Den Watts), following being killed off *EastEnders* a second time in 2005, returned to the British stage in numerous productions, such as in the pantomime *Dick Whittington* as Dirty Rat.

Anita Dobson (Angie Watts) has appeared often on British telly in *Holby City, The Last Detective, The Bill*, and *Hotel Babylon*, among other programmes, as well as a frequent actress on U.K. stages, such as the 2005 West End production of *Hamlet*, playing Gertrude.

Anna Wing (Lou Beale) will be 95 years old on 30 October 2009. She was appointed a Member of the Order of the British Empire (MBE) in the 2009 Birthday Honours for her services to Drama and Charity. She played Grandma in the 2007 film *Son of Rambow*.

Wendy Richard (Pauline Fowler) died on 26 February 2009 after a recurring bout with cancer. She was appointed Member of the Order of the British Empire (MBE) in the 2000 Queen's Birthday Honours. In 2007, Richard was awarded a British Soap Award for Lifetime Achievement for her role in *EastEnders*.

Bill Treacher (Arthur Fowler) left the series in 1996 after the character was killed off. He has since made several films, including *The Musketeer, Tale of the Mummy* and *George and the Dragon*. He also had a guest starring role in the ITV police drama *The Bill* in 2006.

Susan Tully (Michelle Fowler) left *EastEnders* in 1995 and since the late 1990s she has directed episodes of *EastEnders, London's Burning, 55 Degrees North, The Bill* (1999–2004), *Funland, Secret Diary of a Call Girl* and *Lark Rise to Candleford* (2009).

Gillian Taylforth (Kathy Mitchell) since leaving *EastEnders* in 2000 has played Jackie Pascoe-Webb on ITV's *Footballers Wives* (2002–2006), but more recently as Sgt. Nikki Wright in ITV's *The Bill* (2006–2008).

Todd Carty (Mark Fowler) made his final appearance on *EastEnders* in February 2003. He then went on to play PC Gabriel Kent, in ITV's *The Bill*, and more recently appeared in the fourth series of the U.K. version of *Dancing On Ice*.

Gretchen Franklin (Ethel Skinner) died on 11 July 2005 at the age of 94. Her *EastEnders* character made her final appearance in 2000 in a euthanasia storyline. Ethel had learned that she was terminally ill, and asked Dot to assist her in taking her own life.

Ross Davidson (Andy O'Brien) died on 16 October 2006. After his *EastEnders* character died in a road accident in August 1986, the actor worked as a television presenter and appeared in U.K. soaps *Brookside* and *Hollyoaks*.

Judith Jacob (Carmel Jackson) starred as a prison guard in the drama *Provoked* (2006), which told the true story of a woman, who left India to marry a London-based man. She ended up in prison for murdering her abusive husband.

Nejdet Sali (Ali Osman) after his departure from *EastEnders* in 1989 changed his name to Nej Adamson. He played a sailor in the hit films *Pirates of the Caribbean: The Curse of the Black Pearl* and *Pirates of the Caribbean: Dead Man's Chest*.

Nick Berry (Simon Wicks) left *EastEnders* in 1990 and went on to play the lead role as Nick Rowan in ITV's drama series *Heartbeat* (1992–1998), following which he wrote, produced, and directed the BBC One series, *Harbour Lights*.

Michelle Collins (Cindy Beale) since her EastEnders character was killed off in 1998 has worked regularly in television, Sunburn and Two Thousand Acres of Sky, and on stage, most notably in Daddy Kool (2007) in the West End.

Tom Watt (Lofty) since leaving *EastEnders* in 1988 has worked as a sports journalist on radio and in print. On stage, he starred in the one-man show *Fever Pitch*. He also produced, directed, and presented the Channel 4 children's sports show, *Rookies*.

Michael Cashman (Colin Russell) since leaving *EastEnders* in 1989 is now a Labour politician. He has been a Member of the European Parliament for the West Midlands constituency since 1999, and is also a gay rights activist.

Barbara Windsor (Peggy Mitchell) has been an *EastEnders* fixture for the past 13 years. In 2000 she was made a Member of the Order of the British Empire (MBE) in the Millennium Honours List. On 9 May 2009, she received a Lifetime Achievement Award at the British Soap Awards.

Steve McFadden (Phil Mitchell) joined *EastEnders* in 1990 and since has taken a few breaks, but enjoys the second-longest male tenure after Adam Woodyatt (Ian Beale). In 2007 he appeared in the fact-based film *Provoked*.

Danniella Westbrook (Sam Mitchell) reprised her *EastEnders* character in 2009, after another actress had been cast in the role for several years. She published an autobiography, *The Other Side of Nowhere*, in 2006.

Kim Medcalf (Sam Mitchell) was the second actress to play the character, which she left in 2005. Since then she has appeared on British telly in *The Fixer, Death Becomes Him*, and six episodes of *Harley Street* in 2008.

Sid Owen (Ricky Butcher) has appeared in *EastEnders* from 1988 until 2000, 2002 until 2004 and then again from March 2008. He's also appeared on British telly in *I'm a Celebrity, Get Me Out of Here!* (2005) and in ITV1's prison drama *Bad Girls*.

Patsy Palmer (Bianca Jackson) reprised her role in April 2008. Her first *EastEnders* stint ran from 1993 to 1999. She also co-starred in *McCready and Daughter*. On stage she starred in the one-woman musical *Tell Me on a Sunday*, which toured the U.K.

Lindsey Coulson (Carol Jackson) appeared in *EastEnders* from 1993 to 1999. Her other TV credits include: *Clocking Off, Paradise Heights, Manchild, MIT: Murder Investigation Team, Doctor Who,* and Casualty.

Natalie Cassidy (Sonia Jackson) left *EastEnders* in February 2007. Since then, her theatre work has included *The Vagina Monologues, Bedroom Farce, Gertrude's Secret* (opposite Prunella Scales), and *The Cherry Orchard* (opposite Diana Rigg).

Howard Antony (Alan Jackson) since leaving in *EastEnders* in 1997 has appeared on British telly in *Starhunter, Silent Soul, Seizing Me, Doctors, The Defenders, Tic,* and *Green Street Hooligans 2* (2009).

Martine McCutcheon (Tiffany Raymond Mitchell) left *EastEnders* in 1998 for a singing career after her character was killed off. In 2002 she won a Laurence Olivier Award for playing Eliza in *My Fair Lady,* and in 2003 appeared in *Love Actually.*

Andrew Lynford (Simon Raymond) since leaving *EastEnders* in 1999 has worked as a TV presenter. He also wrote a 1970s musical called *Disco Crazee,* and directed *The Cheeky Chappie, Side By Side by Sondheim,* and *The Curse of the Dirty Dusting.*

Deepak Verma (Sanjay Kapoor) left *EastEnders* in 1998 and since then has appeared on telly in *Holby City* and *White Teeth.* He's developing several film scripts and produced on stage in 2009 a Bollywood version of *Wuthering Heights.*

Paul Bradley (Nigel Bates) left *EastEnders* in 1998, and since then has played a feature role in the U.K. medical drama *Holby City,* where he began in 2005. He appeared in the film *The Pianist,* as well as on telly in *Doctors, My Family,* and *Twisted Tales.*

Lucy Speed (Natalie Evans) had a second stint in *EastEnders* from 1999 to 2004 and since has had various roles on television, stage and in film. Since January 2008, she has appeared as DC Stevie Moss in ITV's *The Bill.*

Shaun Williamson (Barry Evans) left *EastEnders* in 2003, and apparently can't escape the character because his agent in Ricky Gervais's *Extras* calls him only "Barry from *EastEnders.*" In 2008 he played Nathan Detroit in a U.K. production of *Guys and Dolls.*

Tony Caunter (Roy Evans) left *EastEnders* in 2003, and since then has appeared on *Holby City, Down to Earth, Casualty,* and *Doctors.* He appeared in the 1965 film *The Hill* alongside well-known British actors Michael Redgrave and Sean Connery.

Paul Nicholls (Joe Wicks) left *EastEnders* in 1997, and since then has worked in *City Central, The Canterbury Tales* with Julie Walters, and *A Thing Called Love.* Film appearances include *The Trench, The Clandestine Marriage,* and *Bridget Jones: The Edge of Reason.*

Daniela Denby-Ashe (Sarah Hills) left *EastEnders* in 1999 and her credits since then *include My Family, North & South, Torchwood, Is Harry on the Boat?, Office Gossip, Rescue Me, Maxwell, Crooked House,* and *Waterloo Road* in April 2009.

Nadia Sawalha (Annie Palmer) since leaving *EastEnders* in 1999 has worked mostly as a TV presenter on numerous shows, including *Loose Woman* and *Wanted Down Under*, but she's also appeared as an actress in *Casualty* and *The Bill*.

Michael Greco (Beppe di Marco) after leaving *EastEnders* in 2002 starred in the West End production of *Chicago* as Billy Flynn. But he's also embarked on a second career as a professional poker player.

Leila Birch (Teresa di Marco) is currently living in Los Angeles where she has shot pilots for three series. Her British telly credits include *One Night of Shakespeare*, *The Bill* and *Renford Rejects* for Nickelodeon. She also frequently works in U.K. theatre.

Russell Floyd (Michael Rose) after leaving *EastEnders* in 1999 appeared in *The Bill* (2002–2005) *Dream Team*, *Doctors*, and *Casualty*. In 2009 he appeared in two plays: *Maggie's End* in London and *The Bullet* in Brighton.

Perry Fenwick (Billy Mitchell) remains a member of the *EastEnders* cast, which he joined in 1998. His wife is former *Coronation Street* actress Angela Lonsdale, who played Emma Taylor, the wife of popular character Curly Watts.

Martin Kemp (Steve Owen) in 2009 returned to playing bass in the 1980s pop group Spandau Ballet for a world tour. In February 2007 he starred in the low-budget British film titled *Back in Business*. In 2008 he founded his own production company.

Sylvester Williams (Mick McFarlane) recently finished his second feature film screenplay, which he hopes to get produced for the American market. He continues to operate an East London drama school, Characters, which trains young actors.

Hannah Waterman (Laura Beale) since leaving *EastEnders* has appeared in *Doctors*, *Holby City*, *The Bill*, and a recurring role in *New Tricks*, which also starred her father. She has appeared in *The Vagina Monologues* and *Tom, Dick and Harry* in the West End.

Nick Bailey (Dr Anthony Trueman) since leaving *EastEnders* in 2005 has appeared in *Doctors*, Manchester Passion, and *Beautiful People*. In January 2006, he was also a contestant on *Soapstar Superstar*.

James Alexandrou (Martin Fowler) left *EastEnders* in 2007 and has since concentrated on theatre, touring the U.K. and Norway with the British Shakespeare Company, playing Romeo in *Romeo and Juliet* and also appearing in *All Quiet on the Western Front*.

Ian Lavender (Derek Harkinson) since leaving *EastEnders* in 2005 played the narrator in *The Rocky Horror Show*, a patient in *Casualty*, and in late 2007, he toured in the comedy play *Donkey's Years*. In 2009 he spoke at Wendy Richard's funeral.

John Bardon (Jim Branning) is recovering from his stroke in June 2007 and has made three appearances since then on *EastEnders,* with the expectation that his progress will allow him to return full time to the series sometime in 2009.

Laila Morse (Big Mo Harris) remains in *EastEnders*, which she joined in 2000. She has also appeared the British cookery/reality show *Hell's Kitchen*. Her stage name was suggested by brother Gary Oldman's then girlfriend Isabella Rossellini.

Derek Martin (Charlie Slater) continues his *EastEnders* role, which he began in September 2000. He contributes a column to the series' in-house newsletter, dubbed the *Walford Gazette*, for fellow cast members and crew, providing inside information about themselves, gossip, and recipes.

Breinigsville, PA USA
26 August 2009
223014BV00002B/2/P